FALLEN
BLUE
KNIGHTS

Recent Titles in STUDIES IN CRIME AND PUBLIC POLICY
Michael Tonry and Norval Morris, General Editors

FALLEN
BLUE
KNIGHTS

Controlling Police Corruption

SANJA KUTNJAK IVKOVIĆ

OXFORD
UNIVERSITY PRESS

2005

OXFORD
UNIVERSITY PRESS

Oxford University Press, Inc., publishes works that further
Oxford University's objective of excellence
in research, scholarship, and education.

Oxford   New York
Auckland   Cape Town   Dar es Salaam   Hong Kong   Karachi
Kuala Lumpur   Madrid   Melbourne   Mexico City   Nairobi
New Delhi   Shanghai   Taipei   Toronto

With offices in
Argentina   Austria   Brazil   Chile   Czech Republic   France   Greece
Guatemala   Hungary   Italy   Japan   Poland   Portugal   Singapore
South Korea   Switzerland   Thailand   Turkey   Ukraine   Vietnam

Published by Oxford University Press, Inc.
198 Madison Avenue, New York, New York 10016

www.oup.com

Oxford is a registered trademark of Oxford University Press

Library of Congress Cataloging-in-Publication Data
Kutnjak Ivković, Sanja, 1965–
Fallen blue knights : controlling police corruption / by Sanja Kutnjak Ivković.
   p.   cm. — (Studies in crime and public policy)
Includes bibliographical references.
ISBN-13 978-0-19-516916-4
ISBN 0-19-516916-6
1. Police corruption.   I. Title.   II. Series.
HV7936.C85K88 2005
363.25'9323—dc22   2004029057

The cartoons in this book were created by Oton Anton Reisinger.
They appear here with his permission.

9 8 7 6 5 4 3 2 1

Printed in the United States of America
on acid-free paper

Acknowledgments

This book grew out of the dissertation that I wrote in the course of my doctoral studies of juridical science at Harvard Law School. I extend my sincerest gratitude to Philip B. Heymann for being a great mentor. Phil's passion for scholarship and the experience he brings to the often complex process of assessing the real-world implications of scholarly research have had a strong impact on my work. I would also like to express my wholehearted thanks to Mark H. Moore from the John F. Kennedy School of Government, Harvard University. Mark was most generous with his time, enthusiasm, ideas, and support.

In the process of compiling the material for this book, I learned a lot from the people I interviewed: William Bratton (former NYPD commissioner), David Burnham (former journalist with the *New York Times*), Kevin Cloherty (assistant U.S. attorney, Boston), Teresa Guerrero-Daley (Independent Police Auditor for the San José Police Department), Judge Milton Mollen (chair of the Mollen Commission), and Mary T. Cagle (assistant state attorney in charge of racketeering/organized crime and public corruption, Office of the State Attorney, Florida). I thank them all for generously sharing their time and their expertise with me.

This book has also benefited from the comments I received from some of the best and the brightest scholars in the field: David H. Bayley (University of Albany, State University of New York), James B. Jacobs (New York University), Stephen D. Mastrofski (George Mason University), Clifford Shearing (Australian National University), Michael H. Tonry (University of Minnesota), and Samuel Walker (University of Nebraska). I am extremely grateful for their invaluable feedback that helped me shape and improve the book.

Special thanks go to my husband, Zoran Ivković, for his challenging criticisms and unsurpassed support, as well as for his love and companionship. Last but not least, thank you, Dora, for helping your mommy finish her book.

Contents

FALLEN
BLUE
KNIGHTS

1

Police Corruption and Its Control

We entrust police officers with the right to use coercive force when needed, and we expect them to enforce the law. Yet some officers abuse this trust and become notorious law violators themselves: They steal. They accept bribes. They rob drug dealers. They sell drugs. They turn a blind eye when they see other police officers stealing or otherwise violating the laws.

The picture of police officers abusing their office for personal gain is itself disturbing, but the problem of police corruption extends well beyond the rule-violating behavior of a few officers. Police corruption distorts police work, encourages the code of silence, promotes resistance to accountability, and undermines the legitimacy of the police and the government.

To ameliorate the effects of police corruption, society has built an elaborate system of control involving multiple entities. Police agencies are assigned the task of preventing corruption, as well as investigating and punishing their own for corrupt behavior. State and federal attorneys are expected to investigate and prosecute corrupt officers, and courts try and sentence them. Mayors, city managers, and other government officials may hold police chiefs accountable. Independent commissions, once formed, are assigned the tasks of investigating the extent of corruption in police agencies, determining causes of corruption, and proposing solutions to the problems that are uncovered. The media may investigate corruption and disseminate corruption-related information to the public. Finally, in a democracy, the public determines the boundaries of acceptable conduct through the diligent work of various citizen groups, its occasional creation of scandals, and its requests to reform the agency.

As numerous examples from New York (Mollen Commission, 1994) to Los Angeles (Los Angeles Police Department, 2000) and from Japan (Struck, 2000) to Brazil (Buckley, 2000) demonstrate, corruption exists and even flourishes despite current corruption-control mechanisms. How can that be, when millions of dollars are spent every year to maintain the anticorruption system? In this book I analyze why our present corruption-control efforts are ineffective and propose a solution. I develop a novel, functional view of corruption control that embraces both preventive and reactive approaches. Moreover, I propose a pragmatic solution to the problem of corruption control.

Corrupt Behavior and Its Consequences

According to the slippery slope perspective, police officers begin their involvement in corrupt practices by accepting items of small value. Once they cross this line, they find it easier to engage in more serious violations of ethical codes, organizational rules, and criminal laws: "It is claimed that the acceptance of small gratuities such as free cups of coffee by police officers will increase the likelihood of, or lead by degrees to, or is not significantly different from, corruption of the worst kind" (Kleinig, 1996, p. 174).

Disregarding for a moment the merits of the slippery slope argument, we can ask a very sensible question: Is it really so wrong for police officers to accept gifts? After all, we sometimes give our garbage collectors, babysitters, or mail carriers holiday presents. We send our kids to school with gifts for their teachers. Why is treating police to free cups of coffee, half-price meals, half-price admission to movie theaters, or special discounts in stores any different? Is the same generally socially acceptable way of expressing our satisfaction with a gratuity or a favor to be considered a bribe—a completely unacceptable practice—when extended toward a police officer?

A priori, it may appear that nothing makes gifts inherently more morally wrong when given to police officers than when given to teachers or mail carriers. However, the true differentiation lies in what the officers do, how extensive their powers are, and what the nature of their job is. Police officers are public servants entrusted with an extensive set of powers and wide discretion in the exercise of their duties. At the same time, they perform their everyday tasks without direct supervision. Their power and lack of supervision coupled with their frequent contact with people caught violating the law create numerous opportunities for corruption and other types of abuse. Police officers are expected to make objective and unbiased discretionary choices; their decisions on how to proceed at a crime scene should not be affected by who has recently paid for their meal or whether someone has slipped them a $20 bill. Simply put, and viewed from the more benign end of the scale of corruption seriousness, extra fries should not be linked with extra police service.

Although free cups of coffee, half-price meals, and discounts given to police officers on a regular basis can add up to substantial financial expenses for restaurants and stores, and disrupt the equity in the distribution of police services, the true story of police corruption extends far beyond such gratuities. Its complexity is determined by the heterogeneity and scope of corrupt activities, in terms of both the nature and the seriousness of the behavior involved. A restaurant owner pays a regular monthly fee (a "pad") to the police in exchange for protection. Two male police officers demand and receive oral sex from a teenage girl in exchange for not issuing a speeding ticket. While securing a crime scene, a police officer steals a valuable watch. A subordinate police officer fixes a misdemeanor ticket for the sergeant's niece. Several police officers beat up a drug dealer, illegally search his residence, steal his drugs, and sell them on the street. A police chief actively takes part in corruption and eventually becomes a ringleader in a series of burglaries.

What are the consequences of such behavior? They distort police work, undermine the legitimacy of the police, and permeate the fabric of the entire society. To begin with, when police officers spend their time actively engaging in corruption, planning their next corrupt enterprise, or covering up their past corrupt activities, they do not perform what the society expects them to do in the first place—regular police work. The distribution of police services becomes distorted and results in injustice: for some, the provision of better than usual legitimate police services (Knapp Commission, 1972, p. 163), deprivation of legitimate police services for others, and the endowment of illegitimate police services for still others (see, e.g., Knapp Commission, 1972, p. 179; Pennsylvania Crime Commission, 1974, p. 247). The scope and scale of such activities may be considerable. Sometimes the police become serious lawbreakers whose profits from corrupt activities exceed their legitimate income several times over (see, e.g., Knapp Commission, 1972; Mollen Commission, 1994).

When people pay bribes to avoid being arrested, the potential formal sanction by the official criminal justice system—be it imprisonment, a fine, or a suspended sentence—is traded for an informal sanction determined arbitrarily by the police officers: a monetary "fine," that is, a bribe. Therefore, the actual punishment in a case, the ability to avoid enforcement of the law, the costs to clear one's name, and the quality and the informal allocation of police services depend on an individual's ability and willingness to pay. Consistency in the application of the laws is undermined, ultimately resulting in injustice.

Just as the ability to avoid arrest depends on people's willingness and ability to pay, promotion and assignment within the department may depend on the police officers' willingness and ability to pay other police officers "for services rendered, ranging from the payment of a couple of dollars for typing up arrest reports to the payment of hundreds of dollars for choice assignments" (Knapp Commission, 1972, p. 166). In agencies characterized by widespread internal corruption, supervisors not only can demand payment for promotion or desirable assignments but also can "use their ability to reassign officials as a punishment for honesty" (Rose-Ackerman, 1999, p. 63). Promoting a police officer who is less qualified than others but more willing to pay for favors or awarding more desirable assignments on such a basis results in injustice, as does punitive reassignment of honest police officers to worse positions.

In a police agency in which police corruption is officially prohibited but unofficially tolerated, police officers develop cynical attitudes, the code of silence among the line officers strengthens, the overall extent of misconduct increases, organizational changes that limit illegal profit making are subverted (see Murphy & Caplan, 1991, p. 247), orders and rules aimed toward developing more honest policing are opposed (see Murphy & Caplan, 1991, p. 247), and respect for supervisors diminishes (see Burnham, 1974), as does supervisors' overall ability and willingness to control corruption (see Goldstein, 1975, p. 10). Eventually, it becomes more important to know how to hide corruption from the public than to curtail it (see, e.g., Knapp Commission, 1972; Mollen Commission, 1994). The word *accountability* may well enter into daily rhetoric, but the very concept of accountability does not appear to be internalized.

Finally, consequences of corrupt behavior extend well beyond the walls of police agencies. Discovery of police corruption may cause an intense public reaction, even outrage and anger in the face of major violations of ethical expectations (Sherman, 1978, p. 60). Suddenly, our heroes become fallen blue knights. Awareness of corrupt practices may lead citizens to question the requirement to obey the law, when figures of authority do not do so themselves (Murphy & Caplan, 1991, p. 247). Shattering the image of "blue knights" may also lead people to question whether they should provide information to the police. As the President's Commission on Law Enforcement and Administration of Justice (1967b) emphasized almost four decades ago, "citizen assistance is crucial to law enforcement agencies if the police are to solve an appreciable portion of the crimes that are committed" (p. 144). If the public revelations of police corruption eventually trigger a major scandal (see, e.g., Burnham, 1970, leading toward Knapp Commission, 1972), public opinion about the integrity of the police department, the public's trust in the police, and the legitimacy of the police will have been eroded, and the police officers' ability to police themselves will be seriously challenged (see, e.g., Mollen Commission, 1994, Exhibit 3, pp. 1–2).

Controlling Police Corruption

If corruption has such severe, devastating, and far-reaching consequences, why does society fail to put an end to it? Why does corruption persist? Why has New York gone through a century of 20-year cycles of scandal and reform? (See Lexow Committee, 1894/1997; Curran Committee, 1913/1997; Seabury, 1932/1997; Helfand Investigation, 1954/1997; Knapp Commission, 1972; and Mollen Commission, 1994.) Why does corruption recur after reform? Needless to say, there are several complex explanations.

First, corruption is a continuously evolving and very heterogeneous form of police misconduct—from bribery and extortion to burglary, robbery, and opportunistic thefts—and, as such, it is notoriously difficult to control, even when there is considerable resolve to do so. What may work for one form of corruption may be completely inappropriate for another. In addition, forms of corrupt behavior exercised or accepted by the police culture at one point in time may be completely unacceptable or abandoned a decade later (see, e.g., Knapp Commission, 1972; Mollen Commission, 1994).

Second, police corruption is an invisible crime, difficult to detect with regular law enforcement methods, and it requires *somebody* to report a corrupt act to the police. Well, whom would we reasonably expect to step up to the plate and do the reporting?

Police officers and citizens—willing participants in corrupt activities—have no motives to report their own illegal activities. Citizens who are coerced by the police into corruption are unlikely to report it because they have lost their trust in the police and probably doubt their determination to investigate misconduct by members of their own agency. Finally, citizens who are deceived by the police or who are unaware of who the real culprits are would not label the activity as police corruption and, consequently, do not even consider reporting.

How likely to initiate the official process are witnesses to a corrupt transaction? The witnesses most likely to be present at the scene include other police officers. The expectations of their reporting a corrupt transaction are not high, though; the code of silence—the informal prohibition within police culture of reporting misconduct by fellow officers—binds police together. Even if other people who witness the transaction dare report what they observe, they will have to face the hurdle of credibility before they are taken seriously. Even law-abiding citizens, whose word as witnesses should carry substantial weight, might think twice before trying to report police corruption to the very same police agencies riddled with corruption. Why bother? In such agencies, there are only slim chances that justice would be done. In fact, police officers may retaliate against those who report.

Police corruption also remains an invisible crime because police agencies themselves may be uninterested in pursuing corruption proactively or investigating existing cases, especially if they are plagued by pervasive corruption. Everything else being equal, more thorough and systematic investigative efforts are apt to uncover more corruption. Indeed, even if they could find police investigators willing to investigate fellow officers, why would police administrators commit resources and energy toward corruption investigation if the public will interpret negatively whatever the investigation uncovers? The blame would be put on the administrators for allowing corruption to exist in the first place. And that is not all. Police investigators are likely to be viewed as traitors by their fellow officers and face cold shoulders and the code of silence at its worst. Without thorough reform, the bulk of the police corps probably would not be affected at all. In such an environment, very few, either inside or outside the agency, would applaud and truly appreciate the administrators' efforts to investigate corruption. Ultimately, even if they succeeded in uncovering and dealing with corruption, such diligent administrators might well become the first (and perhaps only) sacrificial lambs.

Third, most of the existing mechanisms of corruption control are reactive. Prosecutors and courts typically act only when information about existing cases reaches them, which is very unlikely to happen in a typical corruption case. The final outcome is predictable: Only the tip of the iceberg is ever recorded in the official court statistics. Although the few isolated cases with draconian punishments can serve as deterrents, they nevertheless fail to provide a crucial element of successful deterrence: certainty of punishment.

Fourth, police agencies, prosecutors, and courts all routinely focus on individual cases. Their joint efforts are directed toward investigating corrupt activities, collecting evidence, and making decisions in a particular case. Unless the particulars of the case they are investigating or prosecuting require it, they hardly have the opportunity, time, or determination to examine the underlying causes that lead to corruption or allow the corruption to continue.

Finally, as shocking as it may sound, the reality is that police corruption cannot be eradicated completely. A certain level of corruption will always be present. Thus, investing extensive resources into corruption control in pursuit of a completely corruption-free police agency may backfire. Too much control can undermine effectiveness in carrying out the agency's primary mission (see Anechiarico & Jacobs, 1996) and effectively eliminate discretion crucial for high-quality police work. The true issue becomes, then, not how to eliminate corruption completely but how to keep it under control and at an acceptable level.

The evidence from individual cases and investigations by independent commissions (see Knapp Commission, 1972; Mollen Commission, 1994;

Pennsylvania Crime Commission, 1974) indicates that the existing mechanisms of control, mostly reactive and focused on individual cases, fail where they are needed the most. Corrupt police agencies and their larger environments rarely engage in serious control efforts.

Although there will always be police officers so corrupt that they view themselves as criminals first, the key to successful corruption control is to develop mechanisms of identifying them early and preventing corruption from becoming severe, organized, and widespread. Numerous failures of traditional corruption-control systems suggest convincingly that corruption control should go beyond blaming individual police officers and reacting only to discovery of individual cases.

A Novel Approach to Corruption Control

Historically, reasoning about police corruption and its control extended across three themes: defining police corruption, determining its causes, and prescribing methods of control. The large body of literature on the topic—mostly writings from the 1960s and the 1970s (e.g., Goldstein, 1975; Sherman, 1974; Simpson, 1977)—disagrees about even the basic issues, such as the definition of police corruption (see, e.g., Kania, 1988; McMullan, 1961, pp. 183–184; Meyer, 1973, p. 38; Reiss, 1974, p. 253; Roebuck & Barker, 1973, pp. 8–9; Stoddard, 1974, p. 230). Herman Goldstein, one of the pioneers in the area, wrote,

> There is considerable disagreement about what constitutes police corruption. On the one hand, there is a tendency to define the term so broadly as to include all forms of police wrongdoing, from police brutality to the pettiest forms of questionable behavior. On the other hand, police corruption is sometimes defined so narrowly that patterns of behavior with all the characteristics and consequences of corrupt acts are excluded. (1975, p. 3)

Discussion about the etiology of corruption incorporates a range of explanations, from the rotten apple approach typically advanced by police administrators (see, e.g., Knapp Commission, 1972), structural approaches (see, e.g.,

Roebuck & Barker, 1974; Sherman, 1974), subcultural approaches (see, e.g., Skolnick, 1966), and organizational approaches (see, e.g., Goldstein, 1975; Sherman, 1974) to the symbolic interactionist approaches (see, e.g., Stoddard, 1974) and labeling approaches (see, e.g., Manning & Redlinger, 1977; Souryal, 1975). Yet, very few writings incorporate a range of heterogeneous causes and thus could be regarded as general, comprehensive, and integrated theories of police corruption (see Simpson, 1977). Even Sherman's explanations of corruption (1974, p. 2)—considered to be one of the very few attempts at building a general theory of police corruption (see Simpson, 1977)—are not developed as a concise theory but rather as a series of 14 propositions. Indeed, Sherman wrote that "my goal here is to present a conceptual scheme that is by no means a fully integrated theory, but one that at least accounts for all of the available literature on police corruption" (1974, p. 2).

Explanations of corruption are and should be closely related to the prescribed remedies, but, just as the etiological writings mostly listed potential causes and correlates and hardly resulted in a general theory of corruption, theoretical descriptions of prescribed remedies frequently include a list of potential actions and only occasionally a comprehensive and unified set of closely integrated and connected activities. Recommendations by independent commissions (e.g., Knapp Commission, 1972; Mollen Commission, 1994; Pennsylvania Crime Commission, 1974) go the farthest, but their efforts are curtailed by the fact that no one (other than perhaps the mayor) is responsible for the task of monitoring the implementation of their recommendations and following up once the commissions are long gone.

In this book I advance the existing body of knowledge regarding police corruption and its control in several directions. First, I propose a definition of police corruption that can distinguish between police corruption and other forms of police misconduct. Second, I study the extent and nature of police corruption and provide a critical analysis of the prior studies attempting to measure police corruption. Third, I establish a complex and integrated theoretical framework based on up-to-date evidence from empirical studies of police corruption and from investigations undertaken by several independent commissions. Fourth, I rely on the new functional approach toward corruption control and pinpoint challenges for various agencies of control in performing control tasks. Finally, I propose a novel approach toward corruption control that, if implemented thoroughly and properly, can realistically be expected to control corruption successfully over extended periods of time.

The first part of the book walks the reader through a definition of *police corruption*, its measurement, and its causes and correlates. In chapter 2 I define *police corruption* as an abuse of the police officer's official position for personal gain, determine key elements of police corruption, and establish criteria to distinguish corruption from other forms of police misconduct. In chapter 3 I address the issues related to the measurement of the extent and nature of corruption. A detailed analysis of various methods of data collection and the results of the existing studies illustrate an important point: We simply do not know the true extent and nature of corruption.

In the second part of the book, I examine causes and correlates of police corruption and the existing remedies. In chapter 4 I build a complex network of causes and correlates of police corruption. It incorporates police officers' individual characteristics and explains how the police agency affects police officers' propensity toward corruption. It illustrates the effects of agency-related factors, such as recruitment and selection, training, supervision, and investigation and punishment of corruption. In the chapter I further discuss how societal factors influence corruption by creating opportunities for corruption and a supply of citizens willing to participate in corruption, as well as by failing to secure effective corruption-control mechanisms external to the police agency. In chapters 5 and 6 I critically examine the existing methods of corruption control. The conclusion is clear, if disappointing: For various reasons, these control mechanisms—from the police agency itself to the courts, mayors, media, and independent commissions—do not operate nearly as efficiently and effectively as they might. Rather than trying to prevent corruption, they mostly react only after corrupt behavior occurs. Instead of trying to determine and deal with underlying causes of corruption and, at the same time, prevent and punish corrupt behavior, they primarily investigate and punish past corrupt behavior.

In the last chapter I propose a solution to the problem of effective control of police corruption. The proposed model of corruption control rests on both proactive and reactive approaches. It also relies on the investigation and punishment of corrupt behavior, as well as the identification of causes and correlates of corruption. The idea behind the solution is simple: Corruption can be successfully controlled only if an entity external to the police agency monitors control efforts by the police, detects problems before they escalate, proposes solutions, and disseminates its findings to key political players and to the public. This chapter describes how such an agency could be established, what its functions should be, how it might operate, what problems it might encounter, and, above all, how it could contribute to successful and lasting corruption control.

2

Defining Police Corruption

Newspapers across the world routinely report on corrupt police officers, and some of the stories describe convictions for their behavior. Yet, few legal statutes explicitly define and recognize certain behaviors as corrupt. The corruption-related crimes enumerated in newspaper accounts for which police officers could be convicted include the more typical ones, such as bribery and extortion, and more unusual ones, such as robbery and theft.

Could these diverse violations fit under the umbrella of a single form of police misconduct, namely police corruption? What are the important aspects of the definition that would make it applicable to the same corrupt behavior across a broad range of police departments both in the United States and abroad? Must criminal laws be violated for a particular behavior to be classified as corruption? Is acceptance of gratuities covered by the definition? Should noble-cause corruption be regarded as a form of police corruption? Can corruption be differentiated from other forms of police misconduct, such as use of excessive force, planting of evidence, or perjury?

In this chapter, I answer these questions. Unlike definitions based on violations of legal rules, which are jurisdiction-bound and specific, the definition of police corruption I develop here relies on two elements that transcend jurisdictional boundaries: misuse of official position and personal gain. I provide a detailed discussion of the elements related to the definition of corruption: (1) the nature of the corrupt act; (2) the necessity of the agreement; (3) the relevance of the timing of the payment; and (4) the type, value, and recipient of the gain. Finally, I establish criteria to distinguish police corruption from other forms of police misconduct.

A Definition of Police Corruption

One approach to defining corruption is a rule-based definition. Most countries do not have a crime specifically entitled corruption, but even if they did, the definitions would probably vary at least as much as the definitions of street crimes across the world (see, e.g., Newman, 1999). Furthermore, behavior typically understood as "corruption" is often classified as bribery and extortion, but, depending on the legal system, it may also be classified as theft, fraud, tax evasion, or racketeering (see, e.g., Weld, 1988). Some countries "may not even define some of the acts (e.g., bribery) as criminal at all" (Newman, 1999, p. 20). Similarly, what corrupt behavior is prohibited by internal agency rules varies from agency to agency (see Barker & Wells, 1981) and across time within the same agency.

The definition of police corruption developed in this book highlights a common thread: the police officer engaging in corrupt behavior motivated by the achievement of personal gain.

> Police corruption is an action or omission, a promise of action or omission, or an attempted action or omission, committed by a police officer or a group of police officers, characterized by the police officer's misuse of the official position, motivated in significant part by the achievement of personal gain.

The discussion that follows focuses on several key factors: (1) the corrupt act, (2) an agreement between the corrupter and the corruptee, (3) timing of the payment, and (4) the potential personal gain resulting from the transaction.

Corrupt Acts and the Abuse of Official Duties

Police corruption includes police officers' actions, omissions, or attempts to do so that result in abuse of their official duties and are motivated in significant part by gain (Table 2.1). Police officers who knowingly do something they are not supposed to do or do not do something they are supposed to do (e.g., a police officer revealed an undercover operation to a drug dealer or did not arrest a citizen caught violating the law) abuse their official duties. When these actions or omissions are significantly motivated by gain, they are classified as distortive corruption. Police officers who knowingly do something they are supposed to do or do not do something they are not supposed to do (e.g., efficiently issued a passport to a qualified applicant or did not require additional unnecessary documentation from an already qualified applicant) did not abuse their official rights through the mere action or omission. When these proper actions or omissions are motivated in significant part by personal gain, however, they nevertheless represent an abuse of an official position and are classified as nondistortive corruption.[1]

A special subset of behaviors that should be covered by the definition includes acts such as burglary, robbery, and theft that can be committed by any person, regardless of status as a police officer. The key criterion that includes such acts not only within the general realm of police misconduct but also within police corruption is that the police officers abuse their official roles to carry them out. Thus, although all cases of burglary or theft committed by police officers fall under the broad category of police misconduct or deviance, only cases in which police officers abused or misused their office or official position to commit the act qualify as police corruption (see, e.g., Goldstein, 1975, pp. 3–4). For example, if police officers who arrested drug dealers used knowledge obtained from the arrest about the remote location where the drug dealers keep their drug supplies (outside the police agency's jurisdiction) to steal the drugs from that location, the act (burglary) should be classified as police corruption. By contrast, if off-duty police officers stole a

---

1. Examples of nondistortive corruption discussed in the text and listed in Table 2.1 can be identified in some European and Asian countries, for example, where issuance of licenses, permits, and passports traditionally has been entrusted to the police (that is, to the Ministry of the Interior). By contrast, in the United States such tasks are not handled by the police.

Table 2.1 Gain-Motivated Actions and Omissions and the Corrupt Outcome

	Action	Omission
Distortive corruption (Officer did something he or she was not supposed to do; did not do something he or she was supposed to do)	Revealed an undercover operation to a drug dealer To meet arrest quotas, arrested a willing scapegoat provided for by a restaurant owner Issued a permit to an unqualified applicant	Did not arrest a citizen caught violating the law Did not issue a ticket to a traffic offender Did not issue a license to a qualified applicant
Nondistortive corruption (Officer did something he or she was supposed to do; did not do something he or she was not supposed to do)	Efficiently issued a passport or liquor license to a qualified applicant	Did not require additional unnecessary documentation from a qualified applicant

TV set from a house (based on information obtained through cousins who are not police officers), the act should not be classified as police corruption, even though it was committed in the jurisdiction of their police agency.

Agreement

Although the agreement between the citizen and the police officer may be an *important* factor in corruption control, it is not a *necessary* element of police corruption. The agreement itself can be explicit or implicit (a police officer knows or should have known that the payment is provided in return for the service provided or service to be provided) and can include both distortive and nondistortive corruption. The key issue, however, is the voluntariness with which citizens participate in the transaction: This voluntary element in an agreement may be challenged in some cases. Corrupt practices range from those on the completely voluntary side of the scale (e.g., a citizen offers a bribe for nondistortive corruption) toward more questionable ones (e.g., a police officer demands a bribe once a citizen has been caught violating the law) to those that are obviously not voluntary (e.g., a payment extorted through the use of force, threat to use force, or abuse of discretion).

A citizen who bribes a police officer to expedite a liquor license application and a citizen who bribes a police officer to avoid a traffic ticket both agree with the transaction and perceive that they are better off as a consequence of that transaction. In both cases there was a quid pro quo agreement between the police officer and the citizen.[2] Although the voluntariness of the citizen's bribe-giving action in the first case, an instance of nondistortive corruption, is beyond dispute, the actual voluntariness of the second citizen's action may be questioned. Because in an instance of distortive corruption a police officer chooses one line of conduct instead of another (which would be more harmful to the citizen, either in monetary terms or in terms of reputation), there is overt pressure on the citizen to comply with the request (if initially made by the police officer). Refusal to participate induces the risk of experiencing the harmful effects of proper police conduct and perhaps even the exaggerated effects resulting from retaliatory misuse of authority.

Despite the fact that corruption and excessive force have traditionally been separated in the literature, primarily as a consequence of the ostensibly differing motivations, descriptions provided by various independent commissions (see, e.g., Knapp Commission, 1972, p. 91; Mollen Commission, 1994, p. 4; Pennsylvania Crime Commission, 1974, p. 225) and descriptions of court cases (see, e.g., Buder, 1982; Miller, 1999; Neuffer & Freedenthal, 1989) clearly indicate that the modus operandi of corruption can be the use of force, the threat to use force, or the abuse of an official position. For example, the Pennsylvania Crime Commission, which investigated allegations of corruption in the Philadelphia Police Department and reported similar findings in terms of the extent of corruption, wrote,

> Some Philadelphia policemen have extorted money and narcotics from drug offenders to avoid arrests; they have solicited and accepted bribes. . . . The most common form of narcotics related police corruption is the so-called "shakedown," where an officer receives money, drugs, or other payment in lieu of

---

2. However, when the Hobbs Statute (18 U.S.C. 1951) is used to prosecute for extortion, prosecutors need not prove quid pro quo; it suffices to prove that the police officer received money because of his office (Jarrett, 1988, p. 213).

an arrest of a drug offender. If the "arrangement" is initiated by the suspect, it is a plain case of bribery; if the officer suggests it, he is committing the crime of extortion in addition to ignoring his law enforcement duties. (1974, pp. 225, 227)

The Knapp Commission uncovered extortion as well: "Police officers have been involved in activities such as extortion of money and/or narcotics from narcotics violators in order to avoid arrests; they have accepted bribes; they have sold narcotics" (1972, p. 91). Although the Knapp Commission and the Pennsylvania Crime Commission reported extortive behavior of police officers three decades ago, including gain-motivated use of force in the definition of corruption may be even more crucial today. The Mollen Commission concluded that the nature of corruption in New York City has changed and become more aggressive.

> While the systematic and institutionalized bribery schemes that plagued the Department a generation ago no longer exist, the prevalent forms of police corruption today exhibit an even more invidious and violent character: police officers assisting and profiting from drug traffickers, committing larceny, burglary, and robbery, conducting warrantless searches and seizures, committing perjury and falsifying statements, and brutally assaulting citizens. This corruption is characterized by abuse and extortion, rather than by accommodation—principally through bribery—typical of traditional police corruption. (1994, p. 4)

In addition to the scenarios in which the agreement is highly questionable because of the force used or threatened, there are also those in which there was no agreement at all—scenarios in which police officers obtain valuables (i.e., "personal gain") without the permission of the owners and without the use of force against the citizen at all. Given the nature of their work, police officers are often first on the scene of a crime or accident, and they have numerous opportunities to obtain illegal personal gain by stealing property. Therefore, the owners may not be aware that their property has been stolen because they may not be at home or may be intoxicated, injured, or unconscious. The modus operandi of these crimes may vary with time; the Pennsylvania Crime Commission and the Knapp Commission described predominantly *passively* opportunistic forms (using unexpected opportunities that presented themselves), whereas the more recent forms detected by, among others, the Mollen Commission in the 1990s may be characterized as predominantly *active and planned* activities with an active search for a target. Another example illustrates this point: corrupt police officers in Miami, known as the River Cops, "started by stealing drugs from the motorists stopped for traffic violations and worked their way up to major rip-offs" (Dombrink, 1994, p. 66).

Timing of the Payment

The payment could be negotiated or received before or after the corrupt act. Should the behavior be classified as corrupt regardless of when the payment was negotiated or made? Does it matter whether the payment was negotiated before or after the corrupt act?

Certainly, the payment made *before* the action is performed should be covered by the definition of corruption. Cases in which the police officer made an arrangement and received payment *after* performing the action in question are more controversial. If the police officer engaged in distortive corruption and was later paid for it (as might be the case with repeat players, for example, the police officer did not arrest a known drug dealer caught with drugs on him on several occasions and the drug dealer paid after several such incidents took place), the behavior should be classified as police corruption. This behavior may be as serious as the corrupt behavior characterized by the agreement made and payment provided before the police officer's action. The only actual difference is whether the agreement was made before or after the activity took place.

The most controversial case is when police officers performed their official duties exactly as they were supposed to (e.g., arrested a known felon, or protected an important person at a dinner engagement) and received a monetary reward from the citizen afterward (without having a prior agreement). Despite the fact that most other professionals and service providers are allowed to accept tokens of customers' satisfaction (e.g., tips, gratuities) for the quality of the legitimate service provided, police officers are not allowed to do so, nor should they be. The logic behind this choice is simple: To attain unbiased and nondiscriminatory enforcement of laws (and/or other functions in the fulfillment of the police role), the government should be the only source of police officers' income. If individuals or groups pay for their services instead of, or in addition to, the government, the explicit or implicit expectation formed by the paying citizens (and possibly others) is that the recipient police officers will provide more favorable (i.e., more lenient, more efficient) treatment at some future time.

The United States is an example of a country that prohibits the mere acceptance of payment with the knowledge that it was offered for the official action before or after the act was performed (18 U.S.C. Section 201), regardless of whether the payment had an impact on the decision (i.e., distortive versus nondistortive corruption). Section 201 recognizes two possibilities: the payment that has influence on the official act (payment "to influence an official act") and the payment that does not require the official to be influenced by it in order to fulfill the *actus reus* (payment "for or because of any official act performed or to be performed"; Title 18 U.S.C. § 201). The District of Columbia Court of Appeals elaborated on the difference between a bribe (Section 201(b)) and illegal gratuity (Section 201(c)) in *United States v. Brewster* (1974):

> The bribery section makes necessary an explicit quid pro quo which need not exist if only an illegal gratuity is involved; the briber is the mover or producer of the official act, but the official act for which the gratuity is given might have been done without the gratuity, although the gratuity was produced because of the official act.

In addition to the differences in terms of severity of punishment (15 versus 2 years of imprisonment), bribes and gratuities differ in two other aspects: (1) "a former public official can receive a gratuity but not a bribe; and (2) a bribe can be paid to someone other than the public official, while the gratuity must go directly to the public official" (Weingarten, 1988, p. 63).

Gain

TYPE OF GAIN Traditionally, reasoning about corruption is focused on monetary gain or gain that has monetary value, as is demonstrated by most cases of police corruption reported to the investigators, tried by the courts, and broadcast by the media.

> In Freemansburg, Pennsylvania, District Attorney John Morganelli charged Police Chief Robert Nichols and Officer James Attinello with bribery and obstruction of justice for reportedly accepting a $600 bribe to drop drunken driving charges. (Heidorn, 1994, p. B6)

> A police officer and his former partner pleaded guilty on Monday to charges that they demanded payoffs from drug dealers using a bodega near a Brooklyn housing project. (*New York Times*, 1995)

> A New York City police officer was arrested yesterday after he accepted $2,200 from an undercover investigator posing as a drug dealer who needed an escort to deliver $100,000 in drug profits. (*New York Times*, 1993)

> A 7-year officer was charged with stealing money in three searches at the homes of suspected criminals. (Torpy, 1996)

> Sorrentino, 53, agreed Monday to resign and pay a $200 fine in exchange for pleading guilty to stealing the bootleg videocassettes from a police evidence room and returning them to Super Kmart for a $350 refund. (Viviano & Kaempffer, 1999)

> Authorities have accused Smith of stealing at least 5 kilograms of cocaine from a police evidence room from 1995 to 1998. (Main, 2003, p. 12)

Money and material goods seem to be the dominant motives for corruption. The price tag for services may be readily available (e.g., servicing a police officer's private car free of charge by a car mechanic in exchange for a kickback), but it may be more convoluted to price some other services (e.g., not issuing a speeding ticket to the sergeant's niece in exchange for favorable treatment by the sergeant or a favorable letter of recommendation for the next promotion cycle). Money or monetary gain may be a key factor in the definition of corruption, but, as a newspaper article can reveal ("Two city police officers were convicted last night of receiving a bribe, having a 16-year-old Queens girl perform oral sex on them, in return for not arresting her on minor drug and vehicular traffic charges" [*New York Times*, 1986]), the bribe need not be only money or something of monetary value.

Excluding from the definition of police corruption corrupt behavior that is motivated and/or rewarded by nonmaterial gain would omit a potentially severe form of corrupt behavior, one that has serious consequences on the internal relationships within a police agency. Corrupt behavior along the lines of fixing a sergeant's niece's speeding ticket in exchange for future favorable treatment or promotion has evident potential for strengthening the code of silence, developing a police culture that approves of and supports misconduct, and undermining official authority in the police agency.

VALUE OF GAIN Any discussion about the value of gain as an element of the definition of police corruption necessarily leads toward the examination of value boundaries. In particular, should an amount of money or value of a gift given or service provided be specified as a boundary above which any monetary gift, other gift, or service should be regarded as a bribe? Although the value of individual, small gifts—half-price meals, free cups of coffee, and free admissions to performances—may not be large, if such gifts are given on a regular basis (see Ruiz & Bono, 2004, p. 51) and to a large number of police officers (see Pennsylvania Crime Commission, 1974, p. 263), their value can be substantial.

Gifts provided to police officers, regardless of value, have a potential impact on the officers' use of discretion in the future; consequently, the acceptance of such gifts represents corrupt behavior. It is difficult to believe, as Kania (1988, p. 47) argues, that police officers should be able to make a proper decision as to whether to accept a gift each and every time; despite the lack of obvious signs, not all gifts are merely sincere gratitude for a job well done, particularly when they are provided before the job is done. In fact, the commission reports show a number of instances in which the purpose of the bribe was expressly to influence the outcome (Knapp Commission, 1972; Mollen Commission, 1994; Pennsylvania Crime Commission, 1974). Even if the gifts are given after the job is performed, there is still a possibility that the gifts will have an impact on the future behavior of police officers, especially if the gifts are given on a *regular* basis, if they are given simply because the recipient is a police officer, or if the value of the gratuity is disproportionate to the service performed (Coleman, 2004, pp. 39–41).

Gratuities disrupt the equitable delivery of police services (see, e.g., Coleman, 2004; Ruiz & Bono, 2004). Yet, the police should not only perform their duties impartially but also should maintain the appearance of impartiality (see Coleman, 2004, p. 41). Prohibiting acceptance of smaller gifts might be supported by the public at large because, as survey results suggest (see, e.g., Prenzler & MacKay, 1995; Sigler & Dees, 1988), even acceptance of petty gifts undermines public confidence in the impartiality of the police. A natural consequence of this viewpoint is the acceptance of the "except-for-your-paycheck-there-is-no-such-thing-as-a-clean-buck" disciplinary philosophy (cited in Goldstein, 1975, p. 3). A reason for such exclusive disciplinary philosophy may lie in the "slippery slope argument," according to which the acceptance of gratuities leads to corruption.[3] Once police officers cross this line by accepting a free cup of coffee or a free meal, they already are engaged in police misconduct; it is henceforth increasingly easier to continue with illegal behavior than it would have been, had that first step not been taken. According to Sherman, in the process of gradually increased involvement in misconduct (from petty to serious), a police officer develops a career as a grafter and, as an integral part of that process, the police officer will have "worked up a ladder of increasing self-perceived social harm of offenses, neutralizing any moral objection to the (crime-specific) graft at each rung of the ladder—each stage of his moral career" (1974, pp. 199–200).

Although small gifts, free drinks, and half-price meals seem to be peripheral to the corruption problem, the importance of the chief's decision regarding the legitimacy of gifts of small value exceeds their value. If the chief and the administration set the boundary to the lowest possible level by forbidding the acceptance of *any* gifts, they are creating a scenario riddled with potential difficulties. First, such a solution leads toward substantially increased costs of control, which is highly problematic in view of limited personnel and resources. As a practical matter, police administrators may not be

3. For a discussion about the slippery slope argument, see, for example, Coleman, 2004; Kleinig, 1996; Sherman, 1974.

able (or willing) to enforce this rule earnestly and systematically, which in turn sends a message to the troops that the administration is not serious about rules in general and rules about corruption in particular. At the same time, such a practice inevitably undermines the administration's own authority. For example, in a highly publicized case in the 1970s, Assistant Chief Inspector Seedman of the NYPD treated his spouse and another couple to a dinner in an expensive restaurant. The restaurant picked up the bill, and Seedman left only a large tip. Police Commissioner Murphy, who prior to this occurrence took a strong stance against free meals and even free cups of coffee, generated considerable animosity among police officers by commenting that Seedman did not commit any serious wrongdoing. Such inconsistent actions not only provide fertile ground for the growth of police officers' cynicism and the decline of trust and confidence in the leadership but also lead to a further increase of hostility and undermine the administration's ability to handle the troops.

> It was difficult for police officers to take seriously Commissioner Murphy's stern warnings against receiving "any buck but a pay check," when they apparently did not apply to one of the Commissioner's top aides. Several police officers commented wryly to Commission investigators that at last a meaningful guideline had been established for free meals: "It's okay—up to $84.30" [the amount of Seedman's bill]. (Knapp Commission, 1972, p. 171)

Second, the prohibition of this widespread practice compels the majority of otherwise honest police officers to participate in the code of silence to a greater degree than they otherwise would have. That is, they become more willing to tolerate serious misconduct (including serious corruption) by other police officers because they have broken rules themselves.

Third, a complete prohibition of small gifts, free drinks, half-price meals, and discounts may be especially problematic in the cultures in which such gifts are an accepted part of everyday life. A chief may have a difficult task to convince police officers, especially those engaged in community policing, why they need to have higher ethical standards than teachers and postal employees.

Thus, although accepting any gifts, regardless of their value, should be regarded as police corruption, the reality is that enforcement of such official rules is at the very least challenging. At the same time, it is equally challenging to draw the line by determining a particular amount that would separate ethical from corrupt behavior and to find an acceptable justification for that line.

RECIPIENT OF GAIN Although a substantial portion of corrupt activities revolves around personal gain obtained through payment made directly to the officer or through another police officer, it is easy to contemplate a case of corruption in which the recipient of the gain is a third person. For example, when a police officer decides not to issue a speeding ticket to a member of the admission board of the private school to which his daughter has applied, the primary beneficiary of the whole transaction is not the police officer but his daughter. Are cases in which the beneficiary is a third person substantially different from the cases in which the recipient is the police officer?

Regardless of whether the gain is realized by the police officer or by some third person, it is a personal gain. The only crucial difference between the behavior that results in direct gain for the police officer and the behavior that results in gain for someone else is merely the recipient of that gain, and other elements in *mens rea* and *actus reus* remain identical. Of course, there may be differences from the control perspective: Behavior resulting in gain for a third party may be more challenging to trace, and it may be harder to establish a connection between the action and the gain.

From the perspective of developing a definition of police corruption, a pertinent question is whether there are instances of corrupt behavior in which the police department (rather than an individual officer) would reap the benefits, which in turn would render "personal gain" an insufficient characterization of gain in the definition of police corruption and instead call for the inclusion of "personal or organizational gain." The majority of authors in the literature on police corruption discuss the gain resulting from corrupt activity in terms of explicit personal gain (see, e.g., Goldstein, 1975, p. 3; McCormack & Ward, 1987, pp. 29, 35; Meyer, 1976, pp. 54–55; Moore, 1997, p. 46) or implied personal gain (i.e., the definition does not include the specification that the act has a motive of personal gain, but it is implicit in the definition that the gain, whether money and/or goods, is a result of the police officer's individual misconduct and is to be used personally by the police officer; see, e.g., Barker & Wells, 1981, p. 30; Lundman, 1980, p. 5; Mc-Mullan, 1961, p. 184; Misner, 1975, p. 46; Roebuck & Barker, 1974, p. 424). Although several authors have expanded their definitions to cover potential organizational gain (see, e.g., Bracey, 1995, p. 545; Carter, 1990, p. 88), organizational gain does not appear to have been defined precisely in the literature. I am defining it as any gain that contributes toward the realization of the legitimate organizational goals as prescribed by the agency (e.g., fight crime, solve community problems).

Two situations are plausible. First, a police officer who engages in corrupt activities (e.g., acceptance of free meals from restaurant owners) that do not contradict legitimate organizational goals (e.g., develop better relationships with the community) and, in fact, to a degree help achieve those organizational goals will probably expect to reap both personal gains (a free meal by restaurant owners, promotion)[4] and organizational gains (develop better relationships with the community). Second, a police officer who engages in activities that constitute a serious violation of official duties (e.g., violation of a defendant's constitutional rights during interrogation, perjury, planting of evidence, fabrication of evidence) to achieve a legitimate goal of the police department (e.g., law enforcement) may not expect any personal gain for himself. Police officers attempt to rationalize this noble-cause corruption in the following way (Moore, 1997, p. 63):

> I did something wrong, but justice demanded it, not tolerated it but demanded it, because I could put the guy away who otherwise wouldn't be successfully prosecuted. I, the police officer, wouldn't gain personally from it; I didn't get anything from it. I only acted for the community in the community sense of justice to accomplish this goal.

Should noble-cause corruption—perjury, falsification of evidence, planting of evidence, and similar activities conducted for the purpose of achieving a legitimate organizational goal when legitimate means are perceived to be

---

4. Unlike Bracey (1995, p. 545), who considers promotion, peer support, and approval of superiors as organizational goals, I evaluate these gains as of a personal nature and clearly beneficial for the individual police officer.

too limiting[5]—be covered by the definition? As long as activities are at least motivated in significant part by the achievement of personal gain, they should be covered. If the police officer is not motivated in significant part by the achievement of personal gain, but only by organizational goals, then such behavior should not be covered by the definition. In other words, the definition of corruption that relies on the achievement of personal gain should not be expanded to include the achievement of an organizational gain as well.

The two key arguments supporting this choice are related to substantial differences in causes and control efforts. First, unlike regular corruption (primarily motivated by the achievement of personal gain for the police officer), noble-cause corruption may be a result of strong pressures by the community and the department's war-on-crime philosophy (and tacit approval of such practices). As a consequence, efforts to control noble-cause corruption may focus on changing the boundaries of acceptable conduct among the police officers and their police departments, modifying public opinion, and changing the rules that govern the conduct of police officers during investigations.

Second, although a violation of someone's constitutional rights, motivated with the purpose of achieving "higher justice," may have very serious and troublesome consequences, the abuse of official duty in order to achieve personal gain involves something inherently more deviant and would prob-

---

5. However, I consider control of noble-cause corruption to be crucial in the development of a police agency of high integrity. Because of the pressures from, and the approval of, the community to enforce certain laws regardless of the costs, pressures from the police department to satisfy such requests by imposing arrest quotas, and the police officers' widely shared beliefs that it impossible to win the war on crime without bending the rules (Sparrow, Moore, & Kennedy, 1990, p. 51) and that the protection of constitutional rights is an obstacle that limits the realization of substantive goals (instead of sharing the perception that the protection of constitutional rights *is* one of the substantive goals), the overwhelming majority of police officers are tempted to engage in morally dirty means in order to achieve morally right ends. Therefore, it is not surprising that a substantial number of police officers resolve the Dirty Harry dilemma (Klockars, 1991) in the wrong way and, consequently, end up entangled in the web of the code of silence, unable to report more serious misconduct performed for less noble reasons, and often feeling that the sanctity of the law has been violated.

ably be viewed as substantially more serious. Indeed, the public usually reacts with outrage to instances of known classical, distortive corruption, and the resulting scandal, if certain circumstances are conducive (see Sherman, 1978), may lead to a thorough examination of the whole police department by outside investigators or independent commissions (e.g., Knapp Commission, 1972; Mollen Commission, 1994; Pennsylvania Crime Commission, 1974). The key to such a reaction is that the behavior—regardless of whether it is committing perjury to fix a case, planting evidence on a drug dealer to extort a payment, or falsifying evidence to put the blame on a person not guilty of a crime in exchange for a payment from the guilty person—violates the basic trust society has bestowed on police officers.

On the other hand, the same community would probably disapprove much less of actions done for the sole purpose of helping the community. The police officers are perceived to protect "the nice community" ("us") against the criminals ("them") and the costs—for example, violating the defendants' constitutional rights—are acceptable as long as the goal is achieved and "us" does not succumb to "them." Police officers are allowed to use deceptive tactics, violate constitutional rights, entrap, and use similar questionable means, as long as none of these actions involves "us." Not only society but also police officers seem to be more tolerant of noble-cause corruption than of regular corruption. For example, a study by Barker, Friery, and Carter (1994) suggests that police officers differentiate between the lies told with the purpose of achieving the police mission or goal and the lies told in support of illegitimate goals (to further the act of corruption or to protect the officer from organizational discipline, civil, and/or criminal responsibility). Although 60% of the surveyed police officers approved of deviant lies told for legitimate purposes, only 8% approved of deviant lies told for illegitimate purposes (Barker et al., 1994, pp. 155, 161).

The underlying assumption in noble-cause corruption is that official organizational goals are the ones being enforced. An interesting situation emerges when the unofficial and actual organizational goals enforced by the agency are not necessarily those prescribed in the organizational charter. In departments troubled with pervasive organized corruption, the dominant coalition running the agency can substitute the official organizational goals of the agency (e.g., enforce the law, fight crime) with the informal organizational goals (e.g., attainment of personal wealth by the members of the department; see Sherman, 1978, p. 5). In the cases in which one of the un-official organizational goals is related to corruption, a police officer engaged in corrupt activities will achieve personal gains, both material (direct benefit from a corrupt transaction) and nonmaterial (support from peers and super-visors), as well as organizational gains (e.g., increase it's members' personal wealth). However, because such corrupt activity would result in an organizational gain and, at the same time, personal gain for the police officers involved, it is not necessary to expand the definition to require that the gain be either personal *or* organizational. Rather, the requirement of personal gain is sufficient to characterize virtually all instances of police corruption in the police departments that feature increased personal wealth for their members as one of their unofficial organizational goals.

Conclusion

The definition developed in this chapter allows boundaries to be drawn between police corruption and ethical behavior, on the one hand, and between police corruption and other forms of police misconduct on the other hand. When police officers do something they were supposed to do or do not do something they were not supposed to do, they have engaged in proper conduct. When their primary motivation for such behavior is achieving illegal personal gain, they have abused their office and engaged in corruption.

By contrast, when police officers do something they were not supposed to do or do not do something they were supposed to do, their behavior has crossed from the proper or ethical into questionable conduct, regardless of the motivation. Table 2.2 helps differentiate between police corruption and other forms of police misconduct. First, whenever there is misuse of position and illegal gain is achieved as a result of an agreement between the police officer and the corrupter, such as the traffic violator who pays money to a police officer in order to not receive a ticket, the police officer engaged in corruption. Second, when there is misuse of position and the police officer achieves illegal gain as a result of the use of excessive force or a threat to use force, such as a prostitute forced by an explicit threat of force to pay the police officer for protection and thereby avoid arrest, the police officer has also engaged in corruption. Finally, whenever there is misuse of position and

Table 2.2 Plausible Combinations of Key Factors Determining Corruption

Misuse of position	Agreement	Use of force	Illegal gain	Classification
+	+	−	+	Police corruption
+	+	−	−	Other forms of police misconduct
+	−	+	+	Police corruption
+	−	+	−	Use of excessive force
+	−	−	+	Police corruption
+	−	−	−	Other forms of police misconduct

illegal gain is achieved as a result of neither an agreement between the police officer and the corrupter nor the use of force or threat of force, but rather through theft or burglary, the police officer has also engaged in corruption.

When there is a misuse of position that is not motivated by personal gain, the police officer has engaged in other forms of police misconduct, but not police corruption. Three scenarios are possible. First, if there is a misuse of position, no illegal gain was attempted or achieved, and the police officer used excessive force, such activity is typically called *police brutality* or *use of excessive force*. Second, if there is a misuse of position, there is no illegal gain, but there is an agreement between a citizen and a police officer, such activity should be classified as other forms of *police misconduct,* but not as police corruption. Third, if there is a misuse of position, but no illegal gain, agreement, or use of excessive force, such activities — sleeping on duty, "milking" calls — should be classified as other forms of *police misconduct.*

At this point, police corruption is defined and the criteria are established to set police corruption apart from other forms of police misconduct. The next logical step in pursuit of corruption control is to determine the size and nature of the problem. In particular, information should be gathered to gauge how widespread corruption is, what forms are more prevalent, and what the level of organization is. If the information collected at that stage is used as a benchmark for future comparisons, the impact and success of present and future control efforts can be measured as the need arises. The next chapter discusses these measurement issues.

3

Measuring Police Corruption

Despite the need to know the exact nature and extent of corruption, the measurement of police corruption—or, for that matter, any other type of corruption—is surprisingly underdeveloped.

> Unlike for most other crimes, there are no official data on the corruption rate. How much corruption is there? Is the rate rising or falling? Is there more corruption now than in previous decades? Is there more corruption in one city than another, in one government department than another? Has corruption decreased after passage of a law, announcement of an investigation or arrests, or implementation of managerial reforms? Corruption cannot be estimated by examining the *Uniform Crime Reports* or the National Crime Victimization Survey. Thus, it cannot be determined whether any particular anticorruption strategy or spate of strategies is working. We are data deprived. (Jacobs, 1999, p. 76)

This chapter is based on my paper "To Serve and Collect: Measuring Police Corruption," *Journal of Criminal Law and Criminology, 93*, 593–650 (2003).

The situation regarding the measurement of police corruption, however, may not be as bleak. Although there are no nationwide statistics of the official rates of corruption, there are several sources or methods used to estimate the extent of corruption: surveys, experiments, sociological field studies, independent commissions, internal agency records, and the records of the criminal justice system. Whereas each is inherently limited, it may capture a snapshot of the extent and nature of corruption in a particular jurisdiction, at a particular time, and limited to the respondents participating in the study.

The existing data sources yield substantial variation in their estimates of how widespread corruption seems to be, from just a few police officers engaging in serious corruption (e.g., Baueris, 1997; Knowles, 1996; Martin, 1994) to at least 20% or most of the police officers being corrupt (e.g., Barker, 1983; Knapp Commission, 1972; Reiss, 1971). The differences stem from an interplay between the method used, stage in the criminal justice funnel, sample collected, behavior defined as corrupt, wording of the questions, the time frame of the study, and, last but not least, differences in the actual extent of corruption. Unfortunately, without resorting to triangulation (i.e., the use of several methods), it is virtually impossible to determine the degree to which the measurements generated by the applications of a particular method match reality.

In this chapter I systematically examine the results of existing studies on the extent and nature of police corruption and analyze in detail the pros and cons of various methods of corruption measurement. I organize the discussion in the chapter around methods; it begins with surveys and experiments, continues with sociological field studies and independent commissions, and finishes with internal agency records and records from the criminal justice system. Discussion about each method is accompanied by a review of studies that used the method.

The Actual Extent and Nature of Corruption

The practical impossibility of measuring the true extent and nature of corruption, on the one hand, and the pressing need to obtain relevant information, on the other hand, have prompted social scientists to use various methods of estimation: surveys, experiments, case studies, interviews, and observations.

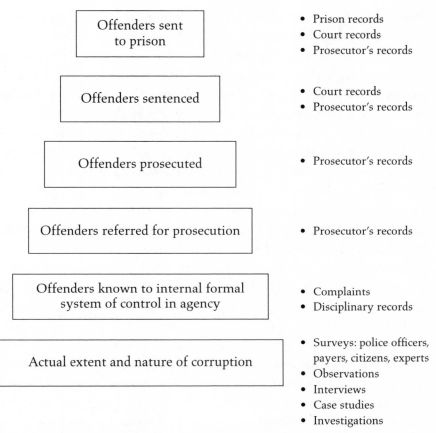

Figure 3.1 The Funnel of Police Corruption and the Data Collection Methods

Figure 3.1 illustrates the levels at which corruption could be measured, starting with the estimates of the actual extent and nature of corruption (bottom) and ending with offenders sent to prison (top). As suggested by the figure, in the real world the number of cases and offenders decreases as they move through the formal systems—both the internal formal system of control in the agency and the criminal justice system.

Surveys

Surveys of police officers that ask them to report their own or their fellow officers' involvement in corruption are rare because the validity of such studies is questionable and the difficulty in gaining adequate access is often

insurmountable. Police officers have no incentive to report their own corrupt activities and thus risk losing their jobs or facing prosecution in criminal court. Moreover, because they are accepted members of the police subculture and are likely to share and support the code of silence, they have no
motive to report fellow officers' misconduct that is protected by the code,
even if guaranteed confidentiality or anonymity by the researchers.

A few surveys of police officers prompted them to report the extent to
which other police officers in their agencies engaged in corruption. As a consequence of the sampling techniques and the methodology used, their results are at best limited to the populations from these agencies and cannot
be extended to other agencies. The most comprehensive is a survey by Mc-
Cormack and Fishman, who tested the degrees of "police improbity" (behavior that can be considered unethical, dishonest, or corrupt) in six police
agencies (Fishman, 1978). In a sample of 755 police officers, even in the clean-
est of the six departments, a certain percentage of fellow police officers,
though smaller than in the departments perceived to be corrupt, engaged in
such behavior (Fishman, 1978, pp. 28–33).

In an attempt to lessen the impact of the code of silence on the willingness to share the true extent and nature of police corruption, Barker asked
only police rookies to report on the frequency of corruption in their agencies (Barker, 1983). Between 9% and 31% of the police officers said that at
least *some* of their fellow officers engaged in serious corruption (e.g., a case
fix, opportunistic thefts, shakedowns, direct criminal activities, or internal
corruption; Barker, 1983, p. 34).

Several other studies tackled the challenge of measuring police corruption by asking police officers about the frequency of corruption in their agencies. The police officers in a Department of Justice–sponsored, three-state
study of police behavior were asked to report what types of misconduct they
had most commonly observed during the past year and during their whole
careers (Martin, 1994, p. 32). A few respondents (fewer than 1% in both Illinois and Ohio; Martin, 1994, p. 33; Knowles, 1996) said that they had seen a
police officer accepting a bribe, stealing property, or purchasing stolen merchandise in the past year. By contrast, more than 80% of the police officers
(81% in Illinois and 87% in Ohio; Martin, 1994, p. 33; Knowles, 1996) said
that they had seen a police officer accepting free coffee or food from a restaurant in the past year—behavior evaluated to be among the least serious.

Another potential source of information about police corruption is *citizens*. Some of them have experienced corruption as participants; some have observed corrupt transactions by others. Analyzing aggregate answers about their own involvement in corruption (as bribe givers) and especially, if possible, comparing them with the police officers' answers could be informative. However, a problem with public surveys is that attitudes can be based on actual experiences or on general opinions about the police (which can be shaped in significant part by the media or a few highly publicized cases).[1] Furthermore, both citizens and police officers may try to project the "socially acceptable" image instead of revealing their actual opinion, if doing so would clash with what they perceive is expected of them.

The results of public surveys provide quite a divergent picture about police corruption, depending on the respondents and the time and place in question. The reported attitudes, thought to be highly correlated with true corruption rates, have an implausibly wide range: Fewer than 2% of White citizens nationwide in the 1960s perceived that most of the police were corrupt (President's Commission on Law Enforcement and Administration of Justice, 1967b, p. 148); 22% of respondents in "Bay City," California, in the 1970s thought that there was at least some bribery of the police (Crawford, 1973, p. 170); and 93% of New Yorkers in the 1990s perceived corruption to be widespread (Krauss, 1994).

Similar surveys across the world suggest that perceptions about the extent and nature of corruption differ widely. One of the public opinion surveys with the widest application is the Gallup International 50th Anniversary Survey (Gallup International, 1996). People in 37 countries were asked to estimate the extent of corruption of various public officials, including the police. While only approximately one third of the respondents in Western European countries and in Israel reported that police corruption was widespread, that opinion was shared by more than two thirds of the respondents in Eastern European countries, Asian countries, and Latin American countries. Moreover, these regional averages hide substantial differences within each region. For example, the one third of the respondents in the 14 West-

1. See Lasley (1994, p. 245), for a discussion about the impact of one highly publicized case (the Rodney King case) on the attitudes of the public in South Central Los Angeles.

ern European countries who described police corruption as widespread included percentages as low as 9% in Finland and 11% in Denmark to as high as 61% in Turkey and 73% in Belgium (Gallup International, 1996).

Another approach in survey methodology is to ask citizens to report incidents in which they offered a bribe to police officers or were victims of corruption. Interestingly, although the U.S. Department of Justice's Bureau of Justice Statistics (e.g., 1994) has been conducting the National Crime Victimization Survey on representative samples of U.S. households for more than a quarter of a century, none of the questions ask about victimization by the police or participation in corruption.

Despite its origin and primary orientation toward questions related to the respondents' victimization, another survey, the International Crime Victim Survey (ICVS Working Group, 1997; van Dijk, 1997), has a few self-report questions related to corruption. In addition to asking respondents whether they were asked to pay a bribe last year, the questionnaire also inquires about the governmental agency that requested the bribe (van Dijk, 1997). Combining the answers to these two questions provides a crude estimate of the percentage of the respondents who said that they were asked to pay a bribe to a police officer last year in a particular country.

Three sweeps of the survey have been conducted over 8 years, resulting in 93 surveys in 56 countries with a total of 136,464 interviews (ICVS Working Group, 1997). The most important lesson from the results of the most recent, third ICVS from 1996 and 1997 is the variation in the extent and nature of corruption (Table 3.1). Of the respondents who said that they were asked to pay a bribe last year, those who said they were asked to pay a bribe by a police officer varied from almost 0% in the Netherlands, Switzerland, France, and Sweden to 71% in Argentina. The fact that 100% of the respondents from the United States who said that they were asked to pay a bribe had paid it to a police officer is an excellent example of the problems with the validity of survey methodology. Because the behavior studied appears to be quite rare in the United States (1.5% of the respondents said that they were asked to pay a bribe), further breakdown of bribe payers (by the type of officials to whom the bribe was paid) relies upon a very small number of respondents. Therefore, assuming that the sampling procedures produced representative samples, the countries in which a higher percentage of the respondents said that they bribed a police officer exhibit a smaller margin of error and thus probably have a higher degree of internal validity. When percentages are very small, however, the question of to what degree these percentages generalize to the entire population remains unanswered.

A cross-country comparison of the percentage of respondents who said that they were asked to pay a bribe to a police officer (out of all the respondents) also yields interesting implications about the perceived extent of police corruption across the world. A very small percentage of the respondents from Western Europe (1% or less) reported being asked to pay a bribe to the police, but the percentages are dramatically higher (between 10% and 20%) in some Eastern European, Asian, and Latin American countries. Broadly speaking, countries with reputations in the international business community for corruption, as indicated by a low score on the 1999 Corruption Perception Index (Transparency International, 1999) in Table 3.1, also have a higher percentage of the respondents who said that they were asked to pay a bribe to a police officer last year.

Of course, these rates capture only those corruption incidents initiated by a governmental employee; by their mission, victimization surveys of the general population cannot capture corruption incidents initiated by citizens. Aside from the Gallup International and the ICVS, most of the existing citizen surveys are conducted locally, usually in a particular city. For example, of 116 people surveyed in Reno, Nevada, approximately half said that "if [they] run a small business, such as a coffee shop or a movie theater, [they would] offer police officers free gifts such as coffee, meals, or free movie tickets" (Sigler & Dees, 1988, p. 18). Moreover, one third of those who said that they would offer gratuities to the police also said (explicitly) that they would expect special favors in return (p. 18).

Recent surveys also suggest that the public still has a relatively positive opinion about police performance, while, at the same time, it perceives that police officers engage in corruption. For example, a survey of citizens in Philadelphia in 1987 revealed very positive ratings of the police service, despite the fact that one third of the respondents thought that police officers often took bribes (Moore, 1997, p. 62). On the eve of a corruption scandal in New York in 1994, a *New York Times* poll showed that, while 93% of the citizens perceived that corruption is either "widespread" or at best "limited," approximately half estimated that the police are doing a "good" or "excellent" job (Krauss, 1994). Another poll conducted in June 1994 indicated that the

Table 3.1 The 1996–1997 ICVS Survey Results on Bribe Payment

	Percentage of respondents asked to pay a bribe last year	Percentage of respondents asked to pay a bribe to a police officer	Percentage of respondents asked to pay a bribe to a police officer last year	CPI 1999 score
Canada	0.8	20.0	0.16	9.2
United States	1.5	100.0	1.50	7.5
Austria	1.5	50.0	0.75	7.6
England and Wales	0.2	0.0	0.00	8.6
France	2.9	0.0	0.00	6.6
Malta	4.3	21.7	0.93	-
Netherlands	0.7	0.0	0.00	9.0
Scotland	0.6	0.0	0.00	8.6
Sweden	0.4	0.0	0.00	9.4
Switzerland	0.0	0.0	0.00	8.9
Albania	14.0	8.1	1.13	2.3
Belarus	12.5	20.9	2.61	3.4
Bulgaria	19.3	54.6	10.54	3.3
Croatia	15.4	44.4	6.84	2.7
Estonia	4.0	36.4	1.46	5.7
Georgia	30.6	30.0	9.18	2.3
Hungary	3.9	34.5	1.35	5.2
Latvia	14.3	12.1	1.73	3.4
Lithuania	13.4	32.6	4.37	3.8
Macedonia	7.7	9.3	0.72	3.3
Poland	7.7	30.7	2.36	4.2
Romania	12.0	13.6	1.63	3.3
Russia	19.0	52.1	9.90	2.4
Slovak Rep.	14.1	32.7	4.61	3.7
Slovenia	1.5	18.8	0.28	6.0
Ukraine	12.9	25.6	3.30	2.6
Yugoslavia	17.5	40.5	7.09	2.0

Table 3.1 Continued

	Percentage of respondents asked to pay a bribe last year	Percentage of respondents asked to pay a bribe to a police officer	Percentage of respondents asked to pay a bribe to a police officer last year	CPI 1999 score
India	23.3	18.3	4.26	2.9
Indonesia	33.8	52.2	17.64	1.7
Kyrgyz Rep.	21.8	24.0	5.23	2.2
Mongolia	5.2	14.8	0.77	4.3
Philippines	4.6	34.0	1.56	3.6
Botswana	3.0	21.1	0.63	6.1
South Africa	7.6	46.1	3.50	5.0
Zimbabwe	7.2	30.6	2.20	4.1
Argentina	29.3	71.4	20.92	3.0
Bolivia	26.0	43.6	11.34	2.5
Brazil	17.9	49.7	8.90	4.1
Costa Rica	11.1	23.7	2.63	5.1
Paraguay	13.8	28.4	3.92	2.0
Average	12.6	36.4	4.59	

public had a more positive opinion about the average police officer than about the NYPD as a whole. Although 73% of the citizens stated that the average police officer was "very honest" or "somewhat honest," 43% of the citizens perceived that there was widespread corruption in the department (cited in Giuliani & Bratton, 1995, p. 22).

Surveys extending over various types of respondents (e.g., police officers, members of the public, and citizens who participate in corrupt activities) potentially increase the validity of the results.[2] For example, surveys of

2. For example, by assessing the extent of corruption on the basis of only the answers provided by the officials in the Cambodian public official survey, one would conclude that corruption is not widespread (unofficial payments received in 10% or less of their contacts).

households, businesses, and public officials within the same country developed by the World Bank Institute serve as diagnostic tools to provide guidance on the extent, nature, causes, and costs of corruption in a particular country and contribute toward measuring the effects of subsequent anticorruption reforms. According to the World Bank, these surveys "are being or have been implemented with assistance from the World Bank in numerous countries including Albania, Georgia, Latvia, Russia, Slovakia, Ecuador, Bolivia, Paraguay, Thailand, Benin, Ghana, [Cambodia], and Nigeria" (World Bank, 2000a, p. iii).

The reports currently available reveal some interesting patterns. Specifically, the results from the Latvian study indicate that citizens evaluated the traffic police as among the most corrupt agencies in the country (Anderson, 1998, p. 16). Similarly, businesses and public officials alike said the traffic police most frequently extracted bribes when given the opportunity (33% of the time according to the enterprises and 39% of the time according to the households; Anderson, 1998, p. 13). Regular police were perceived as somewhat more honest (Anderson, 1998, p. 16) and did not top the list of Latvian agencies most likely to extract bribes. According to the samples of households, enterprises, and public officials, the Cambodian police ("law enforcement and securities") were also ranked as among the country's more corrupt government agencies (World Bank, 2000a, p. 13). Although the frequency of contact with the police was moderate (11–15% of the households and 16–31% of the enterprises had a contact last year), the frequency of bribes, given the opportunity (i.e., contact), was reportedly extremely high (80% or more), among the highest of all Cambodian government institutions (World Bank, 2000a, p. 15). Similarly, Albanian enterprises estimated that the traffic police were among the most corrupt governmental agencies (World Bank, 2000b). In particular, "more than 50 percent of the firms that use the fol-

---

However, the addition of the Cambodian household survey and the enterprise survey clearly shows that public officials underestimated the extent of corruption. In particular, citizens and enterprises estimated that bribes occur in at least 40% of the contacts (53% for urban households, 43% for rural households, 44% for domestic enterprises, and 68% for foreign enterprises; World Bank, 2000a, p. 14).

lowing governmental services [one of which is the traffic police] admit that bribes are a part of the delivery of the service" (World Bank, 2000b).

Experiments

Scientific experiments are rather rare in the study of police corruption. To some extent, random integrity tests conducted by a police agency's internal system of control tend to resemble experiments. They are conducted with the intent to induce the same change for each participant in the "experiment" and to allow the "researchers" to observe the subject's reaction. Unlike questionnaires, which utilize hypothetical cases, random integrity tests are conducted in real-life conditions. In fact, they are usually modeled to resemble previous realistic cases as closely as possible.

However, proactive investigations are *not* scientific experiments; whereas experiments are controlled scientific explorations of human behavior, proactive investigations are fact-finding missions. Moreover, proactive investigations always have serious real-world consequences: Police officers may be fired if they take money from the wallet planted in the back seat of their cruisers.

In the aftermath of the Mollen Commission, the NYPD's efforts to deal with corruption included random integrity tests (see Giuliani & Bratton, 1995, p. 41). Instead of targeting specific officers under suspicion, these tests are "targeted on the basis of statistical information, indicating precincts and tours of duty that might be prone to corruption" (p. 42). Noted former New York City Mayor Giuliani and former NYPD Commissioner Bratton,

> IAB will significantly expand its random and targeted integrity testing programs over the next year. The goal is to conduct sufficient integrity tests to establish a statistically valid sample of police corruption in the NYPD. There will be tests conducted on all tours and in all precincts. The base line established by integrity testing will be compared with integrity testing results in future years as one means to gauge the rise or decline of corrupt activity among police officers. (1995, p. 42)

Because most formal internal systems of control typically perform reactive functions[3] and, moreover, publicizing information regarding corruption is often not aligned with the incentives provided to various members of the agency, the data describing the use of proactive investigations are generally unavailable.

Nevertheless, I provide two examples. Both integrity checks were conducted by the NYPD shortly after the respective scandals and investigations by independent commissions. Bahn reported the results of an internal study conducted by the NYPD in the 1970s in which the department found that "illicit police activity is a minor occurrence, but that its frequency is high enough (twelve percent to thirty-four percent in one series of *experiments*) to warrant attention" (emphasis added; cited in Bahn, 1975, pp. 30–31). The integrity tests in the NYPD in the 1990s did not uncover many instances of the forms of police corruption the department tested for. Of 1,222 police officers tested in 1995, only 11 (0.9%) failed the test and were dismissed. A similar percentage failed tests in 1996 (24 of 1,320) (Baueris, 1997, p. 12). The degree to which these rates represent actual rates of corruption depends largely on how well the integrity tests were designed, the way they were performed, and the systems used to select the targets.

Sociological Field Studies

Typical sociological studies of the police are case studies. They focus on one or a few police agencies and use a combination of methods, such as observation, interviews, and analyses of documents. The potential strength of such studies is that checking and rechecking the information obtained via

3. For example, the Knapp Commission and the Pennsylvania Crime Commission investigated police agencies characterized by widespread corruption. Both commissions reported that the departments they investigated (the NYPD and the Philadelphia Police Department, respectively) did not utilize proactive techniques to control corruption (Knapp Commission, 1972, p. 208; Pennsylvania Crime Commission, 1974, p. 483). The Mollen Commission (1994, p. 11), which investigated the NYPD two decades after the Knapp Commission, pointed out that the NYPD pursued a decidedly proactive approach in pursuit of every investigation of organized and continuing criminal activity (e.g., drug dealing and prostitution) *except* police corruption.

various methods increases the internal validity; an inherent limitation is that the depth of the information required limits the number of agencies covered by each study.

Although very few of the existing studies focused primarily on police corruption, a substantial number of police studies or studies of communities in general contain community descriptions and depict the relationship between the police and the community members (see, e.g., Chambliss, 1971; Gardiner, 1970; Whyte, 1955). Consequently, they often report the extent of police corruption.

After 7 years of interviews and nonparticipant observation, Chambliss described "Rainfall West" as a corrupt city dominated by a complex web of relationships among legitimate businesses, illegitimate organizations, local journalists, politicians, and criminal justice personnel. Similar to the nature and extent of corruption described by the Knapp Commission (1972) and the Pennsylvania Crime Commission (1974), the corruption among police officers in Rainfall West was widespread and highly organized, and it extended to the supervisors as well (Chambliss, 1971, p. 1162). The nature of corruption Chambliss described included typical "pads"—protection of illegal activities (e.g., gambling, prostitution) for a fee and protection of legitimate businesses (e.g., restaurants, cabarets, tow-truck operators) violating the law.

Some studies focus on individual police agencies (see, e.g., Reiss, 1971; Sherman, 1978; Skolnick, 1966; Wilson, 1968). A study involving nonparticipant observation and interviews usually provides a very detailed picture of a particular agency, but it also tends to be a snapshot, taken at one period of time and thus not suited to follow dynamic changes in the agency. The findings are limited to the agencies included in the study, as the President's Commission on Law Enforcement and the Administration of Justice pointed out.

> The Commission's limited studies afford no basis for general conclusions as to the exact extent of police dishonesty or the degree to which political corruption affects police service today. But these studies have shown that even in some of the departments where the integrity of top administrators is unquestioned, instances of illegal and unethical conduct are a continuing problem—particularly in slum areas . . . [t]he

> most common [violations] are improper influence; acceptance
> of gratuities or bribes in exchange for nonenforcement of
> laws, . . . the "fixing" of traffic tickets; minor thefts; and occa-
> sional burglaries. (1967b, p. 208)

Originating as one of the studies submitted to the President's Commission,
Reiss's (1971) study of the police role continued beyond that report to eventually become one of the major studies of the police. Its observations of sit-
uational transactions and distributions of surveys to citizens and police
officers provided valuable insight into the police role. Although he reported
some variation across the three selected research sites (Boston, Chicago, and
Washington, DC), Reiss (1971, p. 156) suggested that the rate of crimes
committed by the police officers across the three cities tended to be of the
same magnitude.

> Counting all felonies and misdemeanors, except assaults on
> citizens, the rate of criminal violation for officers observed
> committing one or more violations was 23.7 in City X, 21.9 in
> City Y, and 16.5 in City Z per 100 officers. . . . Excluding any
> participation in syndicated crime, roughly 1 in 5 officers was
> observed in criminal violation of the law. There was some
> variation among the three cities in the crime patterns of po-
> lice officers and the rate of violation.

The crime rate per 100 police officers, collected from observations, self-
reports, and allegations of misconduct by other police officers, is a compos-
ite score of various types of crimes. Because Reiss provides a list of rates by
the type of crime or dishonest practice, the rate of corrupt criminal violations can be estimated from the overall rate (Reiss, 1971, pp. 157–159). According to the definition of police corruption provided in chapter 2, offenses
that can be classified as corruption include "officer accepts money to alter
testimony report," "officer receives money/merchandise on return of stolen
property," "officer takes money/property from deviants," "traffic violation:
officer gives no citation and gets money," "officer takes merchandise from
burglarized establishment," and "officer receives money or merchandise
from a business." It follows that the rates of serious, criminal corrupt beha-

vior per 100 police officers (calculated from the data provided by Reiss, 1971, pp. 157–159) were 22.8 in City X, 20.5 in City Y, and 15.6 in City Z.

Among the less serious forms of corruption, acceptance of gratuities and free meals was common; even while the observers were present, 31% of the observed police officers did not pay for their meals (Reiss, 1971, pp. 161–162). Self-reported surveys of citizens led toward a similar conclusion.

> Within each of the cities, one-third (31 percent) of all busi-nessmen in wholesale or retail trade or business and repair services in the high-crime areas openly acknowledged favors to policemen. Of those giving favors, 43 percent said they gave free merchandise, food or services to all policemen; the reminder did so at a discount. (Reiss, 1971, p. 161)

The only comprehensive study of police corruption was conducted by Sherman in the 1970s. The focus of the study was not police corruption per se but the role scandal plays in the control of police corruption and the re-form of police agencies. However, Sherman tried to "measure changes over time in the quantity of *organization* generally present in corrupt activities" (1978, p. 188) in four cities (New York City; Oakland, CA; Newburgh, NY; and "Central City") and, therefore, did not focus on measuring the extent and nature of police corruption.

Independent Commissions

A typical independent commission is formed as a reaction to a scandal that developed in the aftermath of public revelations of corruption allegations (see, e.g., Fitzgerald Commission, 1989; Knapp Commission, 1972; Mollen Commission, 1994; Pennsylvania Crime Commission, 1974). Its general pur-poses are to determine the extent and nature of corruption, find factors con-tributing to corruption in an agency, and propose solutions for reform. The task of determining the extent of corruption is performed through corrup-tion investigation, "one of the most difficult investigative tasks which any law enforcement agency can undertake" (Pennsylvania Crime Commission, 1974, p. 31).

The work of independent commissions can be particularly challenging in the absence of political independence. For example, the Pennsylvania Crime

Commission (1974, p. 754) was "never able to remove the taint of conducting a politically inspired investigation." Depending on the level of political independence, support from the city and the police administrator, and the actual functions assigned, commissions can vary greatly in their views about police corruption, available resources,[4] and the energy devoted to the search for patterns of corruption (instead of individual cases), all of which can affect their ability to measure corruption.

The commission's legal authority is an instrumental factor in overcoming the power of the code of silence and the reluctance of police officers to provide information. Indeed, when a commission has the power to grant immunity and issue subpoenas, it is more likely to get a more accurate estimate of the extent and nature of the corruption problem. However, as the Pennsylvania Crime Commission (1974, p. 741) discovered, having the power to subpoena witnesses and grant them immunity is not in itself a guarantee of obtaining truthful testimony (see also Fitzgerald Commission, 1989, p. 78).

The ability to enlist experienced police investigators contributes to the accuracy of corruption estimates. Using former police officers from the agency under investigation is beneficial because it provides internal information about corruption in the agency. However, it is at the same time sensitive because relationships may still exist between such potential investigators and current members of the agency (see, e.g., Pennsylvania Crime Commission, 1974, p. 763).

A common feature of the independent commissions described in Table 3.2—the three most influential commissions investigating allegations of corruption in the United States over the last three decades (Knapp Commission, 1972; Mollen Commission, 1994; Pennsylvania Crime Commission, 1974) and the two most recent Australian commissions (Fitzgerald Commission, 1989; Royal Commission, 1997)—is that, just like sociologi-

4. Unlike the Knapp Commission, which had support from the city, the Pennsylvania Crime Commission experienced serious problems. In fact, even the constitutionality of its formation was challenged. The problems later presented themselves by way of difficulties in finding investigators, administrative support, and equipment (see Pennsylvania Crime Commission, 1974, p. 762).

cal field studies, they relied on a combination of data collection techniques and multiple sources. Unlike sociologists, who focus on particular subject matter and do not persist if they are denied access to a particular location, independent commissions typically have the advantage of the legal authority necessary to gain access to at least some data sources.

The extent and nature of corruption reported by various commissions varied from widespread corruption of the "grass-eating" variety (characterized by police officers "simply accept[ing] the payoffs that the happenstance of police work throw their way" [Knapp Commission, 1972, p. 4]) in the 1970s (which included supervisors as well; Knapp Commission, 1972, p. 44; Pennsylvania Crime Commission, 1974) to the less frequent forms of corruption of the "meat-eating" variety (characterized by police officers "aggressively misus[ing] their police powers for personal gain" [Knapp Commission, 1972, p. 4]) discovered by the Mollen Commission in the 1990s. Of course, because they are formed as an outcome of a scandal resulting from public allegations and revelations of corruption, independent commissions are bound to find corruption ranging somewhere from the isolated or widespread but less serious forms to the more concentrated and more serious forms.

How accurately do these findings match the actual extent and nature of corruption? The use of extensive resources and the reliance on multiple data sources (e.g., police officers, citizens, and informers) increase the probability that the commission's findings are reasonably close estimates. However, the corruption picture painted by an independent commission does not necessarily mean that the commission "got it right." The findings may differ from reality by a substantial margin for a variety of reasons: political pressures, limited resources and authority, ability and skill to "turn" police officers, reliance on a particular definition of corruption, and the search for behavior of a predetermined type. For example, the Knapp Commission reported finding predominantly widespread corruption of the "grass eater" variety. David Burnham, a well-known Pulitzer Prize–winning journalist whose article in the *New York Times* triggered the establishment of the Knapp Commission, argues that the Knapp Commission was just beginning to discover more serious and violent forms of corruption when the necessary funds for its operation were depleted (Kutnjak Ivković, 2000).

Table 3.2 Data Sources and Methods of Investigation by the Independent Commissions

Sources	Methods of investigation	Findings	Comments
Knapp Commission (1972), New York, USA			
Police officers (POs)	Examination of documents: financial disclosures, documents from businesses, complaints to Knapp, corruption cases, records of known criminals, PD's documents	Organized and systematic corruption; PD-wide phenomenon (p. 64)	For a long time, no power to compel testimony by granting immunity
Turned police officers		Receiving money from gamblers, narcotics violators, legitimate businesses, tow truck companies, grocery store owners, prostitutes	No power to subpoena witnesses
Businesses			Lawsuits
Citizens			
Informants	Surveys: construction industry, store owners	Information from many sources → enough repetitive similarity to indicate such patterns existed (p. 43)	
Underworld figures			
PD's documents	Interviews: police officers, business community, people in illegal activities, citizens in high-crime areas, others	"Grass eaters" dominant; "meat eaters" relatively rare	
Case files		"Pads" v. "scores"	
Complaints	Field investigation: surveillance, informants, undercover agents, turned police officers (5)	Supervisors involved (own pads)	
POs' financial disclosures			
Field investigations	Private hearings: 183 witnesses		
	Public hearings: 9 + 5 days and 15 witnesses		
Investigations by others	Investigation by others		

Pennsylvania Crime Commission (1974), Philadelphia, USA

Sources	Methods	Findings	Obstacles
Police officers	Examination of documents: difficulty with access	Corruption ongoing, systematic, and occurring at all levels of the PD	POs and citizens did not cooperate; willing to take chances "downtown"
Turned police officers	Interviews: police officers, business community, people in illegal activities, citizens in high-crime areas	More than 400 POs involved	Problems with access, equipment, manpower
Businesses	Direct observation	Receiving money from liquor violators, gambling, prostitution, narcotics, business notes, car stops	8 separate lawsuits against the PD
Citizens	Field investigation: surveillance, informants, undercover agents, turned police officers (2)	"Clean" v. "dirty" graft (p. 13)	Constitutionality challenged
Informants	Public hearings: 5 weeks scheduled, but canceled	Extortion, planting of evidence, perjury	No cooperation from mayor and commissioner
Underworld		Supervisors involved	
PD's documents			
Field investigations			

Mollen Commission (1994), New York, USA

Sources	Methods	Findings	Obstacles
Mollen staff	Examination of documents: PD's documents, corruption cases, corruption complaints	Minor corruption ("grass eaters") no longer systematic	Support from the mayor and commissioner
PD's documents	Observation: own knowledge, own investigations	"Meat eaters"—serious corruption—rule rather than exception among corrupt POs	
Corruption case files	Interviews: police officers; FBI, DEA, IRS; people in illegal activities; citizens in high-crime areas; defense attorneys; DAs & U.S. Atty's offices	"Crew corruption"—groups of POs that protect and assist each other in criminal activities (p. 17); more akin to street gangs: small, flexible, fast-moving; corruption pacts	
Corruption complaints			
Police officers			
Turned police officers			
DA's office			

(continued on next page)

Table 3.2 Continued

Sources	Methods of investigation	Findings	Comments
Mollen Commission (1994), New York, USA			
U.S. Atty's office	Field investigation: surveillance, informants, undercover agents, turned police officers (6)	Patterns of corruption: theft, robbery, drug dealing, extortion, shakedowns, perjury, falsifications	Focus not exclusively on corruption
FBI, DEA, IRS			Noble-cause corruption included
Defense attorneys	Private hearings: over 100 witnesses	Police violence and brutality	The role of the public exposure, humiliation by the surveillance evidence, and possible prison sentences helped obtain cooperation (p. 40)
Citizens	Public hearings: a few weeks	Supervisors: willful blindness	
Criminals			
Field investigations			
Royal Commission into the New South Wales Police Service (1997), New South Wales, Australia			
Police officers	Examination of documents: corruption complaints, corruption cases	A state of *systemic* and *entrenched* corruption, (p. 33); well organized	
Turned police officers			
Citizens	Observation: own knowledge, own investigations	A very serious state of corruption that is widespread and of long-standing origin (p. 101)	
Criminals	Interviews: police officers, citizens, people in illegal activities	Types: thefts of drugs and money; shakedowns of drug dealers; regular payments from drug dealers, gambling operations, clubs, and brothels; assaults	
Complaints			
Corruption cases	Surveys: police officers	"Process corruption" (noble-cause corruption)	
Field investigations	Field investigation: surveillance, informants, undercover agents, turned police officers, citizens		
	Public hearings: 327 days and over 800 witnesses	Supervisors: unaware/unwilling to respond	

Fitzgerald Commission (1989), Queensland, Australia

Journalists	Interviews: police officers, citizens, people in illegal activities	Corruption by prostitutes, gambling, drug dealers	Openness: apart for one brief setting, all the evidence heard in public restored public confidence, increased confidence in the commission, encouraged public cooperation, asserted that nobody is beyond scrutiny, avoided rumors
Police officers		Thefts	
Turned police officers	Field investigation: surveillance, informants, undercover agents, turned police officers	Focus more on identifying the organizational and policing structures and work practices that make corruption possible than on mapping corruption in a particular area (Finnane, 1990, p. 167)	Perceived as one of the most successful commissions (Finnane, 1990, p. 159)
Citizens			
Criminals	Public hearings: 238 days and 300 witnesses		
Field investigations			

Internal Agency Records

In the early 1990s, the NYPD (a department of 35,000 police officers) recorded approximately 2,700 allegations of police corruption annually (Mollen Commission, 1994, p. 87), decreasing to 1,922 in 1995 and 1,726 in 1996 (Baueris, 1997, p. 12). Are these numbers—amounting to the annual rate of 5 to 8 allegations per 100 police officers—an accurate estimate of the actual level of corruption in the NYPD in the late 1990s?

A short answer is no, not really. One way of checking is to compare the rates of complaints with the expected rates of complaints based on the findings of a reliable source. For example, at the time when the Knapp Commission reported widespread corruption in the NYPD, the results of Cohen's study of corruption complaints recorded by the NYPD (1972, p. 66) suggested fewer than 1 corruption complaint per 100 police officers annually.

This discrepancy clearly illustrates the perils of relying on complaints to measure the extent of corruption. Indeed, although even the Knapp Commission's rates can easily be *underestimates* of the true extent and nature of corruption (see Kutnjak Ivković, 2000), the results of Cohen's analysis (based on the agency's disciplinary records) clearly are even further removed from it. As Simpson concluded (1977, p. 57), Cohen's "figures apparently bear little relationship to reality as indicators of the true level of corrupt activity."

A more current comparison of the findings of the Mollen Commission and the NYPD's allegations of corruption also indicates such discrepancies. The Mollen Commission identified the presence of small groups of police officers engaging in aggressive forms of corruption and crime in general. The rate of 8 corruption complaints per 100 officers per year[5] may not seem exceedingly low for a department in which the majority of police officers are not corrupt, but, because of the nature of their crimes, the corrupt officers probably generated a lot of corruption-related activities, and the resulting rates should have been considerably higher. The cover-up activities carried

5. The Mollen Commission reported that there were approximately 2,700 corruption allegations filed with the department each year (1994, p. 87). Because the NYPD had approximately 35,000 officers at the time, that yields the rate of 8 complaints per 100 officers.

out by the department, also discovered by the Mollen Commission (1994), lend support to this hypothesis.

Another set of very strong reasons for the official internal rates being at best problematic estimates of the actual corruption is related to the agency's procedures and practices for handling complaints. When citizens decide to file a complaint, even several complaints against the same police officer (sometimes as many as 17, as was the case for one corrupt police officer in New York; Mollen Commission, 1994, p. 14), the police agency can ignore the complaint and the problem completely and consequently discourage the less persistent complainants (see chapter 4). Even when agencies investigate complaints, they substantiate just a small percentage of all complaints (typically below 20%)[6] and thus (un)intentionally discourage further complaints.

Criminal Justice System

The next level at which estimates about the extent and nature of police corruption seemingly can be made is the formal criminal justice system: cases referred for prosecution, cases prosecuted, cases with convictions, and cases with imprisonment (see Figure 3.1). Cases are referred for prosecution from various sources: individual citizens, federal investigative agencies (e.g., FBI, IRS), local investigators (e.g., local police), other governmental institutions (e.g., INS), and independent commissions.

One of the most prolific sources of referrals for the police corruption cases should be the police agencies themselves. Yet, in addition to the possibly heavy workload of the internal affairs investigators (see, e.g., Mollen Commission, 1994, pp. 85–86), a typical police agency not only has no motives to investigate complaints diligently and refer cases of police officers who violated penal statutes to the prosecutors but also actually has incentives to conceal cases. For example, the Mollen Commission (1994, pp. 96–98) re-

---

6. Starting from the President's Commission in 1967, which reported that 50% of the departments sustained 10% of complaints or less (President's Commission on Law Enforcement and Administration of Justice, 1967b, p. 196), a common finding across the studies is that the rate of sustained complaints is generally between 0% and 25% (Pate & Hamilton, 1991, p. 42). The national average of sustained cases across municipal law enforcement agencies is only 10.1% (Pate & Fridell, 1993, pp. 113–120).

ported finding 230 cases of serious corruption concealed by the NYPD. Similarly, prosecutors—the recipients of information concerning police corruption—also can be less than eager to prosecute police corruption cases. State prosecutors and local prosecutors both develop long-term relationships with police officers because they need to rely on their help in the investigation of *all* criminal cases. Moreover, local prosecutors may have to rely on the local police to investigate their fellow officers.

Although there are no nationwide data available for *state* prosecutions of police corruption cases, some limited, jurisdiction-specific data on state prosecutions exist. It is possible to assess the degree to which the data on prosecutions are similar to the data about the actual extent of corruption by comparing the available data on state prosecutions with the findings of independent commissions about the nature and extent of corruption (under the assumption that the findings of independent commissions were in the worst case only underestimates of the actual corruption).

Both the Knapp Commission (1972) and the Pennsylvania Crime Commission (1974) found corruption of a grass-eating variety to be widespread in the 1970s. The Knapp Commission (1972, p. 252) reported that, in the $4\frac{1}{2}$ years they focused on, prosecutors had initiated only 136 cases involving 218 defendants (approximately 30 cases per year) from the NYPD, the largest police department in the country. Among the 137 completed cases, one third were dismissed or acquitted, while two thirds (91) either pleaded guilty or were convicted (p. 252). In the end, only 20% of police officers sentenced for corruption received a prison sentence of more than 1 year (p. 252).

Similarly, the Pennsylvania Crime Commission (1974, p. 52) reported that, in the department of 8,303 sworn police officers in 1974, there were only 43 arrests for police corruption over a 6-year period (1968–1973), an average of 7 per year (p. 446). Moreover, almost half of the arrests were made in 1 year, as a consequence of a statement by one police officer (p. 446). Of the sentenced police officers, 40% were sentenced to prison (p. 446).

These numbers clearly indicate that prosecution and conviction rates as estimates of the extent of corruption are the tip of the iceberg. Although, as the Mollen Commission (1994, p. 150) found for New York, both federal and local prosecutors may have become less reluctant to prosecute corrupt police officers in the 1990s, a few studies indicate that state and federal prosecutors can have different levels of activity. Upon engaging in a case study of the Philadelphia Police Department, Dombrink concluded that "compared with federal prosecutors, whose record of thirty-one convictions in thirty-six federal district court cases between 1983 and 1986 was formidable, local prosecutors had fared less well historically with police corruption cases in the Pennsylvania courts" (1988, p. 211).

Another example, documented in Malec and Gardiner's study (1987) of corruption cases prosecuted in Chicago and Cook County from 1970 to April 1987, indicated that the prosecutions for police corruption in Chicago were quite rare. In a police department with more than 10,000 sworn police officers, there were 114 police corruption cases over a period of 16 years. Furthermore, the number of all corruption cases (not just police corruption cases) prosecuted by federal prosecutors exceeded the number of corruption cases prosecuted by local prosecutors by a factor of 10 (412 and 40, respectively; Malec & Gardiner, 1987, p. 273).

One might imagine that obtaining data about police corruption at the federal level would be possible because of the central role the Department of Justice plays. Unfortunately, although questionnaires are sent each year to the U.S. Attorneys' Offices to inquire about the data on indictments, convictions, and prosecutions awaiting trial, the available data refer to the federal cases involving abuse of public office for *all* government employees (U.S. Department of Justice, 1995). Although the classification "abuse of public office" includes crimes such as bribery, extortion, and conflict of interest (U.S. Department of Justice, 1995) and, consequently, broadly fits the definition of corruption from chapter 2, it is not possible to identify only the cases involving police officers. Although indictments and convictions increased since the 1970s (Figure 3.2), the overall numbers of between 1,000 and 1,500 indictments and around 1,000 convictions in recent years tend to be rather small in comparison with the millions of government employees (Burnham, 1996, p. 327).

Because the Department of Justice does not separate cases in the database according to the defendant's occupation, police officers cannot be separated from other public officials indicted for corruption. However, the Department of Justice divides all corruption cases into seven program categories, only one of which potentially refers to police corruption: federal law enforcement

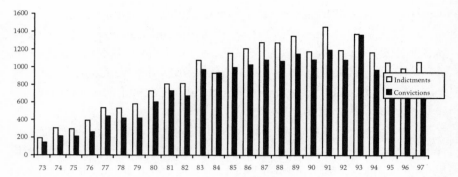

Figure 3.2 Persons Indicted for Offenses Involving Abuse of Public Office (Sourcebook of Criminal Justice Statistics Online)

corruption.[7] The data from Transactional Records Access Clearinghouse indicate that the FBI, the Customs Service, and the IRS made the most frequent referrals for prosecution (Kutnjak Ivković, 2000). Most of the referrals were subsequently declined (Table 3.3) because of "weak or insufficient evidence" or "lack of evidence of criminal intent" or because "no federal offense was evident." Most of the defendants pleaded guilty (89.8%). The overall conviction rate for the cases prosecuted was above 66% (Table 3.3; Figure 3.3). Furthermore, approximately half of the people sentenced were sentenced to a prison term (Table 3.3).

Because there were so few prosecutions for law enforcement corruption each year (35 to 70, depending on the year), these prosecutions or convictions cannot be used for estimates of the actual extent of corruption. In fact, one of the primary functions of these data can be to provide information about the degree of interest the Department of Justice has in corruption issues.

The disadvantages of the use of official data to estimate actual corruption are even more explicit when official corruption data is compared across countries (Table 3.4). The UN World Surveys of Crime Trends and Criminal Justice Systems provide official data (crimes known to the police, prosecutions, convictions, sentences) for various types of crimes, one of which is

---

7. Although two additional program categories, state and local, may be of interest, I excluded them from the analysis because the data available at both the state and local level pertain to all public corruption, and it is not possible to isolate only the cases of police corruption.

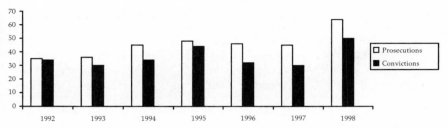

Figure 3.3 Persons Indicted and Convicted for Federal Law Enforcement Corruption
(Transactional Records Access Clearinghouse)

classified as "bribery/corruption." One of the serious challenges of cross-
cultural research is that the definitions of corrupt behavior differ across legal
systems. Furthermore, "bribery/corruption" includes corrupt behavior by all
public officials, not just police officers, as well as corrupt behavior by the public. Therefore, the rates for corruption reported in these surveys are over-
estimates of the rates that would relate only to police corruption.

The data in Table 3.4 suggest that, when the official records are stan-
dardized across countries (as rates per 100,000 inhabitants), the rates varied
from close to 0 to as many as 24 cases per 100,000 inhabitants. Does a higher
rate indicate that the corruption is more widespread, that the law enforce-

Table 3.3 Prosecutions and Convictions for Federal Law Enforcement Corruption

	1992	1993	1994	1995	1996	1997	1998
Referrals for prosecution	86	156	148	131	137	400	186
Referrals disposed of	110	116	162	134	114	346	131
Referrals declined	75	80	117	86	68	301	67
% of disposed referrals	68.2	69	72.2	64.2	59.6	87	51.1
Referrals into prosecution	35	36	45	48	46	45	64
% of disposed referrals	31.8	31	27.8	35.8	40.4	13	48.9
Convicted after prosecution	34	30	34	44	32	30	50
% of prosecutions	97.1	83.3	75.6	91.7	69.6	66.7	78.1
% of disposed referrals	30.9	25.9	21	32.8	28.1	8.7	38.2
Sentenced to prison	16	20	19	19	19	17	28
% of convictions	47.1	66.7	55.9	43.2	59.4	56.7	56

Source: The Transactional Records Access Clearinghouse.

Table 3.4 Official Data on Corruption From the Fifth U.N. World Survey

Country	Recorded cases in 1990	Recorded cases per 100,000 inhabitants	Country	Recorded cases in 1990	Recorded cases per 100,000 inhabitants
Austria	252	3.27	Kyrgyzstan	12	0.27
Azerbaijan	32	0.45	Latvia	35	1.31
Belarus	199	1.94	Lithuania	23	0.62
Bermuda	0	0	Madagascar	10	0.09
Bulgaria	224	2.49	Malta	1	0.28
Chile	30	0.23	Mauritius	10	0.98
Colombia	17	0.05	Morocco	62	0.25
Costa Rica	30	1.07	Qatar	1	0.21
Croatia	56	1.17	Rep. of Korea	204	0.48
Denmark	11	0.21	Rep. of Macedonia	21	1.04
Ecuador	4	0.04	Rep. of Moldova	19	0.44
Egypt	55	0.1	Romania	1,364	5.88
Estonia	3	0.19	Russian Fed.	2,691	1.81
Georgia	80	1.47	Scotland	7	0.14
Greece	59	0.58	Singapore	343	12.68
Hong Kong	1,365	23.93	Slovakia	176	3.32
Hungary	385	3.71	Slovenia	52	2.6
India	1,831	0.22	Sudan	782	3.04
Indonesia	221	0.12	Syrian Arab Rep.	28	0.23
Israel	183	3.93	Turkey	94	0.17
Jamaica	15	0.62	Ukraine	999	1.93
Japan	190	0.15	Zambia	894	11.07
Jordan	29	0.68	Zimbabwe	371	3.96
Kazakhstan	202	1.21			

Countries for which there were no data are not listed in the table.

ment authorities are dealing with corruption more diligently, both, or something else? For example, among the countries with a rate higher than 1 per 100,000 inhabitants, there are countries with a reputation of being relatively clean of corruption (e.g., Austria, which has a high Corruption Perceptions Index score of 7.6). In such cases, it appears likely that the higher rate is the result of more extensive law enforcement activity. On the other hand, in some countries with a rate higher than 1 per 100,000 inhabitants (e.g., Bulgaria and Romania, both of which had a low Corruption Perceptions Index score of 3.3), the higher rate of officially recorded corruption probably indicates that the extent of corruption is wider. Unfortunately, we do not know to what extent this is true.

Conclusion

The first two steps in solving any problem are defining the problem and determining its extent and characteristics. The initial yet crucial steps in designing good control mechanisms for police corruption are no different: Once a subset of behaviors is chosen to be defined as corruption, the next step should be a thorough effort to measure it (and to continue measuring it). Obtaining accurate data about the extent and nature of corruption provides direction for the selection and utilization of appropriate control mechanisms and identifies problem areas that the control mechanisms should target. Subsequently, it also facilitates informed judgment about the effectiveness of the implemented mechanisms. In the absence of reasonably accurate estimates of the extent and nature of police corruption, control efforts are selected on the basis of their general attractiveness and political appeal, and their impact is evaluated almost solely on the basis of successful avoidance of future scandals and other political factors.

A logical source of information about police corruption is someone who knows about it, but all such people (for a variety of reasons) are apt to be predisposed not only to avoid reporting corruption but also to conceal it. Obtaining information from participants in the corrupt transaction leaves them vulnerable to internal discipline (including dismissal) and criminal punishment, as well as public disgrace. Obtaining information from the observers of participants exposes them to informal sanctioning for the violation of the code of silence. Thus, although the participants are the most valuable potential source of information because of their closeness to the activity, they usually are, at the same time, the most reluctant to discuss the topic. This simple paradox drives much of the reality of estimating the extent and nature of police corruption. It is an obvious and severe limitation. It is also a challenge, as the ostensible difficulty in securing the flow of information from the participants themselves creates the need for alternative (though considerably less precise) and often multiple data sources.

Despite its importance, measurement of the actual level of corruption is largely impossible, and the only pragmatic solution is to rely on estimates. Methods used to provide estimates include surveys, interviews, observations, experiments, and case studies. Each of them, regardless of how sophisticated it is in itself, is riddled with inherent problems. Indeed, relying on any single methodology of data collection exposes the resulting estimates to the possibility of severe error, which in turn renders the resulting estimates questionable at best. Setting aside the practical consideration of necessary resources for a moment, increasing the validity of the findings (that is, reducing the likely extent of estimation error) necessitates combining several methods and checking whether the findings they produced are similar or at least consistent.

Moreover, results of the existing studies providing estimates of corruption indicate that the state of police corruption differs across agencies and over time. The latter, of course, adds another level of difficulty, as it suggests that not only measuring but also updating the information may be crucial: The extent and nature of corruption are driven by a number of complex factors, many of which are idiosyncratic, and the snapshot taken in an agency today, even if extremely precise, may be at best a blurry image of the situation in the same agency in the near future.

4

Causes and Correlates
of Police Corruption

For a long time, the dominant explanation of police corruption relied on the characteristics of individual police officers. It was believed that police officers engaged in corruption because of their low moral values. Once their corrupt behavior became public knowledge, the administrators were quick to point to these police officers as "rotten apples." The remedy was to blame them, discipline them harshly (typically by firing them), and proclaim the agency to be otherwise clean.

Yet, by the 1970s there was a body of evidence, including the findings reported by independent commissions (e.g., Knapp Commission, 1972; Pennsylvania Crime Commission, 1974), showing that the issues uncovered in agencies with widespread corruption surpass the problems of a few corrupt police officers. Many deep organizational problems came to light, from inadequate hiring and lack of training in ethics, to relaxed supervision and troublesome investigations of corrupt behavior.

My premise is that police corruption cannot be explained with a narrow set of factors focusing, for example, on the moral values of individual police officers or on the enforcement of laws with no moral consensus. Rather, this chapter features a systematic and structurally rich exposition of the remarkably heterogeneous set of causes and correlates of police corruption and the complex relations among them. The presentation follows a broad classification of the causes and correlates into (1) individual factors, (2) organizational or agency-related factors, and (3) external or society-wide factors.

Individual Factors

If the environment created by a police agency and the society at large is very similar for all police officers in the agency, why do some police officers engage in serious misconduct, and others do not? In other words, why are there "true positivists," profoundly honest police officers like Frank Serpico (see the Knapp Commission, 1972), and "true negativists," profoundly corrupt police officers like Michael Dowd (see the Mollen Commission, 1994)?

Crime has been studied from many perspectives in the criminological literature, and all the resulting theoretical insights agree on a highly intuitive yet very important point: The propensity toward rule-breaking behavior is not dispersed equally in the population, and some individuals are more likely to become involved in such behavior than others. Put differently, neither Michael Dowd nor Frank Serpico was tabula rasa before joining the NYPD.

Propensity Toward Corruption

Everything else being equal, police officers who have a higher level of propensity toward corruption are more likely to act on it than police officers with lower levels of propensity toward corruption. Propensity toward corruption is not static; it is modified under the influence of the officer's personal and individual experiences (accumulated both before and since joining the agency). Through actions or failures to act, both society at large and the police agency as an organization have an impact on the police officer's propensity toward corruption as well.

Mechanisms that were insufficient to keep job applicants from engaging in law-violating behavior prior to applying—strong social bonds (Hirschi,

1969), lack of association with delinquent peers (Sutherland, Cressey, & Luckenbill, 1992), or access to legitimate means of achieving legitimate goals (see Cloward & Ohlin, 1960; Merton, 1938)—continue to affect applicants' behavior once they become police officers (even under the simple assumption that past behavior is the best predictor of future conduct). Applicants who previously engaged in serious law-violating behavior are more likely to engage in serious misconduct after becoming police officers (controlling for what the police agency and the wider environment are doing to control corruption). A review of research studies on predictors for applicants' future performance as police officers indicates that "biographical information about the past behavior of applicants [e.g., a greater number of convictions for more serious offenses, a short duration of prior jobs, being fired before] was the only type of selection criterion with substantial evidence that it predicted later job performance by police officer applicants" (Malouff & Schutte, 1986, pp. 175–177). Previous brushes with the law, regardless of whether they were officially recorded, and otherwise deviant lifestyles indicate more propensity toward rule-violating behavior in the past and suggest that the applicants, if given the opportunity to become police officers, would be more likely to engage in police corruption. The Mollen Commission provides strong support for this hypothesis: Officers who prior to becoming police officers committed a felony and were arrested (yet were hired despite the department's awareness of their criminal record) were three times more likely to be detected as corrupt than those without such records (Mollen Commission, 1994, p. 115).

Propensity toward corruption can be shaped by other prior experiences as well. Generally, rookies who are starting their police careers upon honorable discharge from the military[1] will likely behave somewhat differently than rookies who have had no prior experience in a military or a quasi-military

---

1. In the past, it was quite common for recruits to have a military background. For example, Watts conducted an analysis of the recruits to the St. Louis Police Department. In the study, which extended over five decades (1917–1969), he found that, although the proportion of recruits with previous military service by the time of appointment had changed over time (characterized by a sudden drop from 1925 to 1944 and an equally dramatic increase after 1944), the average proportion of recruits with previous military experience over the whole period was 55% (Watts, 1981, pp. 77, 95).

organization (assuming, of course, that organizational and societal variables are controlled for). In the words of the Mollen Commission, it is "not only because of what educational or military experience provides, but [also] because the successful completion of these endeavors itself reflects a discipline, character, and level of ability" (1994, p. 115).

Among the more experienced rookies, those coming straight out of military service are more likely to be used to the quasi-military bureaucracy of a police department and are probably more aware of the importance of joining the subculture shared by employees of the bureaucracy (see, e.g., McNamara, 1967, p. 203). Britz (1997) reported that individual characteristics of recruits, including their military experience, have a substantial impact on their level of socialization into police culture. As a group, therefore, recruits with prior military experience are likely to try harder to blend into the subculture of a particular police department—even if it is tolerant of corruption—than rookies without prior military experience.

Risk-Propensity Levels

Criminology literature usually views individuals as rational actors who compare the rewards and punishments of criminal behavior.

> At any given moment, a person can choose between committing a crime and not committing it. . . . The consequences of committing the crime consist of rewards . . . and punishments; the consequences of not committing the crime . . . also entail gains and losses. The larger the ratio of the net rewards of crime to the net rewards of noncrime, the greater the tendency to commit the crime. (Wilson & Herrnstein, 1985, p. 44)

Accordingly, the decision to engage in corrupt behavior is a consequence of the calculation of the costs and benefits of law-abiding behavior versus the costs and benefits of corrupt behavior. The costs of corrupt behavior include the cost of violating ethical principles plus the cost of punishment if caught (see Rose-Ackerman, 1978, p. 86). When the sum of the net benefits minus the costs of corrupt behavior exceeds the sum of the net benefits minus the costs of law-abiding behavior, the police officer will have a greater inclination to engage in corruption. Klitgaard (1988, p. 70) used a more formal way to express the calculation: "the bribe minus the moral costs minus [(the probability I am caught and punished) times (the penalty for being corrupt)] is greater than my pay plus the satisfaction I get from not being corrupt."

A crucial aspect of the calculation is the accurate estimation of the actual deterrent threat made by the administration of a police agency. Police officers who are able to estimate the deterrent threat accurately will be more successful in completing their overall calculations correctly (to the extent such calculations can be carried out at all).

Risk propensity can affect the accuracy of these calculations. Brockhaus (1980, p. 513) defines it as "the *perceived* probability of receiving the rewards associated with success of a proposed situation" (emphasis added). Prior life experience may affect a police officer's calculation of the certainty of punishment (i.e., the risk of engaging in corrupt behavior and the punishment itself). The inconsistent application or lack of enforcement of legal rules— be they school rules about tardiness or laws prohibiting underage drinking—by authority figures (e.g., school, local police agency) has a substantial impact on the applicant's calculations of the certainty of punishment. Ceteris paribus, compared with an applicant who did not engage in serious law-violating behavior in the first place, the applicant who engaged in law-violating behavior (especially on more than one occasion) and was not caught may underestimate the probability of being caught.[2]

Although prior experience is likely to continue to have an impact on the rookie's worldview for some time, perceptions about the disciplinary threat by the police agency (the sergeant being the most direct symbol of that authority) and by the criminal justice system at large soon become crucial as well. After a few years of experience, the sergeant's previous history of car-

---

2. Although a number of studies found an inverse relation either between sanction certainty and crime or between perceptions of sanction certainty and self-reported crime (for summaries of these studies, see, e.g., Paternoster, 1987, pp. 173–217; Williams & Hawkins, 1986, pp. 545–572; Zimring & Hawkins, 1973), Paternoster, Saltzman, Waldo, and Chiricos argue that, in the case of perceptions in self-reported studies, the self-reported behavior *preceded* the *perceptions* of sanction certainty; instead of perceived sanctions having a deterrent effect on behavior, they concluded that "what these researchers may actually be describing is an 'experiential' effect, the effect of previously committed behaviors on current perceptions: Behavior ↔ Perceived Sanctions" (1982, p. 56).

rying out and enforcing disciplinary threats, as well as the agency's overall approach toward, and history of, misconduct control will have substantial impact on the police officer's reading of the risks and rewards associated with corrupt behavior. However, how police officers read and understand these disciplinary threats depends on their risk propensity (built through their lifelong experience). Consequently, police officers with low risk-propensity levels tend to overestimate the importance and seriousness of the disciplinary threat, and police officers with high risk-propensity levels are apt to do the opposite. Therefore, everything else being equal, a police officer at the high end of the risk propensity scale would be more likely to engage in corruption than a police officer at the opposite end of the scale.

Organizational Factors

Although no police agency is completely immune from the influences of the larger political, social, and economic environment, the police agency itself has one of the key influences, if not *the* crucial influence, on the level of corruption in the agency. It starts with the recruitment and selection process and continues with training and supervision, incorporating various aspects of rule establishment, communication, and enforcement that stimulate, allow, or prevent police officers from turning their propensity toward corruption into actual corrupt behavior.

The Police Agency as a Paramilitary Bureaucracy

Despite some variation in the degree to which police agencies in the United States rely on the paramilitary mode of policing or embrace alternatives such as community policing, the paramilitary mode still dominates (see, e.g., Walker, 1992, p. 360). A paramilitary-style hierarchical bureaucracy is characterized by numerous rules, clear lines of authority, secrecy, and the view that the war on crime is a primary end of policing.

The attraction of the analogy between the police and the military has its roots in the legitimate use of force, the often unpredictable distribution of the occasions calling for the use of force (Bittner, 1999, p. 171), and the assumption that the personnel have to be under strict command, obedient to supervisors, and in compliance with a voluminous set of rules in order to be prepared for those unpredictable occasions. The emphasis on the military analogy and the related functions of the quasi-military organization—crime control or crime fighting—may give police officers a combat mentality and soldierlike perceptions of their duties.

The Los Angeles Police Department (LAPD), with no external review of complaints at the time, no specialized investigative staff, and no separate office to which complaints could be submitted (see Chevigny, 1995, p. 49), is a paramount example of a police agency that for a long time embraced the paramilitary image and the war-on-crime analogy. In an effort to separate the department from politics and reduce police corruption, William Parker, the former LAPD police chief from 1950 to 1966, resorted to a strong para-military atmosphere and a professional image of the police. Through a se-ries of actions and omissions by the administration and supervisors in the department, the semimilitary approach developed into a hostile approach toward the citizens, characterized by frequent excessive force. The study by Felkenes (cited in Skolnick & Fyfe, 1993, p. 138) suggests that "virtually all Los Angeles police officers see themselves as detached from the public, at war with the press, and underappreciated and disliked by an ungrateful pub-lic." The situation culminated in the Rodney King incident (for an analysis of the situation in the LAPD at the time, see Chevigny, 1995, pp. 35–59) and the establishment of the Christopher Commission (1991), followed by the Rampart area scandal (Los Angeles Police Department, 2000).

An additional consequence of embracing the paramilitary style in polic-ing is the fact that a typical paramilitary organization creates a large set of rules. Because of the extent of these rules, even despite their sincere efforts, police officers unavoidably end up violating some of the existing rules in the course of their careers. Indeed, in one of the earliest studies, McNamara (1967, p. 356) reported that the overwhelming majority (80%) of the police officers surveyed in his study agreed that it is "impossible to always follow the *Rules and Procedures* to the letter and still do an efficient job in police work." Thus, police officers' own rule-violating behavior can tie their hands with respect to reporting the serious rule-violating behavior of their fellow police officers, subordinates, or even their superiors.

The official agency rules, on the one hand, are too elaborate while, on the other hand, they are not elaborate enough. As Bittner noted, there is a sharp contrast between "the existence of elaborate codes governing the conduct of policemen relative to intra-departmental demands" and "the virtual absence of formulated directives concerning the handling of police problems in the community" (1999, p. 176). The results of the study by Franz and Jones (1987) support this argument. Compared with other city officials, police officers in their sample were more likely to say that "departmental procedures stood in the way of their doing the kind of job they would like to do" and were less likely to say that "officer internal procedures and practices help us give good service to our citizens" (p. 157).

Paramilitarism imposes bureaucratic mechanisms of supervision and communication, characterized by limited discretion at the lowest level (see, e.g., Skolnick & Fyfe, 1993, p. 117). As Bittner (1999, p. 176) emphasized, the paramilitary model is inappropriate for the discretionary method of police operation because a typical police organization de facto features discretion at the lowest level of its hierarchy. Furthermore, the supervision model based on the military approach toward discretion is difficult to implement in the police environment, not only because discretion is actually allocated at the lowest level (see Bittner, 1999) but also because of the limited ability of supervisors to invoke any disciplinary action when they are themselves in the position of violating at least some of the numerous rules.

The impact of all these factors, characteristic of the paramilitary style of policing, varies across police agencies, depending on other organizational factors such as leadership, supervision, internal control mechanisms, peers, rules, training in ethics, and recruitment.

Leadership/Administration

Top administrators in each agency have substantial power and control over the functioning of the police agency they head; it's their house. Although the powers of police chiefs are either explicitly or implicitly limited by the mayor, politicians, public, media, civil service rules, police unions, existing laws, and court cases, police chiefs and the administration determine "the rules of the game" within the police agency. They may exert a substantial influence on the recruitment standards, training in ethics, leadership and management style, supervisory accountability and standards, internal control mechanisms, discipline, and rewards.

According to Goldstein (1975, p. 40), the chief's stance on corruption, communicated to the troops through both words and actions, "determines the agency's effectiveness in coping with the problem." Police officers, in a recent nationwide representative sample surveyed by the Police Foundation, seem to share this view about the chief's role: The majority of the respondents agreed or strongly agreed that "a chief's strong position against the abuse of authority can make a big difference in deterring officers from abusing their authority" (Weisburd & Greenspan, 2000, p. 6). The way the chief's message and its sincerity are perceived depends on what the chief reacts to (e.g., acceptance of free coffee versus acceptance of bribes from speeding motorists), over whom the chief's reaction extends (e.g., line officers versus supervisors), with what intensity it is carried out (reflected in the severity of punishment), and how severe the reaction is (e.g., dismissal of the police officers in question or merely a pat on the back).

Although it is highly unlikely that *any* police chief would go to the extreme and openly advocate police corruption as an accepted practice, chiefs may choose not to talk about corruption, hesitate to discuss it, or blame individual police officers. The chief's official denial of the existence of police corruption in an agency characterized by pervasive corruption tends to undermine the police officers' trust and confidence in honest leadership and encourages the opinion that the leadership is corrupt, naive, incompetent, or unable to recognize and control corrupt behavior (see, e.g., Pennsylvania Crime Commission, 1974, p. 393).

Furthermore, police chiefs who protect corrupt police officers once the scandal breaks out or who publicly endorse the "rotten-apple approach" (that is, blame a few individual police officers and deny the existence of any organizational problems) provide the green light for corruption to continue. The Knapp Commission (1972, pp. 6–7) wrote about the rotten-apple approach in the NYPD in the 1970s, as did the Pennsylvania Crime Commission (1974, p. 20) about the Philadelphia Police Department. The Knapp Commission (1972, pp. 6–7) further wrote: "The rotten-apple doctrine has in many ways been a basic obstacle to meaningful reform." The administrators' adherence to the rotten-apple explanation or protection of corrupt behavior within the agency is likely to have serious consequences: Morale of the troops will probably suffer and their confidence in the administration will be undercut (see, e.g., Pennsylvania Crime Commission, 1974, p. 394), integrity and the commitment to integrity will be questioned by the public and the police, and the code of silence will flourish (see, e.g., Pennsylvania Crime Commission, 1974, p. 393).

Although the stance on corruption communicated through words is important, subsequent *actions* corresponding to the stated official view are even more crucial; "the actions of the Department . . . speak louder than formal declarations of policy" (Pennsylvania Crime Commission, 1974, p. 394). An illustrative example is the Seedman incident, in which NYPD Police Commissioner Murphy took a strong stance against free meals and free coffee (Knapp Commission, 1972, pp. 170–171) and then protected a high-ranking aide who accepted free dinner from a very expensive restaurant.

The discrepancy between words and actions may take several forms. First, the chief's own behavior may serve as an example; police chiefs who talk the talk but don't walk the walk, in addition to decreasing their own credibility, send the message that they are not sincere and that the efforts put into corruption control are hypocritical. Although it is difficult to suspect police chiefs of serious corruption, a survey by Rosoff, Pontell, and Tillman (1998) suggests that at least some police chiefs are not immune to such temptations: The police chief in Rochester, New York, was convicted of drug trafficking charges; the chief of the Newark, New Jersey, police department pleaded guilty to stealing $30,000 from the police fund; the police chief of Bristol, Virginia, committed suicide after a grand jury started investigating charges of the theft of $377,000 against him. Another drastic example is that of the former police chief of Newburgh, New York, who not only engaged in corruption himself but also, at the same time, was the leader of a burglary ring at the Sears Department Store. In the end, 15 police officers were convicted, and the chief was sentenced to 11 years of imprisonment (Sherman, 1978).

Second, the chief may behave ethically but fail to perform the traditional managerial functions of planning, organizing, coordinating, and controlling (for the description of these functions, see Moore & Stephens, 1991) in accordance with the official stance on corruption. In terms of planning, the chief may decide to assign a low priority to the issue of police corruption, neglect to control the dominant coalition in the agency and therefore prevent the substitution of the legitimate goals of the department with illegitimate ones, emphasize the ends of policing to the extent that the means become irrelevant, and/or fail to expand the internal affairs office as the incidence of misconduct increases. In terms of organizing and coordinating, the chief might fail to enforce the accountability and responsibility of first-line supervisors; fail to establish adequate mechanisms of supervision (see, e.g., Pennsylvania Crime Commission 1974, p. 395); insist on a complaint process that is too cumbersome, expensive, and complicated; approve vague rules on corruption in the standard operating procedure; neglect to hold police officers (especially supervisors) accountable (see, e.g., Pennsylvania Crime Commission, 1974, p. 395); apply more lenient disciplinary standards to supervisors than to line officers; and provide inadequate resources (budget, personnel) for the centralized internal affairs units and their decentralized units (see, e.g., Knapp Commission, 1972, p. 207; Mollen Commission, 1994, p. 85). In terms of controlling, the chief might develop a performance measure that inadvertently strengthens the code of silence, neglect to develop personnel files that contain both the disciplinary record and the record of rewards, and fail to control the dominant coalition in the agency, which may consider personal enrichment as a primary agency goal.

In sum, the police chief and the administrators are the key figures in the police agency, and their approach toward corruption and their zeal for the enforcement of corruption control play major roles in the creation of an environment intolerant of police corruption. Their actions and omissions have not only a direct impact on corrupt behavior but also an indirect impact on other factors related to corruption, such as supervisors' actions, internal control mechanisms, and peer attitudes.

Resources

Although the resources at the police agency's disposal typically are part of the overall city budget, the police chief and agency administration determine how these resources are allocated within the agency. The decisions both the city and the police chief make are long lasting and affect various aspects of the police agency, including corruption and its control. At the recruitment stage, personnel may be overworked and/or understaffed, and their resources may be severely stretched. Under such circumstances, the personnel may opt to cut corners in the recruitment process (e.g., do less thorough background checks), which in turn may yield a less satisfactory pool of rookies.

Furthermore, first-line supervisors may not be able to provide adequate supervision because of the lack of resources to deal with corruption or to supervise in general; supervisors may be understaffed, overburdened, or untrained to deal with corruption. In such circumstances, even the most honest supervisors may have a difficult time if they want to control the misconduct of their subordinates. For example, the Mollen Commission (1994, pp. 82–83) reported that the deteriorating supervisory conditions in the NYPD in the 1990s included a dramatic increase in the ratio of supervisors to line officers (from 1:10 to 1:30 in some districts), assignment of supervising police officers to two different precincts, the requirement to perform a number of administrative duties, and the necessity of handling calls for service in lieu of busy patrol officers.

The issue of resources can also affect the work of internal affairs units through denial of resources and/or staff to the units assigned to internal control. The Pennsylvania Crime Commission (1974, p. 479) reported that the internal investigative personnel in the Philadelphia Police Department accounted for up to 0.7% of the overall number of sworn officers in the department, while the corresponding percentage in the Internal Revenue Service was 2.8%. In the 1960s, the Internal Affairs Division (IAD) in the NYPD had a ratio of one member of the division for every 533 line officers before the changes introduced by Commissioner Murphy, which improved the ratio to one member of the division to every 64 line officers (Walker, 1992, p. 273). The Knapp Commission (1972, p. 207) reported: "ISB's [Inspection Services Bureau] manpower was kept at a level that virtually made it impossible to do its job effectively." Two decades later, the Mollen Commission (1994, p. 85) noted that the caseload within the NYPD was unevenly distributed between the centralized IAD unit and the field internal affairs units (FIAUs), making the work of the FIAU units impossible.

Corruption-Related Rules

As argued earlier, every police department organized as a paramilitary organization features an abundance of official rules to regulate even the tiniest details of internal organization and impose boundaries on police officers' behavior (Bittner, 1999, p. 172). The Commission on Accreditation of Law Enforcement Agencies (CALEA) standards (1994) prescribe that an agency considered for accreditation should have a written set of rules that specify the standards of conduct and appearance. In adherence to the *nullum crimen, nulla poena sine lege* principle, CALEA's suggestion is establishing the rules of proper conduct or the rules describing prohibited behavior, among other reasons, to discipline police officers for misconduct. The commentary of that same rule (Rule 26.1.1) suggests that the rules should cover "acceptance of gratuities, bribes, or rewards" (Commission on Accreditation of Law Enforcement Agencies, 1994).

Although an agency may enact official rules, the rules themselves can be far from perfect. The ambiguity of a rule may signal the administration's lack of concern about the issue or their inability to conceptualize it, regulate it, and control it. It may also serve as a justification for engaging in such behavior. For example, in a study conducted by Fishman (1978) the percentage of police officers who said that agency rules concerning corruption were not clear was higher in corrupt police departments than in police departments relatively free of corruption.

Written rules prohibiting corrupt behavior, of course, do not mean that corruption will disappear, but they provide legitimacy for the subsequent punishment of police officers who engage in corruption. A key determinant of the extent of corruption is the discrepancy between the rules on the books (the official rules) and the rules that actually govern the agency (the informal rules). Independent commissions investigating police corruption have suggested that a wide discrepancy between the official rules and the informal rules is a strong correlate of corrupt behavior. The Pennsylvania Crime Commission (1974, p. 399) reported a characteristic example. Although the Philadelphia Police Department's official stance was clear (police officers were not allowed to accept any gifts or payments; Pennsylvania Crime Commission, 1974, pp. 240, 399), what precisely constituted a gift was often subject to interpretation, and even "the Commander of the Internal Affairs Bureau and the officer in charge of the Police Academy cannot agree on the proper guideline" (Pennsylvania Crime Commission, 1974, p. 400). However, the informal rules were far clearer, and they overshadowed the official rules. Because not a single police officer from Internal Affairs was assigned to investigate payments of money or merchandise businesses made to the police (Pennsylvania Crime Commission, 1974, p. 394), supervisors did not discipline line officers for corrupt behavior, and no police officers were investigated or punished for accepting free meals despite the apparent widespread practice (Pennsylvania Crime Commission, 1974, p. 339), the informal rules clearly suggested that such practice was acceptable.

Recruitment and Selection

Police agencies characterized by widespread corruption, in addition to being plagued by other organizational problems (e.g., failure of the internal control mechanisms, absence of effective supervision), are also more likely to have continually failed in the recruitment and selection process, which in turn may have resulted in recruiting a higher share of potentially problematic police officers (those who have a criminal record, violent personality, questionable ethical values, a history of drug use, or, in general, a higher propensity toward corruption and deviant behavior). The example of "the River Cops" in Miami in the 1980s illustrates a possible outcome of flawed recruitment and selection practices, combined with other organizational failures.

> It appears that weakened screening procedures combined with the urgent need for new officers, affirmative action mandates, and inadequate supervision permitted a number of marginally qualified individuals to become police officers, including the River Cops. About three fourths of the almost 80 officers dismissed or suspended by 1987 [in a police force of 600–700 at the time] were from the group that experienced more relaxed standards. The number of officers that were eventually relieved from duty rose to 100. . . . Concern is not so much with the number but the seriousness of the charges. Of the 72 initially identified, 20 were involved in conspiracy and/or murder, 15 were selling or using cocaine, and 4 were involved in other types of drug sales. (Burns & Sechrest, 1992, p. 305)

The LAPD's Board of Inquiry also emphasized the role of the accelerated hiring procedures in the selection process. Four of the 14 police officers involved in the Rampart area scandal had red flags (such as criminal records and severe problems with management of their personal finances) in their personnel files before they were hired (Los Angeles Police Department, 2000, pp. 13–24). Similarly, the Mollen Commission studied the records of approximately 400 police officers who were either dismissed or suspended for police corruption over a period of 6 years. It found that approximately 20% of these police officers should never have been hired (p. 113) and, for a large number of them, the information that could have predicted possible future unethical behavior (e.g., prior criminal arrest record) was *readily available* in the applicant's file at the time of hiring (p. 65).

The agency's screening process can go wrong in more than one direction. To begin with, the criteria may be too narrow, and many potentially significant predictors may be omitted from the information set utilized to evaluate the applicants. In addition, the recruitment criteria may emphasize the minimum qualifications necessary to do the policing job while neglecting the criteria used to assess the likelihood that the applicant will be an honest police officer (see Mollen Commission, 1994, p. 115; U.S. Department of Justice, 1989, p. 16). Next, recruitment personnel may be overworked, understaffed, and pressured to lower hiring standards (see, e.g., Mollen Commission, 1994, p. 65) to hire on the basis of political connections or to satisfy community pressure for additional police officers.

Furthermore, the threshold for the criteria established and actually applied to determine the integrity level of the applicants may be set too low; consequently, applicants who might be more susceptible to corruption would be more likely to be hired by the department. The results of the study by Greisinger, Slovak, and Molkup imply that 5% of the surveyed departments accepted applicants with a prior adult felony conviction, 25% with a prior juvenile felony conviction, and 30% with either a prior adult or a prior juvenile misdemeanor conviction (1979, p. 102).

Another possible failure is related to the practice of allowing applicants to become police officers before their background investigations have been completed. For example, the Mollen Commission (1994) reported that 88% of applicants to the NYPD entered the police academy before their background investigations were complete and about one third were put on the streets, with guns and badges, before their background checks were completed (pp. 113–114).

Training in Ethics and Integrity

Police departments can use training and education in police integrity for reinforcing or changing the recruits' ethical values, preparing them for the ethical dilemmas they face in their future work, and sending a message about expected behavior and the consequences of deviating from it. Not surprisingly, all three independent commissions investigating allegations of corruption in New York and Philadelphia found that integrity programs and training offered to recruits and more experienced police officers were inadequate (see Knapp Commission, 1972, pp. 239–241; Mollen Commission, 1994, pp. 10, 56, 108, 119–120; Pennsylvania Crime Commission, 1974, p. 398).

Ethics training programs for recruits may be inadequate in several ways. They may be based on the rotten-apple approach (emphasizing that ethics is primarily a matter of an individual's moral values). They may be inadequate in terms of their content (e.g., focus on legal codes; Knapp Commission, 1972; Pennsylvania Crime Commission, 1974), quality (e.g., boring lectures; Mollen Commission, 1994, p. 119), duration (e.g., very brief; Knapp Commission, 1972, p. 239; Pennsylvania Crime Commission, 1974, p. 397), currency (i.e., outdated; Mollen Commission, 1994), and applicability to real-life situations. All these failures may have a severe impact on recruits' view of the administration (such as cynicism and refusal to take orders seriously; see, e.g., Pennsylvania Crime Commission, 1974, p. 396), the lack of seriousness and sincere commitment toward corruption control, the likelihood of successful control efforts over the recruits, the tendency to succumb to peer pressure (e.g., senior police officers will teach them "how the police work is really done"; see Pennsylvania Crime Commission, 1974, p. 396), and the acceptance of the code of silence. Moreover, inadequate training not only may fail to provide police officers with the skills and knowledge that would enable them to remain honest but also may serve as the first instance at which they are exposed to a police culture that fosters corruption (Mollen Commission, 1994, p. 119).

Training in ethics is supposed to maintain adequate presence throughout police officers' careers, starting from academy training and field training through in-service training and supervisory training. At each of these stages, the department may send a clear message about the lack of seriousness of its effort to teach integrity. By selecting police officers of questionable ethical standards as field-training officers (which is most likely the only option in departments characterized by widespread corruption), the department transmits attitudes tolerant of corruption, permits socialization of recruits into the police subculture, contributes toward the undermining of its own authority, and, subsequently, allows corrupt behavior to flourish (see Knapp Commission, 1972, p. 241; Mollen Commission, 1994, p. 120).

Similar findings were reported for in-service training. The Mollen Commission (1994, p. 108) wrote about the failure of the in-service integrity training in the NYPD, which "did little to enhance the integrity of members of the Department. It did little to encourage officers to resist the temptations of corruption. And, perhaps most important, it did little to transform a culture that tolerates and protects corruption into one that supports and rewards honesty and integrity."

Finally, the department's failure to convey its expectations regarding personal responsibility and accountability and its lack of instructions on how to prevent and identify corruption-related problems through a series of training programs for newly promoted supervisors allows them to continue with any corrupt activities (see, e.g., Knapp Commission, 1972, p. 241; Mollen Commission, 1994, p. 120).

Peers

Police officers' sense of isolation, enhanced by their embrace of the "us versus them" mentality, generates perceptions that nobody understands them, that very few people can relate to their experience (Sparrow et al., 1990, p. 144), that they cannot trust other community members, and that the only people they feel comfortable around are other police officers (see, e.g., Skolnick & Fyfe, 1993, p. 82). As a consequence, an intense sense of solidarity, loyalty, and mutual trust develops among police officers. Indeed, at least 70% of the surveyed NYPD officers in the 1960s agreed: "The police department is really a large brotherhood in which each patrolman does his best to help all other patrolmen" (McNamara, 1967, p. 246).

This potent mixture of solidarity, loyalty, and mutual trust among line officers in a paramilitary environment, characterized by extensive rules and an emphasis on readily quantifiable performance measures such as arrest numbers, invariably culminates in the code of silence, the code of secrecy, the blue wall of silence, or the blue curtain—a set of unwritten rules in the police subculture that prohibit them from reporting on their fellow officers. One of the most vivid metaphors of the code of silence was reported by Blair-Kerr, who was appointed in the 1970s by the former governor of Hong Kong, MacLehose, to investigate former Chief Superintendent Peter Godber's involvement in corruption (Klitgaard, 1988, pp. 107–108):

> On a number of occasions during this inquiry I have been told that there is a saying in Hong Kong:
>
> 1. "Get on the bus," i.e., if you wish to accept corruption, join us;
> 2. "Run alongside the bus," i.e., if you do not wish to accept corruption, it matters not, but do not interfere;
> 3. "Never stand in front of the bus," i.e., if you try to report corruption, the "bus" will knock you down and you will be injured or even killed or your business will be ruined. We will get you, somehow.

New recruits are socialized through transmission of the norms of the existing peer subculture, which in highly corrupt departments may pass on patterns of corruption. However, the rookies are active and reflective participants in the process (see Chen, 2003), and their adoption of the cultural norms depends on their prior personal experience, as well as on the way they perceive organizational and society-wide factors. For example, Chen (2003) found a substantial positive influence from the Fitzgerald Commission and from the increased emphasis on police integrity within the police on the corruption-related views held by a cohort of Australian police rookies.

Stoddard (1974, p. 292) argued that older police officers have a responsibility for screening rookies, teaching them the code, and testing them; failure to socialize rookies into the existing culture and the code would have an adverse impact on their standing in the group and on the continued existence of the code. Rookies and transferred police officers are taught and tested gradually, starting with acceptance of items of small value that would probably cause no serious harm to the record of a rookie if reported, such as a free lunch (see, e.g., Pennsylvania Crime Commission, 1974, pp. 421–422) or a candy bar (see, e.g., Stoddard, 1974, p. 296) and progressing to more serious forms of police corruption. Although socialization does not in itself make any police officer corrupt, it certainly paves the road for corruption.

However, there is no single, uniform police culture (see Chen, 2003). Norms and values can vary greatly across police agencies (see Klockars, Kutnjak Ivković, Harver, & Haberfeld, 1997) and even across the units within the same police agency, as well as across time (see Chen, 2003). Although the degree to which police cultures are tolerant of police corruption could be quite diverse, a police culture may have a negative impact on police officers' attitudes and behavior through enforcement of the norms constituting the "code of silence." The extent of the code of silence could vary as well. For example, the Mollen Commission (1994, p. 53) reported that the code of silence is the strongest in the precincts with most corruption.

> The pervasiveness of the code of silence is itself alarming. But what we found particularly troubling is that it often appears to be strongest where corruption is most frequent. This is because the loyalty ethic is particularly powerful in crime-ridden precincts where officers most depend upon each other for their safety every day—and where fear and alienation from the community are most rampant. Thus, the code of silence influences honest officers in the very precincts where their assistance is needed most.

Compliance with the strong code of silence, which is supportive of police misconduct, is enforced through informal sanctions by the group, ranging from the unpleasant and humiliating but not dangerous ones (such as placing dead rats on the windshield), to more serious ones (such as setting a locker on fire, slashing the tires, threatening with physical harm; see Mollen Commission, 1994, pp. 54–55). In a recent nationwide survey of police officers, the majority reported that "police officers who reported incidents of misconduct are likely to be given a 'cold shoulder' by fellow officers" (Weisburd & Greenspan, 2000, p. 3). It seems that "an atmosphere in which the dishonest officer fears the honest one, and not the other way around," as Frank Serpico, the most famous whistle-blower in the NYPD's history, had hoped (see Knapp Commission, 1972, p. 51), is still unreasonable to expect in agencies experiencing widespread corruption.

Thus, police culture may encourage and even legitimize misconduct by police officers (Sparrow et al., 1990, p. 53). Nevertheless, police culture may also have a positive impact on the police officers' conduct through informal sanctioning of the conduct. Even in highly corrupt agencies, some types of behavior are considered off limits, and police officers who engage in such behavior may expect informal reprisal (e.g., gossip, isolation, labeling) from their colleagues.

The code of silence determines the boundaries of the behavior with which police officers are pressured to comply, affects the socialization of recruits, and limits police officers' willingness to report misconduct by fellow officers. In the police agencies characterized by a strong and extensive code of silence, honest police officers may show great reluctance, if not unwillingness, to report the dishonest behavior of their fellow police officers (see, e.g., Pennsylvania Crime Commission, 1974, p. 432). Although the code of silence and us-versus-them mentality were detected wherever the Mollen Commission (1994, p. 7) found corruption in the NYPD, they were the most prevalent in the crime-riddled precincts, where the strong code helped corruption flourish. Because of group pressure and severe consequences for reporting misconduct (especially in a department characterized by widespread corruption), the code of silence presents honest police officers with a dilemma: They must either report the dishonest behavior and face the consequences or turn a blind eye. Ultimately, the majority of honest police officers in profoundly corrupt departments decide not to report corruption (see, e.g., Mollen Commission, 1994, p. 57). Over time, according to the Mollen Commission (1994, p. 57), "officers view reporting corruption as an offense more heinous and dangerous than the corruption itself."

Police unions and fraternal police organizations are associations of line officers and supervisors that, as the Mollen Commission wrote (1994, p. 66), "can do much to increase the pride and professionalism of our police. . . . Unfortunately, based on our own observations and on information received from prosecutors, corruption investigators, and high-ranking police officials, police unions sometimes fuel the insularity that characterizes police culture." The experience that the Mollen Commission had with police unions resonates with such a view. Only a month after the commission started its work, the Captains Benevolent Association (C.B.A.) initiated a lawsuit with the purpose of dissolving the commission. The commission commented:

While the C.B.A. and its officers are entitled to their opinions, the Commission thought it unfortunate that a police union representing high-ranking members of the Department would attack a Commission whose mission was to investigate police corruption and to recommend means to combat it. The unfortunate result of such action is first to create a negative attitude on the part of its members toward fighting corruption within the Department and at the same time to reinforce the public's cynicism about the members of the Police Department and the officers' sense of insularity against the public. This is particularly egregious coming from the union representing the highest ranking-members of the Department. By contrast, we invited and met with many high-ranking officers of the Department who expressed great concern over the issue of corruption and their readiness to assist in formulating lasting solutions to the problem. (1994, p. 66)

Police unions may experience a conflict of interest: They represent both the police officers who are subjects of the investigations and disciplinary proceedings and the police officers who are witnesses to such corrupt acts. In an effort to protect the accused police officers, they advise other police officers to participate in the code of silence; "the P.B.A. often acts as a shelter for and protector of the corrupt cop rather than as a guardian of the interests of the vast majority of its membership, who are honest police officers" (Mollen Commission, 1994, p. 67). Finally, if police unions choose a strategy that involves attacking a commission, degrading the police agency's own efforts to combat corruption, failing to admit that police officers engage in corruption, and vigorously defending corrupt police officers, they contribute toward the development of the code of silence and a police culture tolerant of corruption.

Supervisors

Because of the quasi-military nature of the police organization, rather than providing help or assistance to line officers, police supervisors are perceived as disciplinarians who apply sanctions "situationally and erratically" (Kappeler, Sluder, & Alpert, 1999, p. 255) and who focus their attention on the police officers' adherence to numerous rules (although they know that it will be impossible for police officers to adhere to all the rules at all times). First-line supervisors (i.e., sergeants and corporals), the part of the administration apparatus that has the closest supervisory capacity and with whom line officers have the most frequent contact, have one of the strongest and most resonant voices in the formation of perceptions that police officers develop about the actual stance on corruption and about the consequences of violations of official rules prohibiting corrupt behavior. In a recent national survey, the overwhelming majority of police officers (90%) perceived the role supervisors play in the prevention of misconduct as important (Weisburd & Greenspan, 2000, p. 6).

The most obvious way first-line supervisors clearly show their subordinates that they will not enforce the official rules prohibiting corruption (if such official rules exist) and that, consequently, official rules are overruled by informal rules is through their own engagement in corruption. The Knapp Commission (1972, p. 177) documented that supervisors either participated and received one-and-a-half value of the regular biweekly or monthly payments given to the line officers or probably had their own "pads" from which patrol officers were excluded. The Pennsylvania Crime Commission (1974) described widespread corruption in which "virtually everyone was involved from captain down either by participating directly in the acceptance of notes or intentionally looking the other way" (p. 426).

In an agency in which they are not directly involved in corruption, supervisors nevertheless may contribute toward creating an environment tolerant of corruption by either failing to take a serious stance against corruption or failing to react in accordance with their declared stance. The Mollen Commission reported about various instances in which supervisors obviously failed to question their subordinates' problematic conduct, including, for example, falsified search and arrest forms (1994, pp. 29, 40) or false maximization of overtime pay (p. 39). This failure to react may provide a lot of mileage for corrupt officers, as the example of Michael Dowd suggests. He was one of the most notorious police officers engaged in the corruption discovered by the Mollen Commission. Despite many obvious signs of his involvement in corruption, none of his supervisors reacted (p. 57). Dowd later told the commission that the lack of supervision and willful blindness of supervisors made him believe that he could "do just about anything and get away with it" (p. 82).

The LAPD's Board of Inquiry (Los Angeles Police Department, 2000, p. 8) also wrote about the obvious breakdown in supervision in the Rampart area (characterized by both corruption and the use of excessive force). The lack of supervision was evident in everyday behavior; "the practice of officers printing or signing a sergeant's name to booking approvals and arrest reports was a particularly glaring illustration of poor CRASH [an anti-gang unit, or Community Resources Against Street Hoodlums] supervision" (Los Angeles Police Department, 2000, p. 61). Similarly, Burns and Sechrest's research about corrupt police officers in Miami suggested that "changes in supervision were put in place in the early 1980s that loosened internal controls and may have helped 'set the stage' for corruption to flourish" (1992, p. 305).

Under deteriorating conditions of supervision, leading sometimes to ratios of supervisors to line officers as low as 1:30 (Mollen Commission, 1994, pp. 82–83), controlling the misconduct of their subordinates may be difficult for even the most honest of supervisors. Burns and Sechrest (1992) linked the corruption scandal that shook the Miami Police Department in the mid-1980s with the (lack of) experience and the type of supervision provided; they reported that, of the police officers promoted to supervisor in 1980 and 1981, only 35% had at least 10 years of experience.

Until yesterday, newly promoted sergeants were peers of the police officers they are now assigned to supervise; they have spent long hours on patrol with them, shared the same police subculture, and probably engaged in some form of rule-violating behavior. All of these factors make them vulnerable and tie their hands in terms of the seriousness and severity of their reaction to corrupt behavior by their former peers. Given that police officers in the NYPD could take the sergeant's exam after only 18 months of experience (Mollen Commission, 1994, p. 83), it is by no means surprising that two thirds of the surveyed NYPD uniformed police officers in 1994 perceived that "sergeants do not have enough confidence to take charge of many situations on the street" (Giuliani & Bratton, 1995, p. 47).

In corrupt police departments, the "heads-must-roll approach" leads toward the belief that the public and the media would react extremely negatively to the uncovered corruption incidents. Consequently, first-line supervisors have very little reason to investigate allegations of corruption and to consistently and systematically punish corrupt officers. In corrupt police agencies, first-line supervisors are neither encouraged nor rewarded by their own supervisors and the administration for taking a stance against corruption and acting accordingly and, in fact, might suffer informal punishment for doing so (see, e.g., Mollen Commission, 1994, p. 13). As the Mollen Commission put it (1994, p. 78), this in reality translates into supervisors being more interested in whether their troops were discreet than in whether they were honest.

Although the official departmental rules in New York have long emphasized command accountability (Knapp Commission, 1972, p. 232), independent commissions reported that supervisors were not held accountable for the behavior of police officers under their command (Mollen Commission, 1994, pp. 128–129; see also Knapp Commission, 1972, p. 232; Sherman, 1978, p. 121). In fact, the commissions regarded the lack of actual command accountability as the most fundamental managerial failure or defect (Knapp Commission, 1972, p. 232; Los Angeles Police Department, 2000, p. 14; Mollen Commission, 1994, p. 128).

Formal System of Internal Control

The formal system of internal control typically includes input structures for the receipt of complaints (both externally and internally generated), investigative structures (e.g., investigations performed either only by the internal affairs office or by the internal affairs office and chain-of-command supervisors), and decision-making structures (e.g., police chief, chain-of-command board). The formal system of control may be completely police operated, that is, internal, as is the case in the overwhelming majority of the U.S. police agencies (see, e.g., Perez, 1994, p. 82).

An agency characterized by widespread, organized police corruption has typically experienced a breakdown of the formal system of internal control. The NYPD (Knapp Commission, 1972) and the Philadelphia Police Department (Pennsylvania Crime Commission, 1974) in the 1970s are textbook examples. The Pennsylvania Crime Commission (1974, pp. 23, 455, 473) found ample evidence of widespread corruption, as well as of weak and ineffective mechanisms of internal control in the Philadelphia Police Department. The Knapp Commission (1972, p. 205) uncovered a similar level of corruption and a similar state of the system of internal control in the NYPD. Although a new system of control was put in place as a consequence of the efforts of the Knapp Commission and former Commissioner Murphy, the gradual erosion of the system over 20 years culminated in the finding of the Mollen Commission that "the New York City Police Department had largely abandoned its responsibility to police itself" (1994, p. 70). Similarly, in addition to studying the NYPD, Sherman (1978, p. 244) studied three other police departments (Oakland, CA; Newburgh, NY; and "Central City") that experienced major corruption scandals in the late 1960s and concluded that all four suffered from failed internal control procedures. These failures have been a consequence of nonwillful omission by the police administrators, supervisors, and internal affairs units in dealing with corruption, as well as a consequence of willful attempts to make detection and investigation of corruption more difficult.

Although the outcome of processing by the formal system of control may include either positive or negative sanctions, the findings of independent commissions typically suggest that the police agencies did not offer any encouragement in terms of positive sanctions for either reporting corrupt behavior of fellow police officers or for uncovering corruption in a supervisory capacity. The Knapp Commission (1972, pp. 167–168, 231–232) and the Pennsylvania Crime Commission (1974, p. 426) found that supervisors (from the rank of captain down) either actively participated in corruption themselves or knew of it and did nothing. Therefore, it is not surprising that they did not encourage reporting. The Mollen Commission (1994, p. 133) found that, although supervisors were typically not involved in corrupt activities, they neither encouraged line officers to report nor were rewarded for uncovering corruption. In fact, the commission wrote: "In recent years, a message had filtered down from top commanders—including Police Commissioners—that disclosure of corruption, even that resulting from vigilant corruption fighting, would be viewed as a management *failure*" (emphasis added; 1994, p. 78).

Reporting behavior was thus perceived negatively, and silence—the radically opposite behavior—was rewarded instead. The Pennsylvania Crime Commission provided an illustrative example of a detective they caught on tape in the process of accepting a bribe. When he refused to cooperate with the commission, the police administration tried to reward him with a pension for his loyal silence (see Pennsylvania Crime Commission, 1974, p. 549).

External Characteristics

Every police department, no matter how coherent and self-contained a unit, is necessarily an integral part of a larger political and social environment. Characteristics of that environment affect the level of police corruption in an agency (see, e.g., Goldstein, 1975; Sherman, 1974, pp. 6–12) both directly (e.g., by providing opportunities for corruption and a supply of willing bribe givers) and indirectly (e.g., through the approval of the police chief's work). At the same time, the larger environment may itself be affected by the level of corruption within the agency. For example, if police officers were unwilling to accept bribes from speeding motorists and instead arrested them for attempted bribery, the public would probably change its behavior and be less inclined to offer such bribes.

Opportunities for Corruption

Police officers in the United States typically share "the American dream" or, in Merton's terms (1938), share the same goals with the majority of the society. Yet, their legitimate means of achieving these goals may be limited because they are members of a (paramilitary) police organization, which puts barriers on career advancement and salary increases. Low salaries are often mentioned as a factor contributing to corruption (see Simpson, 1977, p. 105, for a literature survey); "if public sector pay is very low, corruption is a survival strategy" (Rose-Ackerman, 1999, p. 72). Wilson, for example, argued that higher salaries would increase the status and self-esteem of police officers and might result in a decreased need to subscribe to the code of silence (1963, p. 189).

Although in the 1960s police agencies experienced serious difficulty in recruitment and retention of police officers, partly because of low salaries compared with those earned by most skilled occupations (President's Commission on Law Enforcement and Administration of Justice, 1967b, pp. 134–136), the situation improved by the mid-1970s (see Walker, 1992, p. 309). The effect of increasing already appropriate salaries is unclear, but if salaries do not reach a certain bare minimum, police officers may be more tempted to engage in corrupt activities or, in Merton's parlance (1938, pp. 672–682), to "innovate" while searching for alternative means of achieving legitimate goals when legitimate opportunities are limited. Legitimate opportunities can be further restricted because of police officers' limited opportunities for career advancement: The overwhelming majority of police officers will never get promoted and will walk the beat until they retire (see, e.g., Chevigny, 1995, p. 62).

Thus, their goals and the legal means available to police officers may not match. In the communities in which legitimate opportunities to achieve the American dream are more limited (e.g., low police salaries) or the fulfillment of the American dream is more difficult (e.g., more expensive housing market), more anomie results. Even within the same police agency, police officers could define the American dream differently; an understanding of what constitutes a suitable house varies across the population. A police officer like Michael Dowd (see Mollen Commission, 1994), who wanted to enjoy a lavish lifestyle that a regular police salary could not support, is tempted to "innovate" and engage in corruption to supplement his income and achieve his dream.

By its very nature, policing as an occupation has several characteristics that may provide for illegitimate opportunities and thus contribute to the existence of police corruption. Police officers spend most of their time either working alone (e.g., patrolling the neighborhood) or in the company of their partners. As a low-visibility activity from the standpoint of both the general public and their supervisors, the police job is both difficult to supervise and susceptible to abuse. Furthermore, citizen–police officer interactions may occur in private settings, without other witnesses present during the encounter or in the presence of witnesses who either lack credibility (e.g., drug dealers, prostitutes) or are unwilling to talk because they adhere to the code of silence (e.g., fellow police officers). In addition, the nature of the police job, with its selective enforcement and discretion at the level of patrol officers, generates regular contact with citizens willing to participate in quid pro quo arrangements.

Just as legitimate opportunities for achieving socially acceptable goals are not equally available, Cloward and Ohlin (1960) argued that illegal means are unequally distributed as well. As a rule, police officers generally have some illegal opportunities available simply as a consequence of their occupation (e.g., discretionary work, selective law enforcement), although the quantity and variability of these illegal opportunities may vary across agencies and across time.

Laws without moral consensus and vague or ill-defined laws that police officers needed to enforce were a rich source of opportunities for corruption in the 1970s. The Knapp Commission (1972, pp. 147–148), for example, discussed the laws regulating drinking establishments and found that they were "sound in principle but are so vague and ill-defined that they lend themselves to abuses in practice." Similarly, the Sabbath Law, which regulated the sale of food and other necessities on Sundays, was a very complex statute (Knapp Commission, 1972, p. 149) with rules store owners typically violated (either willingly or through lack of awareness) and thus inadvertently provided opportunities for police officers to shake them down. Another situation that provided fertile ground for corruption was related to construction regulations that required so many permits that a typical construction contractor simply would not be able to obtain all of them (Knapp Commission, 1972, p. 125), which often necessitated involvement in corrupt activities. Still other legal rules the commissions deemed unreasonable were the laws proscribing behavior not perceived to be against morality or constituting serious violations of the law. Examples were readily identified by both the Pennsylvania Crime Commission (1974, p. 413) as the vice enforcement policies and by the Knapp Commission (1972, p. 90) as the gambling laws.

Public Views on Corruption

Community attitudes about corruption may contribute to broadening or narrowing the extent of police corruption. Although the legislature may enact laws prohibiting certain behaviors, the public (or at least a substantial proportion of it) does not necessarily have to disapprove of those behaviors and thereby, implicitly or explicitly, may generate demand for corruption. The Knapp Commission (1972, pp. 72–73) provided an example: Despite the fact that laws prohibiting gambling were passed, both the public and the police officers shared the belief that gambling does no harm, that there is nothing wrong with it, and that the gambling laws should not be enforced at all. Another instance in which the community may behave inconsistently is when, on the surface, the community expects police officers to be "blue knights" who are fully enforcing the law, while, in reality, members of the community bribe police officers to not enforce the law in *their* case. Indeed, speeding motorists—people who otherwise may well be law-abiding citizens—are often the ones who initiate the bribe (see, e.g., Knapp Commission, 1972, p. 157).

Mixed messages may be sent by setting higher ethical standards for police officers than for members of any other profession and, at the same time, by treating police officers according to the standards of other professions. Some of the practices widely used in the business community, such as tipping and doing favors, are not compatible with the police role (see Pennsylvania Crime Commission, 1974, p. 20). Police officers, unlike taxi drivers or waitresses, are not allowed to receive tips for their services. Yet, this practice, as the Knapp Commission (1972, p. 170) reported, "was widely accepted by both the police and the citizenry, with many feeling that it wasn't corruption at all, but a natural perquisite of the job."

By viewing police corruption as a natural part of doing business, as was the case with a number of restaurant and bar owners in New York City and Philadelphia in the 1970s (Knapp Commission, 1972; Pennsylvania Crime Commission, 1974), considerable segments of society resign themselves to the notion that corruption is not only tolerated but also accepted. Such an approach suggests that opportunities for corruption will continue to exist, that police officers should not be concerned with the possibility that a citizen will report the transaction to the authorities, and that the more aggressive corrupt officers (i.e., "meat eaters") are likely to have an easier time finding new opportunities.

Public acceptance or rejection of corrupt behavior may be crucial in an indirect way as well. One of the stages in successful punitive scandals ("dramatization"), according to Sherman (1978, p. 69), depends on public reaction: The public needs to interpret the alleged revelations of corruption as severe cases worthy of serious public concern. A strong public reaction of disapproval may include rage, anger, surprise, and disappointment because someone bestowed with social trust violated their expectations (see Sherman, 1978, p. 60). The Knapp Commission (1972, p. 61) reported that the public expressed shock and outrage when investigations revealed corruption. Sherman (1978, p. 69) analyzed four police departments that experienced substantial, full-blown scandals preceded by "little scandals" within 2 years. With the exception of one city, "little scandals" did not cause substantial public disapproval and, ironically, despite the fact that some of the corrupt activities discovered were more serious than the corruption discovered in the subsequent "big scandals," they did not mobilize external forces to the degree necessary for the reform of these agencies. In fact, they "may have encouraged the police department's definition of its behavior as proper rather than deviant" (Sherman, 1978, p. 33).

Levels of Corruption in the Criminal Justice System and Society at Large

A police officer is a member of society who has been socialized to accept the norms of that society. Unless they are considered for special elite units having a well-known reputation of high integrity,[3] police officers socialized in a highly corrupt society will probably have a difficult time separating the expectations and values of the society at large from those advanced by the police agency. Indian society is a prime example of a country in which corruption is tolerated by the public and is widespread (see Transparency International, 1999). Corruption includes the judiciary as well as the police (see Bayley, 1974). In fact, Bayley (1974) argued that "the practice of bribing may be so common that the rejection of a bribe by an official may cause the briber to wonder if the official hasn't already been won over to the other side or is being purposely malicious" (p. 87). It is, then, by no means surprising that, because the public perceives police corruption to be widespread (especially in the cities), they think that money, viewed as the officer's due, is required if they want help or cooperation from the police (Bayley, 1974, p. 76).

Although the history of policing in the United States is intertwined with political corruption, the first period (from the 1840s to the 1900s) of police history was particularly troublesome. Even the name of the period—"the political era"—emphasizes the close connection between the politics and the police in that period (see Kelling & Moore, 1988). Police administration consulted with the local politicians about police priorities and tasks; police officers were hired on the basis of political connections and promoted based

---

3. Klitgaard (1988, pp. 107–115) provides an example of Hong Kong's Independent Commission Against Corruption (ICAC), which at its peak had a reputation for high integrity in a society accustomed to corruption and tried to recruit individuals of high integrity for its units.

on bribes. Haller (1976, pp. 303–324) argues that corruption was actually one of the main functions of local government and that the police were only a part of the problem. Although police reformers starting from the early 1900s have substantially cut these close connections between local politicians and police agencies, in his study of four police departments experiencing major corruption scandals in the 1970s, Sherman (1978, p. 141) found strong connections between a corrupt political environment and police corruption in the period before the scandal in three of the four departments studied.

External Mechanisms of Control

External mechanisms of control include a heterogeneous group of institutions, from prosecutors and courts to the media and the public at large. Broadly speaking, if external mechanisms operate properly, they signal to police officers that the risks of engaging in police corruption are very high and that, if they do engage in it, they run a high risk of being caught, processed, and punished.

Having both examined police departments characterized by widespread organized corruption, the Knapp Commission (1972, pp. 252–253) and the Pennsylvania Crime Commission (1974, pp. 445, 785) both noted that the reality was such that the criminal justice system protected corrupt police officers, that police corruption was tolerated, and that the risk of detection and punishment was very low. To begin with, the Knapp Commission (1972) found corruption to be widespread in the NYPD in the 1970s. Yet, very few corrupt New York City police officers had been prosecuted and tried for police corruption: The prosecutors initiated 136 Supreme Court and Criminal Court proceedings involving 218 police officers over a period of 4½ years (Knapp Commission, 1972, p. 251). These proceedings resulted in the arrests of only 0.16% of the New York City police force. By the time the commission wrote the report, only 91 police officers had been convicted, of whom 80 had been sentenced (p. 252). Only 31 of the 80 sentenced police officers were imprisoned, and of those sentenced to prison, approximately half received a sentence of less than a year (p. 252).

Similar findings were reported by the Pennsylvania Crime Commission (1974). The commission focused on arrests in Philadelphia and reported that in the observed 6-year period 43 police officers were arrested on charges of corruption (p. 446). In the police agency that the commission described as characterized by widespread corruption, the arrested police officers at the time constituted less than 0.1% of the Philadelphia police force (Pennsylvania Crime Commission, 1974, p. 52). Furthermore, only 18 police officers were convicted, and only 3 of them served jail time, leading the commission to conclude: "In the view of its sentencing record, the judiciary has clearly demonstrated its reluctance to take a strong stance against the police offender in corruption cases" (Pennsylvania Crime Commission, 1974, p. 446).

In the course of its investigation of recent cases of police corruption in the Rampart area, the LAPD's Board of Inquiry found that several Rampart officers were involved in severe cases of police misconduct, including planting of evidence. Yet, as the board wrote (Los Angeles Police Department, 2000, p. 27), "Every one of these cases went through that entire system virtually unchallenged by anyone."

Conclusion

A police officer's propensity toward corruption, colored by the way the police officer perceives the ratio of costs and benefits of corruption, is shaped by organizational factors (such as the administration's failure to deal with corruption, weak supervision, low recruitment and selection standards, inadequate training in ethics, presence of a strong code of silence and culture tolerant of corruption, and failure to engage in proactive and reactive investigations of corrupt behavior), as well as society-wide factors (such as attitudes tolerant of corruption and abundant opportunities for corruption).

Frank Serpico—the most famous whistle-blower in the history of the NYPD—and Michael Dowd—the most infamous symbol for notoriously corrupt police officers in the 1990s—are two crowning examples of completely opposite views about and attitudes toward police corruption. They are not only the products of their personal characteristics, of what the police department did or did not do, and of what the society at large and its specific groups and actors did or did not do. Rather, both of them are also the results of a complex blend of individual, organizational, and external factors. However, all ingredients in this complex blend do not seem to carry the same weight. At the end of the day, the most powerful impact on police be-havior has been exerted by the police organization itself. Although individ-ual and external factors remain relevant for the control issues, the organi-zational factors are the ones of paramount importance. The police agency has the power to inhibit all but a few of the most predisposed and deter-mined police officers. Similarly, even the most honest police officers will be more willing to engage in corruption when they perceive that everyone else in the agency is doing it without suffering any negative consequences.

Successful control mechanisms have to take into account all the factors that have an impact on police corruption, from the individual ones to the or-ganizational and external ones. Although ultimately the administrator may decide to address only some factors affecting police officers' propensity to corruption, the decision has to be made after a careful examination of all the factors and a cost-and-benefit analysis of what would work best in the world of limited resources. Part of the decision has to include an examination of what control mechanisms are available, how effective they are, and why they fail to provide long-term continuous control of corruption. In the next two chapters, I focus on such issues to provide an in-depth analysis of what the current control mechanisms are and why they are unsuccessful in the control of corruption.

5

Corruption Control

Detection, Investigation, and Discipline

Although a variety of control mechanisms—from the police agency itself to the courts, mayors, media, and independent commissions—have been put in place to prevent police corruption, police scandals from New York (Mollen Commission, 1994) to Los Angeles (Los Angeles Police Department, 2000) and from Chicago (Warmbir, 2001, p. 6) to Miami (Burns & Sechrest, 1992) suggest that police officers do engage in organized and serious corruption. This chapter and the next chapter analyze the existing mechanisms of corruption control and the reasons for their lack of success. Especially illustrative cases are those of police agencies characterized by widespread and organized corruption.

The classic approach to the analysis of corruption control entails an examination (1) of the control efforts performed by the police agency itself and (2) of the control efforts carried out by institutions and groups external to the agency—legislatures, prosecutors, courts, the media, citizens, mayors, and independent commissions. The resulting strict division into internal, agency-based mechanisms and external, environment-based mechanisms or institutions of control has profound shortcomings, some of which translate into obstacles for successful control.

The first such shortcoming is the failure to recognize that a police department *is* a part of its environment, integrated and submerged into the community at large. Emphasizing the distinction between the police department and its environment undermines their interaction and fosters potential opposition by the members of the agency toward outside influences and control efforts.

Second, the way one institution carries out its control-related activities has a domino effect on the way other institutions perform their respective tasks; the roles performed by various institutions are intertwined and interdependent. For example, successful prosecution of corrupt police officers depends at least partially on the police department's control efforts. If the department does not investigate complaints of corruption and does not engage in proactive methods of control, the prosecutors' investigation and subsequent prosecution will be all the more challenging. Similarly, if the media do not engage in investigative journalism, the public is less likely to learn about corruption.

Third, the emphasis on institutions of control (rather than on control functions) clouds the fact that the responsibility of performing control-related functions may not be assigned to a single institution but, rather, may be shared by several institutions. For example, the task of improving the operation of the existing mechanism of control within the police agency may be assigned not only to the police agency itself but also to a citizen review board or an independent commission. Similarly, the task of limiting the opportunities for corruption is entrusted not only to the police agency itself (through the change of enforcement practices) but also to the legislature (through changes in laws) and the mayor or city manager (through changes in enforcement practices).

Fourth, organizing the critical analysis of control around institutions masks an important difference: Despite their common name, not all institutions within a particular group perform or focus on the same function. In particular, although any "procedure for handling citizen complaints about police officer misconduct that, at some point in the process, involves people who are not sworn officers" could be called "a citizen review" (Walker, 1995,

p. 4), the actual functions assigned to citizen review boards vary, from an emphasis on case-by-case reviews of complaints to a review of the agency's policies and recommendations for change.

With a view toward ameliorating these shortcomings, this chapter and the next center on the functions or tasks of corruption control as the primary organizing themes and treat the role of the institutions performing these tasks as the organizing theme of the second order. The analysis of the functions focuses on three principal topics: (1) what the task is, (2) who is assigned a particular task, and (3) what inherent obstacles and potential problems these institutions may confront in the performance of their tasks.

The discussion of the control-related functions flows from those more likely to be performed by the police agency itself to those more likely to be shared by the police agency and other institutions or exclusively performed by other institutions (Table 5.1). The purpose of this critical analysis is not to show that these mechanisms may operate quite successfully in some jurisdictions but to address an even more important issue: whether these mechanisms can operate effectively and fulfill control functions where they are needed the most—in highly corrupt police departments. Because the first two functions—detection and investigation of corruption and punishment of corrupt police officers—are the most extensive and fundamental, the discussion about existing control mechanisms is naturally divided into two chapters: In this chapter, I focus on detection and investigation of corruption and punishment of corrupt police officers, and in the next chapter I explore other functions (see Table 5.1).

The police agency can perform detection and investigation of corruption in a reactive way, once the agency receives the complaint, or in a proactive way, unrelated to a particular corruption complaint or a resolution of a historical case. I will first analyze successes and failures of various entities participating in reactive investigations (i.e., the police agencies, prosecutors, and independent commissions) and then examine issues related to various entities participating in proactive investigations (i.e., the police agencies, prosecutors, independent commissions, media, and citizen groups). In the second part of the chapter, I provide an in-depth examination of the challenges associated with the police agency's discipline of corrupt police officers and the criminal justice system's punishment of corrupt police officers.

Table 5.1 Control Functions and Institutions of Control

Functions	Institutions
1. Detect and investigate corruption	Police agency, prosecutors, media, independent commissions
2. Discipline/punish corrupt police officers	Police agency, courts (prosecutors)
3. Monitor propensity for corruption	Police agency, independent commissions
4. Cultivate culture intolerant of corruption	Police agency
5. Establish supervision and accountability	Police agency, mayor, public, media, courts
6. Set official policies and enforce them	Police agency, mayor
7. Provide resources for control	Police agency, mayor
8. Control the police agency's efforts to control corruption	Mayor, citizen reviews, prosecutors, independent commissions, media
9. Detect and investigate corruption not investigated by the police agency	Prosecutors, independent commissions, citizen reviews, media
10. Improve the existing system	Police agency, mayor, independent commissions, prosecutors, citizen reviews
11. Limit opportunities for corruption	Police agency, mayor, legislature, media
12. Disseminate true information about corruption	Police agency, mayor, media, independent commissions, prosecutors

Detect and Investigate Corruption

Although detection and investigation of corrupt activities could be entrusted to a number of institutions, from the police agencies themselves to local and federal prosecutors, independent commissions, the media, and citizen groups, this task is assigned primarily and systematically to the police agencies. Following the CALEA standards (Commission on Accreditation for Law Enforcement Agencies, 1994, 52.1.1), police agencies seeking accreditation should assign the investigation of allegations of "corruption, brutality, misuse of force, breach of civil rights, and criminal misconduct" (i.e., more serious allegations) to their internal affairs offices, and the investigation of allegations such as "rudeness on the part of the officer, tardiness, or insubordination" should be assigned to line supervisors.

Regardless of whether the corrupt activity is a violation of internal agency rules (and, therefore, subject to internal discipline) and/or a violation of the laws (and, therefore, subject to the application of criminal sanctions), the common feature is that the investigation is conducted by the agency itself.[1] Nevertheless, both the decision on how to proceed and who has the power to make this decision may differ across police agencies. Because different legal rules govern internal affairs investigation and criminal investigation (see *Garrity v. New Jersey*, 1967), investigation into allegations of criminal misconduct is separated—one investigation conducted by the internal affairs staff (the administrative investigation) and the other conducted by the investigators in the general criminal section (the criminal investigation). Criminal investigation into corruption, like any other criminal investigation, is regulated by the rules of criminal procedure and the rules of evidence. Internal, administrative investigation, on the other hand, is regulated by labor contracts and the police officers' Bill of Rights. The

---

1. Because the legal rules guiding an internal investigation and a criminal investigation differ, internal investigation (leading to the application of internal discipline) and criminal investigation (leading to the prosecution and application of criminal sanctions in a court-guided process) typically are separated within an agency. In *Garrity v. State of New Jersey* (1967, p. 562), the Supreme Court granted certiorari and heard the case involving appellants, police officers in New Jersey boroughs who were questioned during the course of a state investigation. Prior to being questioned, each appellant was warned "(1) that anything he said might be used against him in any state criminal proceeding; (2) that he had the privilege to refuse to answer if the disclosure would tend to incriminate him; but (3) that if he refused to answer he would be subject to removal from office" (p. 562). The Supreme Court held that the threat of removal from public office under the forfeiture-of-office statute, which was meant to induce public officials to waive their privilege against self-incrimination, rendered their resulting statements involuntary and, consequently, inadmissible in criminal proceedings. The majority concluded that they "now hold the protection of the individual under the Fourteenth Amendment against coerced statements prohibits use in subsequent proceedings of statements obtained under threat of removal from office, and that it extends to all, whether they are policemen or other members of our body politic" (p. 562). The *Garrity* decision, however, does not prohibit police agencies from obtaining statements from police officers under the threat of removal from public office and using those statements in administrative proceedings, such as internal disciplinary proceedings.

most noticeable differences between the two pertain to the evidence standards and the extent of the police officer's rights.

The investigation of corrupt activities by the police agency, "one of the most difficult investigative tasks which any law enforcement agency can undertake" (Pennsylvania Crime Commission, 1974, p. 31), could be initiated on the basis of the information obtained through (1) complaints of corruption or information about existing cases of corruption submitted to the police agency by citizens, police officers, or anybody else (i.e., reactive investigation) and (2) the initial collection of information by the agency itself (i.e., proactive investigation).

Reactive Investigation

POLICE DEPARTMENTS' REACTIVE INVESTIGATIONS A reactive investigation includes activities that the agency conducts after receiving a complaint alleging police misconduct. Its purpose is to determine whether the complaint has merit. Unlike the situation in the 1960s, when the overwhelming majority of surveyed police agencies did not have established procedures for investigating, successful completion of the accreditation process nowadays requires police agencies to have such procedures in place (see Commission on Accreditation for Law Enforcement Agencies, 1994, 52.1.1).

Reactive investigations by police agencies can be initiated on the basis of complaints submitted either by citizens or by police officers, both of whom could be participants in or observers of corrupt transactions. It is crucial to examine the degree of citizens' and police officers' willingness to report and the possible obstacles they may face, as successful performance of the first function—detection and investigation of police corruption, particularly reactive investigation—largely depends on the complaints they submit.

CITIZEN-INITIATED COMPLAINTS Citizens who participated in corrupt transactions are one of the best sources of information—as participants, they have detailed knowledge of the incident. However, their ability to recognize the transaction as corrupt and their willingness to report it to the police depend on a number of issues. The cognitive process, from the realization of the corrupt incident until the decision to report (see Felstiner, Abel,

& Sarat, 1980, p. 631), may be different from a similar cognitive process following, for example, incidents of use of excessive force. Indeed, unlike people who were physically abused by police officers and who would have few problems recognizing and correctly labeling the police officers' activity, someone who willingly engaged in a bribe would typically justify his or her decision as the cost of doing business and not explicitly name the transaction as corruption. Conversely, a citizen whose property was stolen by the police would experience no difficulty in labeling the activity as a theft but usually would not be able to blame the police for it (e.g., the property was stolen at the crime scene from an unconscious person or from an empty burglarized residence). Extortion is the one type of corruption citizens are most likely to recognize and label correctly; they provided money or other personal gain to the police because of the force used or threatened.

Even people who recognized and labeled the incident correctly might not necessarily use the official route and file a complaint with the police agency. A person who made a rational decision that it was better to bribe a police officer than to be processed officially has no incentive to change that decision and thereby expose his or her own involvement in not one but two crimes. On the other hand, someone who perceived being forced into such an arrangement has a stronger motivation to disclose the transaction. People may also be reluctant to report because of the lack of evidence to support their claims and the issues of their own credibility, especially if the only evidence in the case is their word against the word of a police officer. Therefore, another frequent facet of the problem is that the overall reputation of the citizen—who may be a prostitute, a drug dealer, or a thief—may be highly questionable, which in turn limits the complainant's ability to challenge the police officer's word and decreases the chances of proving the case.

Citizens who *witness* corrupt transactions or notice obvious signs of corruption (e.g., police tolerance of double- or triple-parked cars on the street in front of a particular restaurant [Knapp Commission, 1972, p. 146]) may be in a better position to label these behaviors correctly than the actual participants, but they may lack the motivation to make the effort to report it to the police or may fear reprisal for reporting. When corruption is accepted by the community at large as a way of doing business or is simply tolerated because of the benefits it brings, as was clearly the case in Philadelphia in the 1980s (Moore, 1997, p. 62) or in New York in the 1990s (Krauss, 1994), people who witness such transactions may be reluctant to report them and, if they choose to report, may be ostracized for doing so.

Like complainants in any other case, citizens willing to complain about corruption, regardless of whether they are participants in the transactions themselves or are mere observers, may experience obstacles created by the police agency to eliminate frivolous and unfounded complaints or simply to discourage citizens from filing complaints for a variety of other reasons. The President's Commission on Law Enforcement and Administration of Justice reported that the police used various methods of discouraging citizens from filing complaints. For example, almost 40% of those who filed complaints against police were arrested for filing false charges, in comparison with the arrest of only 0.3% of those who filed similar charges against private citizens (1967b, p. 195). It is not surprising, then, that only 21% of the complainants surveyed by the U.S. Civil Rights Commission in 1981 felt comfortable filing complaints at the police building, while 44% preferred filing complaints at some other location (U.S. Commission on Civil Rights, 1981, p. 51). Although the situation appears to be gradually improving, potential complainants still face obstacles.

Complaint rates and the number of subsequent reactive investigations by the police agencies may be severely distorted by these barriers. To begin with, potential complainants may not be aware of their right to file a complaint. Similarly, they may not be familiar with the complaint system (see, e.g., Russell, 1978, pp. 52–53). Jones and colleagues reported that citizens' propensity to contact officials (to request a service or file a complaint) is affected by both their need for that service and their familiarity with the system (Jones, Greenberg, Kaufman, & Drew, 1977, p. 148). Russell (1978), for example, found that one of the six typical reasons that citizens in England and Wales did not file a complaint against the police was that they were not aware of the complaint procedure (pp. 52–53).

Furthermore, the procedures and the submission requirements may be complex, and the potential complainants may be required to sign their complaints, swear their complaints, or have their statements certified or notarized. For example, Pate and Fridell (1993, p. 133) found that between one half and three fourths of the police agencies they surveyed require potential complainants to sign their complaints; between 9.1% and 32.0% of the police agencies, depending on the type of agency, require that citizens swear to the complaints; and between 4.5% and 19% of the police agencies, depending on the type of agency, require that complaints be certified or notarized. Furthermore, citizens willing to file a complaint could be threatened with criminal charges of false reports (see, e.g., President's Commission on Law Enforcement and Administration of Justice, 1967b, p. 195). Not surprisingly, less than 5% of all the respondents to the 1996–1997 International Crime Victim Survey who said that they were asked to pay a bribe to a police officer (see Table 2.1 in chapter 2) said that they reported the act to the police.

Viewed from another vantage point, despite their familiarity with the process and their willingness to jump through the hoops, citizens may be reluctant to file a complaint if they do not have at least a minimal level of trust in the police in general, or if they do not believe that the police will follow through with the complaint and open an investigation. This distrust in the police and their ability to police themselves could indeed have a negative impact on the people's willingness to report.

> We saw much evidence of this distrust. Many people—sometimes represented by experienced lawyers—brought the Commission evidence of serious corruption which they said they would not have disclosed to the police or to a District Attorney or to the City's Department of Investigation. Even today, complainants who call the Commission and are told that the investigation has ended often refuse to take down the phone numbers of these agencies. It makes no difference whether or not this distrust is justified. The harsh reality is that it exists. (Knapp Commission, 1972, p. 14)

Furthermore, citizens may be discouraged from reporting because the police are in the position to decide whether to proceed with the investigation in the first place, and they may "discourage citizens through indifference, rudeness, or failure to act on complaints in a timely fashion" (Walker & Bumphus, 1992, p. 13). For example, the survey conducted by the Office of the Independent Police Auditor for the City of San José indicated that 22% of the surveyed community members should have filed a complaint but did not do so for various reasons: "fearing that officers would retaliate, feeling the complaint would not be taken seriously, not knowing how to file a complaint, were too busy, or did not want to get into problems with 'the law'" (T. Guerrero Daley [independent police auditor, City of San José, CA], personal communication, November 14, 2000). Moreover, citizens may be less than eager to complain because the final outcome, if investigated at all, is often disappointing for them—police agencies sustain only a small percentage of all complaints (typically less than one quarter; see, e.g., Pate & Fridell, 1993, p. 42; Perez, 1994, p. 113). Alternatively, they may decide to report the corrupt activity to another body with a more credible reputation, such as the FBI or federal or local prosecutors.

POLICE-INITIATED COMPLAINTS Despite the fact that they are more likely to succeed with their complaints than citizens are (Griswold, 1994, p. 217), police officers' motivations not to report their own misconduct may be even stronger than those of the general public: If confession of a corrupt activity is made, police officers risk not only being prosecuted criminally (and sentenced to imprisonment) but also being processed administratively (and losing their jobs and benefits without the possibility of obtaining subsequent employment in law enforcement).

Although police officers are provided with numerous opportunities to observe corrupt behavior by fellow police officers through their socialization into policing and through their day-to-day activities as trusted members of the informal group (Stoddard, 1974, p. 292), the existence of a strong code of silence—informal prohibition against reporting—keeps them from reporting misconduct to the agency.

> Patrol officers, too, shut their eyes to corruption. Officers from various commands told this Commission that they would never report even serious corruption because they feared the consequences of being labeled a "rat" and lacked confidence in the Department's commitment to uncover corruption and maintain confidentiality. Indeed, so powerful is this code of silence that in dozens of Commission interviews and in recent group discussions held by the Department, police officers admitted that they would not openly report an officer as corrupt as Michael Dowd—though most of them would silently hope

that he would be arrested and removed from the Department. (Mollen Commission, 1994, p. 4)

Recent research studies show that not all forms of corruption are equally protected by the code; perhaps not surprisingly, the more serious forms of corruption (bribery, theft) are less likely to be protected (see Klockars et al., 1997). Nevertheless, in the agencies characterized by widespread corruption, the code of silence is stronger and more encompassing, and even serious forms of corruption may be protected by the code, thus hindering any attempt to report undesirable activities sanctioned by the peer group. For example, at the time the Knapp Commission (1972) found widespread corruption in the NYPD, the commission was warned that the code of silence was strong and that it would be difficult to find a police officer willing to speak frankly and openly or do the necessary undercover work. In fact, the commission found only a few police officers willing to talk (Knapp Commission, 1972). Therefore, in the highly corrupt agencies in which, among other things, confidentiality protections are broken (see, e.g., Mollen Commission, 1994, p. 107) and reporting of fellow police officers' misconduct is punished instead of rewarded (see, e.g., Mollen Commission, 1994, p. 102), it is not reasonable to expect police officers to report misconduct, even when the signs of corruption are obvious, such as driving an expensive car and even forgetting to pick up a paycheck for months (see, e.g., Mollen Commission, 1994).

POLICE AGENCIES AND COMPLAINTS Complaints of corruption, filed by citizens or police officers, are not frequent. An example from the NYPD illustrates that the number of complaints officially registered by the agencies, especially corrupt ones, is unlikely to match the actual number of complaints people wanted to file with the agency. While Cohen (1972, p. 58) reported in the 1970s that complaints regarding gratuities constituted only 5.7% of the complaints for a cohort of active police officers, the Knapp Commission (1972) found widespread corruption in the same agency at the time.

Even when citizens or police officers want to come forward with information about corruption, the agency has a strong motive to keep the lid on corruption as long as the police administrators, the media, citizen groups, and the public at large subscribe to the rotten-apple theory. The theory is grounded on two basic premises: "First, the morale of the Department requires that there be no official recognition of corruption, even though practically all members of the Department know it is in truth extensive; second, the Department's public image and effectiveness require official denial of this truth" (Knapp Commission, 1972, p. 6). The data obtained in the course of independent investigations of corrupt police agencies indicate that the investigated agencies acted in accordance with the rotten-apple viewpoint. For example, the Knapp Commission (1972, pp. 210–213) discovered a file containing allegations of narcotics-related corruption against 72 police officers. Administrators were aware of its existence but took no action pursuant to the information in that file. In fact, they behaved in accordance with one of the notes written on the file, "to get our men out of that" (Knapp Commission, 1972, pp. 210–213).

The failures discovered by the three independent commissions went far beyond what could be explained within the confines of the rotten-apple approach:

- not establishing written guidelines (Pennsylvania Crime Commission, 1974, pp. 455, 459)
- denying resources and manpower to the units assigned to internal control
- assigning inexperienced police officers to undercover work (Pennsylvania Crime Commission, 1974, p. 480) and investigations (Mollen Commission, 1994, p. 85; Pennsylvania Crime Commission, 1974, p. 473)
- fragmenting the system of control and the overall control strategy (Knapp Commission, 1972, p. 205; Mollen Commission, 1994, p. 13)
- failing to coordinate investigative activities (Knapp Commission, 1972, p. 209)
- ignoring the information obtained from field associates (Mollen Commission, 1994, p. 3), other police officers, and the public (Mollen Commission, 1994, p. 15)
- denying access to files (Mollen Commission, 1994, p. 89)
- allowing records to be disorganized (Knapp Commission, 1972, p. 209)

- failing to use turned corrupt officers and polygraph tests as investigative techniques (Knapp Commission, 1972, p. 208; Pennsylvania Crime Commission, 1974, p. 484)
- openly hiding complaints and allegations of corruption (Mollen Commission, 1994, pp. 96–98)
- failing to look for patterns of corruption (Knapp Commission, 1972, p. 208; Mollen Commission, 1994, pp. 101–102)
- targeting petty misconduct (Mollen Commission, 1994, p. 3)
- closing investigations prematurely (Mollen Commission, 1994, p. 88)

It is not surprising that in the 1970s NYPD environment, characterized by many of these listed failures, Detective Frank Serpico's corruption complaint was mishandled; "they [David Durk and Frank Serpico] had gone to First Deputy Police Commissioner John F. Walsh, the Department's top anti-corruption official, to ask for help. They had gone to Arnold Fraiman, the city's Commissioner of Investigation, to ask for help. They had gone to Mayor Lindsay's closest assistant, Jay Kriegel, to ask for help" (Burnham, 1978, p. 10). Perhaps what *is* surprising is that out of this mishandled complaint grew a large scandal, which resulted in the establishment of the Knapp Commission (1972, p. 196).

An illustrative example of the failure to react to citizen complaints is that of Michael Dowd. In May 1992, six New York City police officers were arrested not by the NYPD but by Suffolk County Police (Mollen Commission, 1994, p. 1). The press soon uncovered that Michael Dowd, one of the arrested officers, had been the subject of 15 allegations of police corruption reported to the NYPD over a period of 6 years. None of the previous allegations had been proven by the department, "despite substantial evidence that Dowd regularly and openly engaged in serious criminal conduct" (Mollen Commission, 1994, p. 1).

In fact, the Mollen Commission (1994, p. 88) found that most complaint cases (60–70%) were closed prematurely because the "investigators found insufficient evidence to either prove or disprove the case." This outcome should not be surprising because, as the Mollen Commission discovered, many of these cases were closed *before* the investigators took the basic investigatory steps. Furthermore, the Mollen Commission found the infamous "Tickler File" used to conceal corruption cases: "Many of the Tickler File corruption cases were quite serious in nature, ranging from sale and use of narcotics, protecting drug dealers, accepting payoffs from organized crime figures, to perjury and leaking confidential information." The commission found that approximately 40 cases over the 5 years preceding the investigation had never been recorded in the official records or sent to the prosecutors. Furthermore, the commission discovered that the department simply failed to provide 230 cases of serious police corruption to the prosecutors and also used other mechanisms to conceal corruption cases. For example, approximately 1,500 cases of police corruption were classified as "police impersonation" cases each year and were sent to be investigated outside internal affairs. Ultimately, they "died on the vine" (Mollen Commission, 1994, pp. 96–98).

Similarly, a *Boston Globe* investigation revealed that five Boston police officers most frequently named in citizen complaints were investigated 100 times by the Internal Affairs Division from 1981 to 1990 (Murphy, 1992). In 90 of the 100 cases, they were cleared of all allegations, and in the remaining cases "the officers generally received mild reprimands" (Murphy, 1992, p. 1). These allegations were not trivial and vindictive, as further developments show: Steven Borden was named in 16 complaints before being convicted of drug dealing, and Carlos A. Luna's name appeared in 15 complaints before he was convicted of perjury (Murphy, 1992).

In sum, the available data illustrate that dedicated corruption control cannot rely on corruption complaints as the predominant way of initiating control efforts because of the lack of motivation by citizens, police officers, and police departments to report and investigate instances of corruption and because of the potential obstacles the general public and police officers who are willing to report may encounter.

PROSECUTORS' REACTIVE INVESTIGATION OF MISCONDUCT Although each corrupt transaction has at least two parties, prosecutors do not take an equal interest in both. In the typical corrupt transaction with only two witnesses to the event—the police officer and the citizen—for the prosecutor to obtain sufficient evidence, one of the parties must testify in the case. The prosecutors view the police officer's crime as more serious: "The police are the public officials paid to enforce the law; they, therefore, have violated the public trust and are the more serious offenders" (Dennis & Wilson, 1988, p. 69). As Dennis and Wilson further explain, prosecutors have to convince the bribe giver to testify, and they have additional ways of motivating these parties to participate:

> The task at this point is to induce the payer to cooperate with you and provide information and evidence that will result in the successful prosecution of the police officers. Obviously, most of these persons will not offer their assistance for altruistic reasons, but will only cooperate when they have no choice. Accordingly, it is necessary to employ some type of process in order to make these individuals cooperate. (1988, p. 70)

As suspects and defendants, citizens and police officers alike have incentives to provide as much information about others as possible to obtain better plea-bargaining deals for themselves (see, e.g., Jarrett, 1988, p. 211). However, the truthfulness of the information they provide could be suspect. A possible solution, rarely available in corruption cases, is to obtain corroborating evidence (e.g., drug dealers' and police officers' telephone records, police officers' financial records; see, e.g., K. Cloherty [assistant U.S. attorney, Boston], personal communication, May 17, 2000; Kellner, 1988, p. 46), especially for historical cases. As Trott (1988) argues, there is "the proven rule of thumb that the jury will not accept the word of a criminal unless it is corroborated by other reliable evidence" (p. 130).

Another way prosecutors can learn about corruption is through anonymous tips. Although the motivation of these information providers is not as transparent as that of suspects involved in plea bargaining, checking the accuracy of the information provided through the search for corroborating evidence is a must. For example, when a clean police officer is assigned to a corrupt unit, the prosecutor may receive a tip alleging the officer's involvement in corruption, and the tip is clearly motivated by the desire to get rid of the officer from that unit (K. Cloherty, personal communication, May 17, 2000).

The prosecutors can also obtain information about police corruption in an agency through investigative work and the leads provided by journalists (M. T. Cagle [assistant state attorney, deputy chief for special prosecutions, division chief for racketeering/organized crime prosecution unit, Miami office, Miami, FL], personal communication, May 25, 2000; K. Cloherty, personal communication, May 17, 2000). Jeremiah O'Sullivan wrote about the establishment of larger federal prosecutors' offices and highlighted the media as a source of information for corruption cases (1988, p. 266). Accordingly, Joseph M. Lawless (who wrote about the tactics of the smaller offices) instructed the prosecutors:

> A final, and frequently very fruitful source, is the local press. If a story appears that the state is selling a property to a cohort of the Governor at a bargain price, or that land is being purchased by the state at a highly inflated price, or that bizarre zoning decisions are being rendered that substantially affect property values, you may wish to go out and shake that particular tree to see what may fall out. (1988, p. 274)

Although infrequent in the domain of crime- and police-related stories, several well-known pieces of investigative journalism have triggered prosecutors' attention. One of the most famous examples is that of the former *New York Times* journalist David Burnham in the 1970s, whose story eventually led to the establishment of the Knapp Commission (1972). A more recent example is an investigation conducted by the *Boston Globe* staff (see, e.g., O'Neill, Zuckoff, & Lehr, 1996; MacQuarrie, 1996): The prosecutors' and the department's interests (see, e.g., K. Cloherty, personal communication, May 17, 2000; O'Neill et al., 1996) were piqued when the *Boston Globe* published a series of stories alleging police involvement in numerous counts of theft, extortion, and conspiracy (O'Neill et al., 1996; Zuckoff, 1997). Keeping in mind that investigative journalism takes time and is costly (see, e.g., Burnham, 1978, p. 8), requires skill, and could have serious adverse consequences for the journalists as well as the newspapers (e.g., the everyday working relationship between the journalists and the police department could be severely jeopardized by an investigative piece on police corruption), it is not surprising that the majority of the published stories concerning the police are short summaries of the facts of ongoing cases, as provided by the police department.

The most systematic way the prosecutors, both federal and local, should learn about police corruption in the agency is through the agency itself. When an agency is investigating cases of corruption and is actively collecting information, at the end of each criminal investigation in which the original suspicion was confirmed, the case should be transferred to the prosecutor. However, as the examples of the NYPD over a time span of three decades (Knapp Commission, 1972; Mollen Commission, 1994, p. 98) clearly indicate, corrupt police departments not only fail to actively collect information about corruption but also actually try to hide the information provided by the public and police officers alike. The Mollen Commission (1994, p. 98), for example, discovered that the NYPD failed to provide the prosecutors with 230 cases of serious police corruption.

The common feature of all these avenues of obtaining information about police corruption is that, for various reasons, in reality they do not provide a systematic, continuous source of information to prosecutors, especially not in highly corrupt agencies where such information is needed the most. Checking the accuracy of information and finding corroborating evidence can be a challenge in itself, even when the information is provided and the prosecutor is willing to conduct the investigation. The code of silence among the police, the payers' reluctance to provide information, limited technical surveillance skills and equipment, and jurisdictional limitations render police corruption cases difficult to develop (see, e.g., Dennis & Wilson, 1988, p. 67).

Assuming that these substantial obstacles were overcome (a somewhat unlikely assumption in corrupt agencies) and that the information has somehow been provided to the prosecutors, it does not automatically mean that the prosecutor will open an investigation. In the world of limited resources (see, e.g., O'Sullivan, 1988, p. 268), in which the prosecutor's own success is judged by the number of cases won and the public is more interested in prosecutions of violent street crimes, prosecutors are forced to select cases that have a greater probability of success, given the strength of the evidence, credibility of witnesses, and level of control over the case. There are additional factors that may make a local prosecutor unwilling to proceed with a case concerning police corruption. The number of cases assigned to the prosecutor can effectively discourage any serious long-term investigation of corruption. For example, because of a heavy caseload, district attorneys in New York in the 1970s focused primarily on prosecuting cases that originated elsewhere (Knapp Commission, 1972, p. 257), which they were inclined to pursue because the cases had already been originated, whereas addressing widespread corruption in the city would also have to include the arduous task of investigating the case in the first place.

District attorneys work closely with police officers on ongoing criminal cases. Over time they become more sympathetic to the police in general and develop professional and personal relationships with police officers. Both of these factors may have an impact on the way a prosecutor uses discretion and is willing to open investigations and prosecute police officers from the agency. As the Knapp Commission emphasized, "a district attorney and his assistants, who work daily with police officers, often find it difficult to believe allegations of corruption among policemen who are brother officers of the investigators with whom they work" (1972, p. 256). Consequently, the Knapp Commission recommended the establishment of an independent prosecutor (1972, p. 262).

A national survey of prosecutors in state courts revealed that more than 95% of chief prosecutors were elected locally (DeFrances, 2002, p. 11). The fact that they are locally elected officials, dependent upon public support for their reelection, could affect their zeal to investigate corruption cases. If the constituency is tolerant of police corruption or is not interested in the issue, as seemed to be the case in Philadelphia in the 1980s and New York in the 1990s (see Moore, 1997, p. 63; Krauss, 1994), targeting cases of police corruption will not lead to widespread public support and may undermine the chances for reelection.

In the situation in which "pervasive corruption within a local police department may make the investigation and prosecution of corruption by local authorities politically sensitive if not impossible" (Dennis & Wilson, 1988, p. 67), space potentially opens up for federal prosecutors to step in. The Public Integrity Section of the U.S. Department of Justice (1999) described a number of cases prosecuted successfully in 1998. For example, in one such case the potential payer contacted the FBI and agreed to cooperate in the investigation, and the FBI captured on tape Alex H. Richardson, a former deputy sheriff for Lake County, Indiana, soliciting the payments and accepting $10,000 in cash. Richardson pleaded guilty to a one-count indictment charging him with extortion under color of official right in violation of the Hobbs Act (U.S. Department of Justice, 1999). In another case, while the FBI was monitoring radio communication as part of a drug corruption investigation, the agents overheard a New Orleans police officer "putting a contract" on a woman who submitted a complaint against him (Walker, 2001, p. 3).

Federal prosecutors can rely on the help and sophisticated surveillance skills and equipment provided by the FBI and have the advantage of being able to handle multidistrict cases. However, a few hundred federal prosecutors scattered throughout the United States do not have a realistic chance of continuously monitoring more than 700,000 sworn employees in almost 19,000 state and local law enforcement agencies (Pastore & Maguire, 2000, p. 37). Furthermore, because they typically do not have close professional relationships with the local police officers (relationships that could also be perceived as motivation *not* to investigate corruption), to a certain extent federal prosecutors have limited access to information about corruption in local police agencies either through anonymous tips or through confidential information from police officers. If federal prosecutors rely on the state and local police officers to provide information and to investigate their fellow officers, they might face the same issues experienced by internal affairs units and local prosecutors: In police agencies, especially corrupt ones, police officers' loyalties lie primarily with their fellow officers.

However, citizens may be more willing to provide information to investigators not associated with the police agency under investigation. The Knapp Commission (1972) noted that "the investigators' backgrounds as federal officers aided them in that many witnesses who would refuse to talk to a policeman were willing to talk to an investigator with no apparent ties to the Department. This attitude, which reflected a deep-seated mistrust of the Department's ability to police itself, was repeatedly encountered during the investigation" (p. 45).

Finally, special prosecutors could be established with a limited task and/ or mandate. As their name suggests, one of the greatest obstacles in successful corruption control is their "special," temporary, or limited nature; they are empowered to investigate only a particular case or set of cases within a prespecified time frame. Faced with the findings of widespread corruption in police departments and local prosecutors' lack of willingness to investigate and prosecute cases of police corruption, both the Pennsylvania Crime Commission (1974, p. 824) and the Knapp Commission (1972, p. 262) recommended the establishment of the special prosecutor ("the Office of Special Prosecutor" and "a Special Deputy Attorney General," respectively). The special deputy attorney general proposed by the Knapp Commission would "continue this [Knapp] Commission's role in spotting patterns of corruption and providing impetus for reform as well as to prosecute corruption-related crimes." The special prosecutor was expected to mitigate the deficiencies of the NYPD's internal system and those of district attorneys and supplement them with an ongoing independent anticorruption effort until the regular mechanisms "should be adequate to cope with corruption" (Knapp Commission, 1972, p. 261). Based on the recommendations made by the Knapp Commission, the Office of the State Special Prosecutor was established in the 1970s, only to be dissolved in 1990 (Mollen Commission, 1994, p. 150).

INDEPENDENT COMMISSIONS' REACTIVE INVESTIGATION OF MISCONDUCT A typical independent commission has a powerful but temporary impact; it is established in the midst of political momentum spurred by a scandal that had developed following public revelations of corruption allegations (see, e.g., Knapp Commission, 1972; Mollen Commission, 1994; Pennsylvania Crime Commission, 1974). As discussed earlier, the establishment of a commission and its subsequent work are conditional on the development of a full-blown scandal (see Sherman, 1978), the political pressure created by it, and politicians' reactions. Political conditions in which a commission is assembled determine its potential success. For example, unlike the Knapp Commission (1972) and the Mollen Commission (1994), the Pennsylvania Crime Commission (1974) was "never able to remove the taint of conducting a politically inspired investigation" (p. 754), had no cooperation from the Philadelphia mayor and police commissioner, faced opposition from police officers and citizens who refused to cooperate with the commission (p. 744), and had problems with obtaining access to the department, equipment, and manpower. Moreover, the commission's own establishment was challenged in court (Pennsylvania Crime Commission, 1974, p. 762).

General tasks assigned to the commissions usually are to determine the actual extent and nature of corruption in an agency (see, e.g., Knapp Commission, 1972, p. 273; Mollen Commission, 1994, p. 1; Pennsylvania Crime Commission, 1974, pp. 40–41), find factors contributing to corruption, and propose solutions for reform. Therefore, the purposes of the commissions and their focus "on identifying patterns of police corruption and on defining the problem areas in sufficient detail to lay the groundwork for the remedial recommendations" (Knapp Commission, 1972, p. 273) effectively move the spotlight away from individual cases. The search for patterns involves investigation of individual cases as well, but the commission's temporary nature eliminates the possibility of focusing on individual cases on a continuous and regular basis. The Pennsylvania Crime Commission (1974, p. 3) "came across more than 150 officers who could be indicted . . .; an estimated additional 250 officers who could be dismissed or disciplined . . .; and more than 300 other officers . . . who should be further investigated." However, in the grand scheme of things, the purpose of these investigations of individual cases was primarily to collect supporting evidence about the *patterns* of corruption, as was noted by the Pennsylvania Crime Commission.

> Thus, the Commission was created as an independent fact-finding agency without any prosecuting power or responsibility. Its purpose is to focus attention on general problems in the criminal justice system, with particular emphasis on corruption. The Commission has operated and will continue to operate on the assumption that to focus on individual acts of wrongdoing cannot correct system-wide problems. The specific facts contained in its reports are presented solely to support the validity of the Commission's overall factual findings. (1974, pp. 40–41)

Another problem faced by independent commissions is finding reliable and skilled investigators. The Pennsylvania Crime Commission (1974, p. 763) and the Mollen Commission (1994, p. 11) both used former members of the agency under investigation as investigators. Such an approach is beneficial because it provides internal information about corruption in the agency and probably eases the access. At the same time, it is burdened with loyalty conflicts because of the investigators' relationships with the remaining members of the agency.

> A corruption probe assignment given to an investigator with former ties with the Department under scrutiny places the investigator in a potentially difficult and vulnerable conflict position. Unfair pressures can be brought to bear, because many of the investigator's friends and family may have ongoing relationships with the unit under investigation. (Pennsylvania Crime Commission, 1974, p. 763)

Even if it relies on the police officers formerly employed by the police department, a commission, like any other investigative body, faces obstacles in obtaining information from citizens and police officers alike. Commissions need to find a way to shatter the code of silence among the police, motivate citizens to share information, and gain access to the agency's records. The level of legal authority given to a commission, one of the factors instrumental for overcoming the power of the code of silence and the reluctance of police officers to provide information, could influence the commission's ability to perform its task. However, as the Pennsylvania Crime Commission (1974, p. 741) discovered, having the power to subpoena witnesses and grant them immunity is not in itself a guarantee of actually obtaining truthful testimony, and it can result in resource-draining and tiresome legal battles.

Proactive Investigation of Misconduct

Proactive investigation of police corruption involves a series of self-initiated activities by an organization—the police agency, prosecutor, independent commission, media, or citizen groups—with the purpose of collecting relevant information. A common feature of proactive investigation conducted by any organization is that the organization takes an active role and focuses not on checking the accuracy of a particular complaint and resolving that particular historical case but on investigating predisposition for corruption and the extent and nature of corruption within the police department, with the possibility of building corruption cases by collecting and securing evidence for the prosecution.

This heterogeneous set of proactive methods varies across two dimensions: who the targets are and what the level of intrusion is. In terms of targets, proactive methods range from randomly conducted ones (e.g., random integrity tests on a sample of all police officers), those targeting a particular population (e.g., integrity tests targeting only recruits or rookies), and those focusing on a particular police officer or group of police officers (e.g., an undercover operation when there is reasonable belief that the targets of the operation are committing crimes). Proactive methods also vary with respect to the level of intrusion, ranging from the less intrusive ones, such as the examination of public records, to the more intrusive ones, such as electronic surveillance or undercover operations.

POLICE DEPARTMENTS' PROACTIVE INVESTIGATION OF MISCONDUCT
Police departments, as the frontier and the basis for systematic collection of
information obtained through proactive methods, can use a variety of such
methods, from early warning systems and integrity tests to turned police
officers and full-blown undercover operations. However, just as they have
motives to hide and dispose of outside information alleging corruption (i.e.,
complaints), corrupt police agencies have no motivation to pursue any active information-gathering efforts. As long as finding cases of corruption in
an agency is evaluated primarily in negative terms, regardless of the actual
corruption level, the agency will have very little motivation to engage in
proactive investigations and find patterns of corruption (see, e.g., Pennsylvania Crime Commission, 1974, p. 512). In fact, it is quite likely that these
attitudes actually cripple anticorruption efforts. The Knapp Commission
noted that "because of the 'rotten apple' theory, the Department did not utilize investigative methods such as turning corrupt policemen and allowing
a known corrupt situation to continue over a period of time in the interest
of rounding up all offenders" (Knapp Commission, 1972, p. 208). Consequently, as the Mollen Commission (1994, p. 11) noted, for the NYPD
"avoiding scandal became more important than fighting corruption."

All three influential commissions investigating allegations of widespread and/or serious corruption—the Knapp Commission, the Pennsylvania Crime Commission, and the Mollen Commission—reported that the
investigated agencies (the NYPD in the 1970s and 1990s and the Philadelphia Police Department in the 1970s) failed to use proactive investigative
methods (see Knapp Commission, 1972, p. 208; Mollen Commission, 1994,
p. 101; Pennsylvania Crime Commission, 1974, p. 483) and, instead of looking for patterns of corruption, focused on a very few isolated cases. The
Mollen Commission "found that the IAD's [Internal Affairs Division] investigative system reacted solely to isolated complaints. It did not pursue
patterns of corruption and conspiratorial wrongdoing as was done in investigative commands other than IAD. Of course, such an approach guar-
antees that the full scope of corruption will never come to light" (1994,
pp. 101–102).

The commission further noted that the department failed to use proactive methods that were routinely utilized in all other criminal investigations, that the "Self-Initiated Investigation Unit" (charged with the task of

conducting self-generated investigations) did not conduct a single self-initiated investigation in the period of 5 years, and that the undercover programs were poorly used and had provided information that led to substantiation of only four cases in the period of 10 years (p. 102). Similarly, the Pennsylvania Crime Commission concluded:

> The effectiveness of the Internal Affairs Bureau in rooting out corruption internally is crippled by the almost complete lack of the use of aggressive investigative techniques. Nearly all investigations of corruption in the Department are done in response to complaints or allegations received by the Police Department. Little effort is made to initiate investigations, to expand investigations, or even to follow them up in the most aggressive manner. (1974, p. 483)

PROSECUTORS' PROACTIVE INVESTIGATION OF MISCONDUCT   Prosecutors can resort to a wide range of proactive methods, from the review of mail covers, telephone records, and financial records[2] to the use of electronic surveillance and undercover operations (see Keefer, 1988, p. 139). An advantage of proactive methods, especially undercover operations, is that prosecutors have more control over the quality and type of evidence to be collected than they do in reactive, historical cases. Furthermore, it seems to be easier to find supporting evidence for proactive cases—"cases built upon current events controlled through undercover participants" (Kellner, 1988, p. 44)—because the corrupt transaction could be recorded and, unlike some complainants in reactive cases, carefully selected participants in the undercover stings (typically undercover police officers) should not have credibility problems in the subsequent trials.

The same set of obstacles that may keep local prosecutors from engaging in reactive investigations could prevent them from engaging in proactive investigations as well, ranging from objective factors such as heavy

---

2. Examination of a police officer's financial records, for example, could be a part of either a proactive or a reactive investigation. If used to corroborate the complaint provided by victims, then the focus is primarily reactive. If, on the other hand, it is used as a part of the early-warning system employed by the police agency, then the nature of the investigation is proactive.

caseloads, limited resources, and the difficulty of collecting evidence in corruption cases because of their secretive nature, to subjective factors such as everyday reliance on, and the relationship with, the police and the potential political dependence.

Even if prosecutors were willing to engage in proactive investigations, they would probably face obstacles in trying to gain the trust of the police officers in the agency and breaking the code of silence. The involvement of local police officers in undercover roles has potential advantages in obtaining easier access to the agency and gaining knowledge about the agency and its operation at the outset, but assigning local police officers to investigate their fellow police officers, especially in the police agencies characterized by widespread corruption, potentially jeopardizes the level of trust in, and objectivity of, these police officers. On the other hand, reliance on police officers from other agencies or the FBI for the undercover work could result in the inability to obtain information, in prolonged investigations, and in succeeding in investigating only a very limited subset of cases.

In addition to being a rather minuscule group relative to the number of all police officers employed at the local level, federal prosecutors may also face the same problems in pursuing proactive investigations that they face in reactive investigations, including limited resources and the difficulty of gaining access to the police officers in the agency under investigation.

The findings reported by the two independent commissions in the 1970s—the Knapp Commission and the Pennsylvania Crime Commission—provide support for the argument that one cannot rely on the prosecutors, nor can one be certain that the prosecutors will perform the task of investigating corruption, even if the police agency is not investigating corruption among its own members. In particular, although the two commissions found widespread corruption in the two agencies, the number of cases processed by the prosecutors (cases resulting both from reactive and proactive investigations) tended to be very low. The Knapp Commission (1972, p. 252) reported that prosecutors initiated only approximately 30 cases per year from the NYPD, the largest police department in the country, with tens of thousands of police officers. Similarly, the Pennsylvania Crime Commission (1974, pp. 52, 446) reported that in the Philadelphia Police Department, a department that had 8,303 sworn police officers in 1974 and had been characterized by widespread corruption, there were on average seven arrests per year.

INDEPENDENT COMMISSIONS' PROACTIVE INVESTIGATION OF MIS-
CONDUCT Assuming that an independent commission is established and
endowed with adequate resources and legal authority, its task typically is to
look at the patterns of corruption rather than at individual cases (see Knapp
Commission, 1972; Mollen Commission, 1994; Pennsylvania Crime Commission, 1974). Consequently, a typical commission would be motivated to
engage in extensive proactive investigations. However, as discussed earlier,
the establishment of independent commissions is neither a certain nor a
simple process. Furthermore, what behavior is to be examined and included
under corruption depends on the understanding shared by the members of
the commission and the way the commission's goal has been determined.

Compared with the patterns of investigation pursued by police departments under investigation and prosecutors in charge of prosecuting police
officers in these agencies, the three independent commissions each engaged
in in-depth proactive investigations and employed a variety of proactive
methods. They relied on a combination of data collection techniques and
multiple sources. The commissions thoroughly examined departmental records, surveyed businesses and citizens, interviewed police officers and others involved in criminal activities, used turned police officers, and engaged
in undercover operations (see chapter 3).

THE MEDIA PROACTIVE INVESTIGATION OF MISCONDUCT Aside from
their role in pursuing reactive investigations, the media could play a crucial role in proactive investigations. One of the most famous examples of
corruption-related investigative journalism dates back to the 1970s and involves the *New York Times*. After trying to lodge a corruption complaint
within the NYPD and outside the police department equally unsuccessfully,
Frank Serpico finally had a chance to tell his story to *New York Times* journalist David Burnham, who described how he checked the story:

> I began interviewing literally hundreds of New Yorkers from
> all over the city and from all walks of life. I interviewed—
> usually with a promise that they would not be quoted by
> name—bartenders, restaurant owners, liquor store operators,
> delicatessen operators, tow truck drivers, building contractors,
> parking attendants, supermarket managers, numbers game op-

erators, bookmakers, policemen, detectives, prosecutors, lawyers, judges, blacks, whites, and Spanish-speaking people. From
these interviews, which consumed more than a year of eve-
nings and free moments during the day and from an examination of the handful of corruption cases that were being
prosecuted at that time by the city's five prosecutors, I came
to two conclusions. (Burnham, 1978, p. 8)

Burnham concluded that "corruption did in fact dominate many of the activities of the New York Police Department" and that "corruption, like cooping [sleeping while on duty], had a significant impact on the effectiveness of
the police" (p. 8). Burnham's investigative reports, starting with "Graft Paid
to Police Here Said to Run into Millions" (1970, pp. 1, 18), triggered the attention of the public at large, the police department, prosecutors, and city
officials and created a stir that eventually led to the establishment of the
Knapp Commission (1972). Just as his previous story of cooping (Burnham,
1968, pp. 1, 54) was "a factual, carefully documented report" (Burnham,
1978, p. 8), the story of police corruption traced boundaries of the nature
and extent of corrupt behavior in the NYPD in the 1970s accurately, as his
findings were later confirmed by the Knapp Commission (1972) report.

Similarly, as a consequence of a series of articles based on an investigation conducted by the *Philadelphia Inquirer*, alleging that officers in the
Philadelphia Police Department were accepting payoffs to protect illegal
gambling operations, Pennsylvania Governor Milton Shapp ordered an independent investigation into police corruption by the Pennsylvania Crime
Commission (Heidorn, 1986). The commission found corruption to be widespread and the department to be unable or unwilling to control it (Pennsylvania Crime Commission, 1980, pp. x–xi).

A more recent example of high-profile corruption-related investigative
journalism is an investigation conducted by the *Boston Globe* staff about
corrupt activities—failing properly to account for money seized during
searches and arrests—perpetrated by the officers and detectives of the
Boston Police Department (see O'Neill et al., 1996; MacQuarrie, 1996). The
prosecutors' and the department's interests were piqued when the *Boston
Globe* published a series of stories alleging numerous counts of theft, extortion, and conspiracy (see O'Neill et al., 1996; Zuckoff, 1997), and outside

management consultants (Arthur Andersen Consulting and KPMG Peat Marwick) were hired to evaluate the department's procedures for handling cash and valuables seized during searches and seizures and to examine the department's evidence accounts (Zuckoff, 1997).

Such investigative pieces are rare for a number of reasons. First, the expectation beforehand may be that most police officers are honest and that there indeed is no material for such stories. Second, investigative journalism requires time, skills, and resources. Third, to find some of the data, journalists at least partially depend on the willingness of the police agency to open its doors and provide information, which may be quite challenging, especially in departments characterized by widespread corruption. Burnham summarized some additional problems:

> It is my belief that many reporters in America, perhaps even a majority of them, approach their jobs too passively, because the polite and passive stance is what many of their editors and publishers actually want. It is partly because reporters rarely are given an opportunity to develop enough expertise in a single area to question intelligently the expert and his conventional wisdom. It is partly because some reporters are insecure in their personal lives and desire to be liked by the people and the institutions they are covering. . . . Although there has been some shift in emphasis in recent years, I believe that the nation's newspapers, magazines, and television stations still devote far too much of their energy and manpower recording what officials say and therefore far too little energy and manpower reporting what is occurring in the agencies headed by these officials. (1978, pp. 2–3)

Although newspapers, especially local newspapers in small towns, may lean toward advocacy journalism and have a range of motives for discouraging reporters from investigating and later for refusing to publish the completed stories, their motivation for the publication of investigative reports, in addition to the profit gained through the sale of newspapers, could range widely, from the zeal for the discovery of government conspiracies, to party support and loyalty, to simple revenge. The bottom line, then, is that, although the media generally can be successful in uncovering information about corruption, the sporadic character of such activities makes the media unsuitable as the primary source of information about police corruption.

CITIZENS' PROACTIVE INVESTIGATION OF MISCONDUCT Citizens, either as organized, goal-oriented associations (e.g., the ACLU [the American Civil Liberties Union]) or ad hoc groups (e.g., the neighborhood watch), can be viewed as another potential source of proactive information gathering. The general public plays a crucial role in the development of successful corruption scandals, and public reaction and the resulting pressure have a strong impact on the outcome (see Sherman, 1978). However, the public's reaction to the most transparent cases of police corruption *already* discovered and publicized by the media is unpredictable. Outrage, no matter how desirable for the successful reform of the police agency, is not necessarily the only possible public reaction. In fact, the public may perceive the police to be corrupt but, at the same time, evaluate their performance as excellent (see Krauss, 1994; Moore, 1997, p. 62). The public may even completely disregard the information provided (see, e.g., Sherman, 1978).

Unlike people who suffer when directly involved in some other types of police misconduct, such as the use of excessive force or racial profiling, those directly involved in corrupt transactions, with the exception of extortion, typically not only suffer no harm but also actually reap benefits from the transaction (see, e.g., Hailman, 1988, p. 20; Rose-Ackerman, 1999, p. 53). Therefore, unless police officers overstep the accepted and established informal boundaries and bring the interaction closer to extortion, the general public is unlikely to be motivated to engage in a proactive investigation of police corruption. If anything, they could have strong reasons *not* to engage and thereby to protect their own corrupt activities and allow the beneficial corrupt activity to continue.

Setting aside the citizens who have had some contact with corruption (those directly involved in a corrupt transaction themselves; those whose friends, family members, or associates shared their own corrupt experiences with them) and those whose task it is to control the government (those in groups such as citizen review boards or city councils), citizens would find it very difficult to learn about the corruption if the outer consequences of corruption are not highly visible. Furthermore, they would not be able to obtain the skills and resources necessary for such an investigation. Finally, they would have a difficult time gaining access to the police agency and its officers. Consequently, unless people act as part of an organized association with a clearly defined task of curtailing police misconduct, the general public could at best be sporadic, temporary, and case-driven agents of proactive investigation.

Discipline and Punishment of Corrupt Police Officers

Discipline and punishment through the application of administrative sanctions by the agency and court sentences in criminal cases constitutes the last stage in the process that was initiated by the detection and investigation of corruption. The success and effectiveness of the discipline and punishment of corrupt police officers is thus inextricably linked with the extent and sincerity of the effort invested in the previous stage.

Administrative Discipline

Regardless of whether the police agency learns about corruption through reactive or proactive efforts, the next step in the application of internal discipline should be determining whether the allegation has merit (that is, whether the police officer has committed the alleged policy violation) and, if so, what the appropriate discipline should be. Within the police agency, depending on a particular agency and the severity of the allegation, this task could be assigned either to the officer's chain of command or to the top administrators in the agency (see, e.g., Klockars, Kutnjak Ivković, Haberfeld, & Uydess, 2001). Even if the civilian review board is involved in the process in some capacity, the police chief and the administration within the agency most frequently have the final say.

The point of the whole exercise is to send a clear message to the police officers that the agency is serious about its rules and that it seeks to discipline the rule violators consistently and systematically. However, the same reasons for police agencies' reluctance to investigate corruption or even their inclination to obstruct such an investigation—acceptance of the rotten-apple theory; lack of skills, ability, and resources to deal with corruption; prevention of the discovery of one's own misconduct or that of fellow police officers—could persist in the process of applying internal discipline. Furthermore, this is the second step in the process, and its successful completion in significant part is predetermined by the approach and measures carried out during the investigation itself. Indeed, if there is no detection and investigation or if they are reduced to negligent levels, the agency will be very limited in its imposition of discipline. At best, if the information about corruption leaks outside the agency (despite the agency's best efforts to hide it), and if it then causes a corruption scandal, the few police officers caught in flagrante delicto would be punished severely and swiftly, in accordance with the rotten-apple approach.

Empirically, to test the argument that police departments characterized by widespread corruption punish very few corrupt police officers, one would need to collect disciplinary case outcomes and an estimate of the true extent and nature of corruption in the agency. Obtaining systematic data about the outcomes of disciplinary procedures in corruption cases is challenging in more ways than one. The agencies most interesting and relevant for the analysis are the ones least likely to provide the information: The more widespread the corruption in the department, the more pressure is applied by the agency to hide any information. On the other hand, even when such data exist, reliable estimates of the true nature and extent of corruption are seldom available for these same agencies. In rare instances, independent commissions may come to the rescue, because they have the mandate and power to provide a more accurate estimate of the true extent of corruption and also the power and resources to compile disciplinary records. However, despite their powers, the independent commissions experience considerable difficulties, too.

> Unfortunately, the Department [NYPD] does not maintain summary statistics on corruption case dispositions in terms of the charges brought. To obtain information on corruption cases and the penalties invoked for corruption-related offenses, it is necessary to search the individual disciplinary record of each officer brought to [administrative] trial. In doing so, it is often difficult to determine from the record whether a case is corruption-related or not. (footnotes omitted; Knapp Commission, 1972, p. 229)

Even the simplest steps can be perplexing. The Knapp Commission (1972, p. 230), for example, illustrated difficulties in obtaining even the basic number of corruption-related disciplinary cases: "The Department Advocate's office counted 186 cases, Disciplinary Records Section counted 238, and the Commission staff counted 223." Of the 223 cases, 79 were still pending when the commission counted them. One hundred forty-four completed cases were resolved as follows (Table 5.2): in almost 40% of the cases, the officer was freed of the charges (the charges were dropped, amnesty was granted, or the police officer was acquitted after the hearing), in 32% of the cases the officer was no longer with the force (the police officer resigned before the hearing, was dismissed before the hearing based on the probationary status or conviction in a criminal trial, or was fired after the hearing), and in the remaining 29% of the cases the officer was reprimanded, put on probation, and/or fined.

Without further details about each case, it is difficult to draw any conclusions about the appropriateness and severity of the discipline, but it is possible to draw some inferences about the adequacy of the mere number of these cases. In particular, while the Knapp Commission "found corruption to be widespread" (1972, p. 1) in the NYPD, a police force of 30,000 at the time (p. 69), there were only 223 cases of corruption (or 0.74 cases per 100 police officers) processed administratively in a particular year (p. 230).

Table 5.2 NYPD Corruption Case Outcomes in 1971

Case outcome	Number of cases	Percentage
Charges were dropped, amnesty granted, or police officer acquitted after the hearing	57	39.6
Police officer was reprimanded	4	2.8
Police officer was put on probation (and four were also fined)	5	3.5
Police officer was fined	32	22.2
Police officer resigned before the hearing, was dismissed before the hearing (probationary status; convicted in a criminal trial), or was fired after the hearing	46	31.9
Total number of completed cases	144	100

Source: Based on the data provided by the Knapp Commission, 1972, p. 228.

Furthermore, 40% of the completed cases were resolved without any discipline for the police officer. A statement made by a former police officer before the Pennsylvania Crime Commission, therefore, is not surprising (1974, p. 439):

> Q: Was there a fear of discipline if you got caught taking a safe note?
>
> A: I would say not really. The reason I would say that is because if you were doing something and you had occasion, somebody wanted to give you something, you wouldn't— *nine chances out of ten your superiors wouldn't punish you or wouldn't take disciplinary action against you if you received it.* And maybe they sent a letter, a commendatory letter into the Department for the services you rendered because it makes the Police Department look good, and the people are happy. . . . [emphasis added]
>
> Q: And no disciplinary action was taken against the officer?
>
> A: Usually a verbal reprimand.

Regardless of whether the investigations are appropriate in terms of their frequency and thoroughness, when they are conducted and their findings do point toward the "guilt" of police officers, the police agency may be unwilling to discipline them. For example, recent investigations by the Public Advocate for New York City and the New York City Civil Liberties Union in 1999 revealed that only about one quarter of all the police officers against whom the Civilian Complaint Review Board sustained complaints were actually disciplined (Green, 1999).

Criminal Sanctions

Like police agencies themselves, the criminal justice system should provide boundaries of acceptable behavior and send an unambiguous deterrent message by punishing police officers guilty of corruption. Failure to do so communicates the message that police corruption is tolerated and allows the development of a police culture tolerant of police corruption.

Criminal events described as corruption, like any other criminal events, need to enter into the criminal justice system. The criminal justice system is defined by the President's Commission on Law Enforcement and Administration of Justice as "an apparatus society uses to enforce the standards of conduct necessary to protect individuals and the community" (1967a, p. 7). According to the commission, the system's parts, as described below, are not independent:

> The criminal justice system has three separately organized parts—the police, the courts, and corrections—and each has distinct tasks. However, these parts are by no means independent of each other. What each one does and how it does it has a direct effect on the work of the others. The courts must deal, and can only deal, with those whom the police arrest. (1967a, pp. 8–9)

The same principles apply to corruption: The way the prosecution stage and the adjudication stage will progress depends on the previous stages. One of the most prolific sources of prosecutorial referrals for police corruption cases should be the police agencies themselves; the police agencies should conduct administrative and criminal investigations in parallel and submit the results of their criminal investigations to the prosecutor for further decision making. Yet, as discussed earlier, the more corrupt an agency, the less motivation it has to investigate corruption diligently and refer corruption cases to the prosecutors. Consequently, even if citizens and police officers actually report corruption (which is not likely to happen in a corrupt agency to begin with), a good portion of these cases are likely to be trumped by the agency, because corrupt police departments tend not only to fail to actively collect information about corruption but also to hide information provided by citizens and police officers alike (see, e.g., Knapp Commission, 1972; Mollen Commission, 1994).

In theory, all is not lost because, aside from information obtained through their own proactive work, the prosecutors can learn about police corruption from other sources—individual citizens, police officers, federal investigating agencies (e.g., FBI, IRS), other local investigators (e.g., other local police agencies), other governmental institutions (e.g., INS), and independent commissions and journalists. However, for various reasons discussed earlier, the participants in corrupt transactions—citizens and police officers alike—have no motive to report their own corrupt activities either to the police or to the prosecutors. Furthermore, the observers may lack motivation and skill to collect the information or may be equally reluctant to share that information with the police or the prosecutor.

The prosecutors, just like police departments (albeit for partially different reasons), can also be less than eager to prosecute cases of police corruption. As argued earlier, local prosecutors' decision making about police corruption cases could be swayed by heavy caseloads, close working relationships with the police, sympathy toward the police, reliance on the police to conduct investigations, and fear of losing public support. For example, Anechiarico and Jacobs summarize the intensity of corruption efforts regarding city employees in New York as follows:

> Historically, corruption prosecutions were infrequent and episodic. Even the remarkable Seabury investigations generated few prosecutions. "Mr. District Attorney," Frank Hogan, also failed to prosecute many corrupt public officials. In the 1980s and the 1990s, however, local, state, and especially federal prosecutors have become much more involved in dealing with corruption in New York City government. It remains to be seen, of course, whether these developments are simply a short-lived blip on the screen, or whether they mark the beginning of a new long-term trend. (1996, p. 107)

Federal prosecutors, on the other hand, are too few in numbers to control the overall police in the United States and, as outsiders to the local community, could experience limited access to information. A common feature that could affect both local and federal prosecutors is the inherent difficulty in building a historic corruption case because of the secretive nature of police corruption, the reluctance of participants and witnesses to testify, and, frequently, the lack of credibility of the crucial witnesses in the case. An example from New York in the 1970s (cited by the Pennsylvania Crime Commission) is particularly illustrative.

> Cases against policemen, compiled by other policemen, have an extraordinary tendency to collapse in court. Incriminating

statements are passed over, affidavits for wiretaps are inaccurately drawn, search warrants become inadmissible and the evidence gathered faulty. . . . Cops in trouble are almost always supplied with the best defense attorneys available through the political muscle and, sometimes, the financial assistance of the Patrolmen's Benevolent Association. Long court delays help, too. Prosecution witnesses become less certain. . . . Judges in overcrowded courts feel a greater urgency to dispose of cases in which defendants are in jail and unable to raise bail. Cops are, in 95 percent of their cases, freed on their own recognizance while awaiting their trials. (Pileggi & Pearl, 1973)

Even when prosecutors decide to proceed with the case and try to obtain a conviction, they may need to confront Mr. Prejudice and Mrs. Sympathy among the jurors and judges. For example, the Pennsylvania Crime Commission noted that the criminal justice system did not react severely to police corruption and that "in view of its sentencing record, the judiciary has clearly demonstrated its reluctance to take a strong stand against the police offender in corruption cases" (1974, p. 446). In fact, one of the judges sentenced three police officers found guilty of extorting money from a drug dealer to probation (p. 447).

As the results of opinion polls demonstrate (see Moore, 1997, p. 62; Krauss, 1994), the public may tolerate corruption and, despite its existence, still evaluate the police in positive terms. Members of the public serving as jurors can support the blue knights, refuse to trust the drug dealers' or prostitutes' allegations that the police officers extorted money from them, or actually tacitly approve of the police officers applying a measure of "street justice" and extorting money from "criminals." Furthermore, the public (or at least a substantial proportion of it) does not agree with some of the enacted legal rules, such as gambling laws, and consequently can refuse to find guilty police officers who received money from gambling organizations (see Knapp Commission, 1972, pp. 72–73).

Both the Knapp Commission and the Pennsylvania Crime Commission found police corruption to be widespread and, relative to these findings, the numbers of prosecutions and convictions to be quite low. In particular, the Knapp Commission (1972, p. 252) reported that, in the 4½ years that the commission focused on, prosecutors initiated only 136 cases, involving 218 defendants, from the NYPD. The cases were dismissed or the defendants acquitted in one third of the cases, and two thirds of the defendants (91) either pleaded guilty or were convicted (p. 252). The majority of the convicted defendants (61%) were either set free or given suspended sentences. At the end, only one out of five sentenced police officers received a prison sentence of more than 1 year (p. 252). The findings reported by the Pennsylvania Crime Commission were similar. The commission reported that in the department of 8,303 sworn police officers in 1974 there were only 43 arrests over the preceding 6-year period (1974, pp. 52, 446). Furthermore, only 7 of the 18 sentenced police officers were sentenced to prison (p. 446).

These numbers demonstrate that prosecution and conviction rates are substantially lower than even the crudest estimates of the extent of corruption are. The situation may have changed by the 1990s, as the Mollen Commission (1994, p. 150) indicated for New York, and both federal and local prosecutors may have become less reluctant to prosecute corrupt police officers. By contrast, the findings obtained by Malec and Gardiner's study (1987, p. 267) of all corruption cases prosecuted in Chicago and Cook County from 1970 to April 1987 suggest that prosecutions for police corruption in Chicago were still quite rare. In a police department with more than 10,000 sworn police officers in the early 1990s (Reaves & Smith, 1999, p. 16), only 114 police corruption cases were recorded over a period of 16 full years (Malec & Gardiner, 1987, p. 273).

Even at the federal level, prosecutions of police corruption cases and, ultimately, convictions of corrupt police officers are very infrequent. The overall number of indictments and convictions in federal cases involving abuse of public office for *all* governmental employees (including police officers; U.S. Department of Justice, 1995) oscillates from 1,000 to 1,500 indictments and around 1,000 convictions per year (see Table 3.1 in chapter 3), and it tends to be small in comparison with the millions of government employees (see Burnham, 1996, p. 327).

Based on the existing data, it seems that, in terms of deterrent effects, prosecutions and convictions of corrupt police officers are not certain, swift, or severe. The general message that the criminal justice system sends to police officers is that it is not very likely that they will be caught and, even if caught, they will not receive severe punishment.

Conclusion

Although the task of detecting and investigating corruption and disciplining corrupt police officers is shared by the police, prosecutors (both local and federal), the courts, the general public, and the media, the police are typically expected to carry the bulk of it. However, the primary reliance on the police can turn out to be a very risky proposition. In police agencies characterized by widespread corruption, in which systematic and organized corruption control is most needed, internal control mechanisms are most likely to be neglected and sometimes even openly sabotaged. Highly corrupt police departments do not send a strong deterrent message to their police officers that corrupt behavior is prohibited and that violations of these norms will be punished swiftly and with certainty.

Despite the crucial role of detection and investigation of corruption and discipline of corrupt police officers in corruption control, this is just one function in the overall system of corruption control. In the next chapter I examine other functions within the system, so diverse in nature that they have to be performed by various entities—the police agency itself, the mayor or city manager, prosecutors, courts, the media, and the general public.

6

Corruption Control

Other Functions

Corruption control is complex. It involves a number of heterogeneous functions, from providing resources for corruption control to monitoring propensity for corruption. The functions are so diverse that they have to be performed by various entities: the police agency itself, the mayor or city manager, prosecutors, courts, the media, and the citizenry. Some functions can be carried out by more than one entity, and others have to be performed by very specific ones. For example, although investigations of corrupt behavior can be conducted by the police agency, prosecutors, or the media, only the courts can mete out punishment in criminal cases. Moreover, it frequently takes several institutions to carry out a certain function. For example, the task of controlling the police agency's efforts to control corruption is shared by the mayor, independent commissions, and the media. The resulting relationships are often intricate: The way one institution carries out its tasks can have both a direct and an indirect impact on the effectiveness of other institutions and their ability to carry out their control tasks. Indeed, if the police agency or the prosecutors do not engage in thorough and systematic investigations of corruption or prosecutions of corrupt police officers, courts will have very few cases to process.

In the previous chapter I covered two corruption control functions: investigation of corruption and discipline and punishment of corrupt police officers. Although these two functions are necessary for effective police corruption control, they are by no means sufficient. In this chapter I continue with a detailed analysis of the functions that are most likely to be assigned to the police agency (i.e., monitor propensity for corruption, cultivate a culture intolerant of corruption, and establish supervision and accountability), an inquiry into the functions more likely to be shared by the police agency and other agencies (i.e., set official policies and enforce them, provide resources), and an examination of the functions most likely or exclusively performed by institutions external to the police agency (i.e., control police agency's control efforts, detect and investigate corruption the police agency is not investigating, improve the existing system of control, limit opportunities for corruption, and disseminate true information about corruption). For each function, the format of the presentation is the same: description of the function, followed by an analysis focusing on institutions that have the responsibility of carrying it out, the way they should carry it out, and the inherent obstacles and potential problems they may experience in the process.

Each of these functions is crucial for corruption control, but carrying them out is hardly free of obstacles or failures in implementation. Such problems range from the administrators' lack of motivation or skill to direct resistance against the idea that a function has to be performed to facilitate successful corruption control. The ultimate result is that the highly corrupt police agencies—that is, those in greatest need—are the least likely to carry out corruption functions effectively.

Monitor Propensity for Corruption

Police officers' individual experiences have a continuous impact on the way they perceive, interpret, and react to the disciplinary environment created by their agencies. Although police agencies have recently started introducing early warning systems (which allow them to monitor police officers' propensity for misconduct in general and police corruption in particular; see

Walker, 2001), for a long time the assumption was that the propensity for misconduct is static. Administrators and policy makers believed that thoroughness during the recruitment and selection process resulted in future police officers with high moral values. However, just as it was assumed that their individual experiences shaped police officers' propensity for corruption *before* they joined the police, it is perfectly reasonable to assume that their individual prior life experiences will have an effect on the way police officers perceive and evaluate their environment *after* they join the police agency.

Regardless of whether the agencies adopted an incorrect view about propensity for corruption consciously or whether they drifted toward it because of their lack of ability or desire to control police corruption, a number of things can go wrong in the areas of recruitment and selection, supervision, and internal formal control.

Recruitment and Selection

Police agencies may fail to screen out applicants with higher risk-propensity levels because of negligence, inability to deal with the recruitment and selection process, or willful enforcement of lowered standards. First, the recruitment personnel could be overworked (see, e.g., Mollen Commission, 1994, p. 115), understaffed, or of questionable integrity or competence (U.S. Department of Justice, 1989, pp. 16–40). Second, the established recruitment criteria could be inadequate in terms of content (e.g., not including ethics-related issues) or standard thresholds (e.g., acceptance of applicants with prior felony convictions or drug abuse problems). Third, the established criteria could be neglected or could be enforced at a lowered standard. The example of "the River Cops" in Miami in the 1980s illustrates the dangers associated with inappropriately relaxed selection standards (e.g., failure to disqualify for illegal drug use, lowering of driving standards, mail certification of employment, acceptance of the GED rather than graduation from an accredited high school, tolerance of poor credit history; see Burns & Sechrest, 1992). Similarly, the results of the Los Angeles Police Department Board of Inquiry investigation portray the impact of the relaxed recruitment standards and the related consequences: Of the 14 police officers who engaged in serious corruption in the Rampart area, 4 had evidence of criminal records, inability to manage personal finances, and histories of violent behavior and narcotics involvement in their *pre*-employment records (Los Angeles Police Department, 2000, pp. 13–14).

Fourth, background investigation could be superficial. Applicants might sometimes be hired as police officers even before the background investigation is completed. The Mollen Commission (1994, pp. 112–113) studied the records of approximately 400 police officers who were either dismissed or suspended for police corruption over a period of 6 years and reported that, based on the information already in the applicant's case file at the time of hiring, approximately 20% of these police officers should never have been hired. Similar evidence was uncovered in the course of investigating the Rampart Area corruption scandal (Los Angeles Police Department, 2000, pp. 13–14).

Supervision

First-line supervisors are in the best position to monitor the corruption-propensity levels of their subordinates. The example of the Miami Police Department in the early 1980s highlights the importance of this monitoring: Although the actual rate of misconduct probably increased over time, the annual number of reprimands per 100 officers and the number of officers who received a loss-of-time punishment decreased drastically in 1980–1981, compared both with the previous period (1974–1975) and the later period (1985–1986) (Burns & Sechrest, 1992, p. 305). Burns and Sechrest reason that "changes in supervision [in the Miami Police Department] were put in place in the early 1980s that loosened internal controls and may have helped 'set the stage' for corruption to flourish" (p. 305).

Although the idea of supervisory monitoring may work reasonably well in organized and relatively clean agencies, supervisors may be unable or unwilling to monitor their subordinates where monitoring is required the most—in highly corrupt agencies. Both the Knapp Commission (1972) and the Pennsylvania Crime Commission (1974) reported that the supervisors in the NYPD and the Philadelphia Police Department, two departments labeled as highly corrupt in the 1970s, knew or should have known about the extent of corruption among their subordinates (and, therefore, about their propensity for corruption) but did very little to control it. The Mollen Commission, investigating allegations of corruption in the NYPD two decades later, reported various instances in which supervisors obviously failed to question problematic conduct by their subordinates. This failure to react could be quite protective of corrupt officers, as suggested by the aforementioned example of Michael Dowd (one of the most notorious police officers engaged in corruption, discovered by the Mollen Commission): Despite the abundance of signs of his involvement in corruption, *none* of the supervisors reacted (Mollen Commission, 1994, p. 57). Instead, his supervisor said that one day he could "easily become a role model for others to emulate" (Mollen Commission, 1994, p. 81).

As the examples of two departments found to be corrupt in the 1970s demonstrate, supervisors sometimes also participate in corruption themselves (see Knapp Commission, 1972; Pennsylvania Crime Commission, 1974). In such cases, they usually have no interest in monitoring the misconduct of their subordinates. Ironically, if they monitored the misconduct of their subordinates, they did so for quite the opposite reasons: to obtain additional illegal gain for themselves, to protect their own misconduct, and/ or to cover the misconduct of other subordinates.

Even if supervisors are willing to monitor the propensity for corruption, they may be unable to do so because of the generally deteriorating conditions of supervision (as was the case in New York City in the early 1990s; see Mollen Commission, 1994), dramatic increase in the ratio of supervisors to line officers, assignment of additional administrative responsibilities, the informal practice of answering the calls for service in lieu of busy patrol officers, or the responsibility of supervising police officers in two different districts (see Mollen Commission, 1994, pp. 82–83).

Internal Formal Control

Because the propensity for corruption changes over time and even the best recruits can gradually become highly corrupt police officers, a police agency needs to perform additional monitoring efforts. The findings of the three independent commissions investigating allegations of corruption in Philadelphia and New York in the 1970s and 1990s (see Knapp Commission, 1972, p. 208; Mollen Commission, 1994, p. 101; Pennsylvania Crime Commission, 1974, p. 483) illustrate that these police agencies, plagued with corruption or experiencing serious corruption-related challenges, failed to use proactive methods to monitor the propensity for corruption. Particularly illustrative is the aforementioned case of Michael Dowd, a NYPD police officer who drove a red Corvette, led an openly lavish lifestyle (Mollen Commission, 1994, p. 81), occasionally forgot to pick up his paycheck, and was a subject of 15 unsubstantiated allegations of police corruption over a course of 6 years. If early warning systems were even close to operational, red flags should have been raised much sooner, particularly in that there was "substantial evidence that Dowd regularly and openly engaged in serious criminal conduct" (Mollen Commission, 1994, p. 1).

Similarly, the Rampart scandal in the LAPD, uncovered in 1999, forced the agency to examine its own mechanisms of accountability. The agency concluded that its internal procedures had collapsed, including standard personnel evaluations, which were found to be worthless (Los Angeles Police Department, 2000). Furthermore, Oettmeier and Wycoff (1997) found police personnel evaluation systems in a number of police agencies to be inadequate and generally unrelated to the actual work of police officers.

Cultivate a Police Culture Intolerant of Corruption

By creating a culture intolerant of corruption, police agencies provide some of the essential requirements for its successful control: They establish clear boundaries of acceptable behavior and encourage police officers not to tolerate corrupt behavior. Not surprisingly, highly corrupt police agencies are typically characterized by a culture exceedingly tolerant of police corruption. The majority of honest officers do not report corruption because they lack confidence in the department's commitment to deal with corruption or they fear retribution for reporting. In fact, reporting corruption is sometimes perceived as a more serious "offense" than the corruption itself (Mollen Commission, 1994, p. 57).

> Even the officer caught in illegal conduct is very reluctant to talk about other corrupt activity involving police. That does not mean that on occasion some officers will not report other

officers or that some police officers will not make anonymous calls about misconduct. However, the term, code of silence, does describe the generally understood and accepted
standard of behavior. As a result, officers who are unwilling
to participate will react strongly against even the slightest
hint of improper conduct in order to place their fellow officers
on notice that they do not want to be involved in any way.
(footnotes omitted; Pennsylvania Crime Commission, 1974,
p. 432)

Overall, the findings of the three independent commissions clearly indicate
that the police departments did very little to change the existing police culture, which was tolerant of serious forms of police corruption. The Mollen
Commission (1994) summarizes this point nicely:

We found a police culture that often tolerates and protects
corruption. We also found that the Department completely
abandoned its responsibility to transform that culture into
one that drives out corruption. It made little effort to change
the attitudes that foster corruption among the rank and file,
supervisors or commanders; and it made little effort to convince anyone that its occasional pronouncements on integrity
were more than obligatory rhetoric. (p. 107)

Establish Supervision and Accountability

Although effective supervision teaches police officers how to react to in-
tegrity-challenging events, monitors their propensity for corruption and
their overall performance, determines boundaries of tolerated behavior, and
provides information for investigations and application of discipline for violations of the official rules, the administration in the agency is not relieved
from monitoring the performance of these same supervisors and holding
them accountable for their own conduct, as well as that of their subordinates. Indeed, whereas the accountability of the supervisors is internal (i.e.,
to the administration within the police department), the accountability of the

administration—the chief and other top commanders within the agency—
is primarily external (i.e., to the mayor and other politicians, as well as to
the public).

Internal Accountability

Although all three commissions investigating allegations of corruption in
the Philadelphia Police Department and the NYPD from the 1970s to the
1990s reported weak supervision and numerous problems leading toward
ineffective supervision, the Mollen Commission—the most recent one—
was the most vocal in arguing that supervision was in a state of crisis. The
commission reported "a widespread breakdown in supervision which fueled
and protected corruption" (Mollen Commission, 1994, p. 80). Similarly, in
the course of investigating the Rampart Area scandal, the LAPD Board of
Inquiry concluded that "the lack of effective supervision in Rampart was,
frankly, glaring" (Los Angeles Police Department, 2000, p. 14).

The Knapp Commission (1972, p. 232) reported that, despite the long-
established command accountability on paper, the NYPD did not succeed in
translating it into an operating routine. The same was still the case 20 years
later; the Mollen Commission (1994, p. 13) reported that they found "a total
lack of commitment to the principle of command accountability. This was
allowed to happen because no formal institutional mechanisms were ever
adopted to ensure its perpetuation and enforcement." In particular, the administration rarely included assessments of the supervisors' success in
corruption-control efforts in their performance evaluations and typically
neither punished failures nor rewarded successes in corruption control
(Mollen Commission, 1994, p. 77). The perception shared by the supervisors—that it is better for one's career to hide corruption than to uncover
it and deal with it—seems to have been an accurate reading of the policies
set forth by the administration (p. 78).

Thus, such a state of affairs can rarely be blamed exclusively on the
supervisors themselves; just as police supervisors should be responsible for
the performance of their subordinates, the police administration within an
agency should be responsible for the performance of the supervisors. In particular, by not providing adequate resources, by putting little or no emphasis
on issues of corruption control, and by overburdening the existing super-

visors with additional tasks, the administration sets the stage for weakened and ineffective supervision and creates potential for subsequent growth of misconduct. Indeed, the Mollen Commission did not hesitate to blame the NYPD administration for the poor state of supervision:

> The Department's management is largely to blame for this state of supervision. Indeed, it is the Department's past Police Commissioners and top managers who, through their inaction and silence, permitted this situation to exist. It is the Department's top commanders who let supervisors off the hook and let command accountability wither. It is true that past Police Commissioners had other important priorities and concerns and they carried these out with skill and efficiency. But that does not excuse their failure to maintain strong supervision and command accountability.

By not holding supervisors accountable for their own misconduct, the misconduct of their subordinates that they should have known about, or their failure to supervise, the administration conveys to the supervisors that the official rules establishing their accountability are little more than dead letters on paper. In fact, some of the supervisors in the NYPD in the 1990s knew that they would not be held accountable and did not even perceive that rooting corruption out was part of their responsibilities (1994, p. 80).

External Accountability

The police are accountable to the public and to elected public officials for performing tasks assigned to them and for the means they use to complete these tasks. Police chiefs can be held accountable for their own misconduct and the misconduct of their employees they knew or should have know about, as well as the general state of affairs in the agencies they are leading and managing. Although police chiefs have substantial influence over a number of organizational issues—recruitment, training, leadership and management style, supervisory accountability, internal control mechanisms, discipline, and rewards—their powers are limited by the legal framework in which they operate and the civil service systems whose decisions in personnel issues they are bound to accept (see, e.g., Greisinger et al., 1979; Walker,

1992, p. 369). Even more important, police chiefs can be held accountable by the city manager or mayor, special oversight agencies, citizens, and courts for the tax dollars they spend and for the way their agencies exercise the authority delegated to them (see Moore & Stephens, 1991, p. 36).

There are various methods of achieving a police chief's accountability on a systematic basis. The first method is accountability to public officials, namely, the mayor or the city manager and other politicians. Because of the fear that the line between interfering and holding police chiefs accountable is thin, "Mayors and council members are frequently reluctant to intervene publicly in police affairs lest they be accused of improper political interference" (Moore & Stephens, 1991, p. 36). Furthermore, mayors may feel that they do not possess the level of expertise necessary to oversee the police. Walker summarized these problems:

> Mayors and city council members have displayed either staggering indifference to police problems or have themselves been the ultimate source of police problems. Most of these elected officials have not cared about police misconduct. Additionally, even today those who are well intentioned lack expert knowledge about the very complex aspects of policing and police administration. . . . Through all of the nineteenth century and much of the twentieth, these elected officials thought about the police primarily in terms of the potential opportunities for graft or patronage. (2001, p. 9)

The way the chief has been selected has an impact on the extent of political bargaining the chief has to undertake and the extent to which the public and the mayor can hold him or her accountable (Guyot & Martensen, 1991, p. 436). The nature of the police chief's contract also affects his or her relationship with the city manager and the standard of accountability to which the city manager can hold the chief. A police chief who serves at the pleasure of the city manager or mayor, as is traditional, obviously needs to be more responsive to the manager's requests. However, as Guyot and Martensen (1991, p. 439) argue, city managers only occasionally dismiss chiefs without good cause and frequently do not dismiss the chiefs they should have dismissed because they do not have the political strength to do so in the presence of a powerful police union supporting the chief. In an agency characterized by widespread corruption, the police union strongly supports the chief who not only allows them to engage in corruption but also resists any attempts by the city manager or the public to replace the chief or even challenge the chief's integrity and accountability.

In addition to the hiring decisions and the threat of dismissal, the mayor can hold the chief accountable through budget submissions and annual reports. Budget submissions are not a very effective and easy way of obtaining information about corruption control because more than 90% of the typical police operating budget is devoted to personnel issues (Guyot & Martensen, 1991, p. 442). Using annual reports as a corruption-related accountability tool is not a big hit either. Because the chief primarily has to prove that the goals of the agency—crime fighting, problem solving, and the like—are being achieved, annual reports contain statistical data (e.g., crime rates, clearance rates, and response times) about the realization of these goals and very little information about potential corruption. Although they often contain data about complaints and discipline, such practice is less prevalent in the agencies characterized by widespread corruption. Even if they do provide the data, the degree to which these statistics reflect the true state of affairs in the agency is highly questionable.

Therefore, the existing frameworks make mayors reluctant to ask questions about police misconduct and police chiefs reluctant to provide answers to such questions if asked. The only two sources of information provided on a regular basis—budgets and annual reports—focus on the overall performance of the police agency and are probably too broad for the mayor to determine any patterns, changes in the actual police behavior, and possible problems in the area of police corruption (see, e.g., Moore & Stephens, 1991, p. 39). Consequently, the traditional approach toward police organization and management, according to which the goals are set externally and the police chief is entrusted with finding the means to fulfill these goals, has been challenged (Moore & Stephens, 1991, pp. 22–45). In fact, the only systematic study that examined police policy formation, conducted in Rochester, St. Louis, and Tampa, reveals that in slightly less than half of the cases police chiefs made the policy alone, and in close to 40% it was a joint decision by the city administrator and the police chief (Mastrofski, 1988).

Another source of police chiefs' accountability is the public. Moore and Stephens (1991) argue: "Through media coverage of their activities, the police are also held directly accountable to the public" (p. 339). As discussed earlier, however, whether the media will learn about police corruption and decide to run the story depends on a number of factors. The media can play crucial roles in the development of scandals and subsequent reforms in some cases, as was the case with the *New York Times* in New York City in the 1970s (Burnham, 1970; Knapp Commission, 1972) and the *Boston Globe* in Boston in the 1990s (O'Neill et al., 1996; MacQuarrie, 1996). However, another question is whether they can continuously require accountability on a regular basis. Their decision to publish stories also depends on the public reaction these stories are likely to provoke and, if the citizens tolerate corruption of their blue knights, no scandal will emerge (Sherman, 1978). The absence of a scandal usually means no calls for accountability.

The courts can also hold a police chief accountable. They establish the boundaries and punish the police for violating the rules through evidentiary rulings in criminal cases, verdicts in criminal cases, and decisions in civil liability cases. However, neither the evidentiary rulings in criminal cases nor the decisions in civil liability cases apply to the typical bribery type of corruption. As discussed earlier, prosecutors can be less than eager to try corruption cases, and judges and juries may perceive police officers to be too trustworthy and thus be less likely to sentence them. The Knapp Commission (1972) and the Pennsylvania Crime Commission (1974) pointed out a stark discrepancy between their findings on the extent and nature of corruption and the actual number of police officers prosecuted and sentenced for corruption. Although the situation may have improved recently (see, e.g., Mollen Commission, 1994, p. 150; but see also Malec & Gardiner, 1987, p. 267), still, the courts seem to rarely hold police officers accountable for corrupt behavior.

Consequently, it is not surprising that the relationships between mayors and police chiefs (determined also to a large degree by the selection process and the type of government) and other sources of accountability are "fragile, shifting, and episodic" (Moore & Stephens, 1991, p. 38). Furthermore, the pressures for accountability typically focus on individual cases and their resolution, rather than on broad improvements and changes in the existing system. The rare exceptions occur when revelations of corruption result in a scandal of such proportions that an extensive investigation and dramatic changes are necessary.

Set Official Policies and Enforce Them

Federal and state statutes (e.g., 18 U.S.C. §201 for bribery; 18 U.S.C. §1951 for extortion) prohibit most forms of corrupt behavior. However, the police agency needs to establish that a felony conviction automatically serves as grounds for dismissal of police officers. Also, it needs to enact internal agency rules that stipulate what appropriate and inappropriate conduct would be, establish the rules of the disciplinary process, and determine possible disciplinary outcomes for police officers who violate official agency rules. Whether an agency will have a set of written rules seems to be related to its size (Barker & Wells, 1981), with smaller agencies less likely to have written official rules in place.

Compared with rules dealing with the use of excessive force, rules prohibiting corrupt behavior in general are relatively straightforward. The more challenging part, however, lies in drawing the line between allowed and prohibited behavior for corruption of authority. Absolute prohibition of the acceptance of any gifts of small value, for example, is a simple yet unenforceable solution, and prohibition of the acceptance of gifts above a certain value is difficult to design in an equitable way (see chapter 2). Although two thirds of the agencies in the study by Barker and Wells (1981, pp. 8–16) had no rules dealing with corruption of authority (e.g., accepting a free cup of coffee, free meals from restaurants, or holiday gifts), slightly less than half of the agencies had no rules at all prohibiting serious corruption, including kickbacks; opportunistic thefts; shakedowns; protection of illegal activities; traffic, misdemeanor, or felony fix; involvement in direct criminal activities; and internal payoffs.

Setting up the policy and wording the actual rules can be assigned to the chief and the agency administration, or the task can be a joint endeavor undertaken by the chief and the mayor. A study focusing on Rochester, St. Louis, and Tampa suggests that in a similar percentage of cases (between 40% and 50%) the policy was made either by police chiefs alone or in a synchronized effort by the city administrator and the police chief (Mastrofski, 1988). Whereas each of these two players could have reasons for not wishing to establish a strict policy on the issues of police misconduct in general and corruption in particular, the establishment of official agency rules and the chief's strong stance on corruption are merely the first steps on the road to successful control; they are far from sufficient. The more crucial issue is whether the official rules are enforced. Clearly, not every rule can be enforced, and there will be a discrepancy between the official rules and the informal rules in each agency. What matters is how wide that gap is and what rules get enforced.

As discussed earlier, the administration's actions or omissions create informal rules that trump the official ones in several ways. First, the chief's own involvement in corruption clearly denounces any official prohibition of corrupt activities. Second, the chief may behave ethically but fail to perform any of the traditional managerial functions of planning, organizing, coordinating, or controlling (see Moore & Stephens, 1991, p. 38) in accordance with the official stance on corruption (see chapter 3 for details). The Knapp Commission provided an illustrative example involving a highly-ranked administrator, the tolerance of whose actions (the acceptance of a free dinner for four persons from a very expensive restaurant) by the former Commissioner Murphy spoke louder than the official policy prohibiting such conduct (Knapp Commission, 1972, p. 171). Thus, the chief can often override the official rules through lack of enforcement, application of more lenient punishments, or even promotion of police officers regardless of the complaints against them.

One of the administrators' most important failures is not punishing officers who are caught engaging in corruption. As noted earlier, by failing to detect corrupt behavior or by not being serious about detecting and investigating misconduct and disciplining the violators, the police agency trumps the rule prohibiting such behavior and de facto legitimizes it. The Pennsylvania Crime Commission focused on such discrepancies between the official rules and the unofficial rules in the Philadelphia Police Department in the 1970s. The department's official rules and the stance on corruption were clear (police officers were not allowed to accept any gifts or payments), but the informal rules clearly suggested that the practice of receiving gifts or payments was acceptable: No investigator from the internal affairs office was ever assigned to investigate payments of money or merchandise that businesses had made to the police (Pennsylvania Crime Commission, 1974, p. 394), supervisors did not discipline line officers for corruption, and none of the police officers was investigated or punished for accepting free meals, despite the apparent widespread practice (p. 339).

Provide Resources for Control

The city manager or city government has an indirect impact on the allocation of resources for corruption control in the police agency; the police operational budget is part of the city budget (or the budget of a larger unit),
determined by the city government. The police chief makes the decisions regarding consumption of the money from the budget allocated to the police
and thus has direct input regarding the resources for corruption control.

The city manager, city government, and the police chief might be less
than eager to allocate substantial resources to corruption control. To begin
with, if corruption is widespread in the larger environment, there is little
motivation to designate substantial funds to corruption-control mechanisms. Furthermore, by virtue of being political players and/or being dependent on public support, even if they are not engaged in corruption themselves, they may be concerned that the public, tolerant of corruption among
the police, could evaluate the allocation of significant resources to corruption-control efforts as a waste of resources.

Finally, further allocation of resources would probably reveal corruption
to be more widespread than the public is likely to assume. As discussed earlier, if they rely on the rotten-apple approach, and if they believe that the
public subscribes to the rotten-apple theory, police chiefs and mayors may
feel that the discovery of corruption would have an adverse impact on the
public image of the agency. The Mollen Commission (1994) connected the
rotten-apple approach to the administrators' denial of resources for corruption control.

> From the top brass down, there was an often debilitating fear
> about police corruption disclosures because it was perceived
> as an embarrassment to the Department, and likely to en-
> gender a loss of public confidence. . . . This attitude infected
> the entire Department, manifesting itself in different ways
> throughout the ranks. It encouraged the Department's top
> managers to allow corruption controls to wither through neg-
> lect and denial of resources, and to allow the principle of com-
> mand accountability to collapse through lack of enforcement.
> (pp. 70–71)

Regardless of the motives, the final result could well be that police chiefs provide only very limited resources to the corruption-control system. For example, the Mollen Commission (1994, Exhibit Six, p. 12) reported that the NYPD in the 1990s "allocated little of its billion-dollar-plus budget to anti-corruption efforts," resulting in even basic equipment and resources being routinely denied to corruption investigators. Operating two decades earlier, the Knapp Commission (1972, p. 28) and the Pennsylvania Crime Commission (1974, p. 416) both found that providing insufficient resources for undercover work was problematic, especially if cash was not provided to pay informants. One of the witnesses testifying before the Pennsylvania Crime Commission argued that the police officers who were more likely to pay for information from their pockets were at the same time the ones more likely to be taking "notes" (p. 416). The commission further wrote: "Not only is little money available to support the Department's vice policy, but good undercover vehicles are essentially unavailable, and plainclothesmen are expected to use their own private vehicles for which they receive a substantial gas allowance" (p. 417).

In corrupt police departments, the internal affairs office, one of the pillars of a typical corruption-control system, could be plagued by inadequate manpower (in terms of numbers, training, and experience). For example, the Knapp Commission (1972, p. 206) evaluated that the NYPD did not provide adequate resources to the Internal Affairs Division: The number of investigators assigned to internal affairs was "kept at a level that virtually made it impossible to do its job effectively" (p. 207). In fact, the internal affairs office suffered a cut of almost 50%, which resulted in only 45 police officers assigned the task of policing the remaining 30,000 sworn officers in the department (see Knapp Commission, 1972, p. 208). The Pennsylvania Crime Commission (1974, p. 479) addressed the same issue.

> According to the testimony of Chief Inspector Scafidi there were approximately 58 police personnel working for the Internal Affairs Bureau, as of July 10, 1973, which represents an increase of about ten over the previous eighteen months. This total is a mere 0.7% of the entire Police Department. There is, of course, no magic number of personnel needed to do the job, but the number in Philadelphia appears to be inadequate. By

way of rough comparison, the Internal Revenue Service of the federal government assigns approximately 2.8% of its more than 72,000 personnel to the Inspection Service Division, a ratio four times greater than that of the Philadelphia Police Department. The Crime Commission believes the Police Department should greatly increase the number of policemen assigned to internal investigations.

While investigating allegations of police corruption in the 1990s, the Mollen Commission (1994, p. 3) also found that the resources provided for corruption-control efforts were inadequate. An interesting twist was the allocation of resources for internal affairs activities. The Internal Affairs Bureau (IAB) had more than 150 officers (90 of whom handled cases) and dealt with only 5% of the corruption cases (133) each year, and it assigned 95% of the cases (2,569) to the 270 officers in the field internal affairs units (FIAUs; Mollen Commission, 1994, p. 85). The outcome was that the investigators in the IAB handled 2 new cases per year, whereas the investigators in the FIAUs handled an average of 18 cases, reaching up to 30 or 40 cases in high-crime precincts (p. 85). The official explanation for this massive discrepancy was that the most serious, complex, and time-consuming cases were assigned to the IAB. In fact, the Mollen Commission found the opposite to be true. It further concluded that the volume of serious cases sent to the FIAUs suggested that the department sent many of these cases to the FIAU to die (p. 90).

An additional staffing failure is the assignment of investigators who have limited investigative experience or no specialized training. For example, because the former chief of the Philadelphia Police Department, Inspector Scafidi, did not get a large number of experienced plainclothes investigators (according to the Pennsylvania Crime Commission, in order to minimize the chances that they were involved in corruption themselves), their experience in undercover work was limited (1974, p. 480). The commission further reported that the police officers assigned to do internal investigative work received little specialized training before they undertook their tasks (p. 474), primarily because the department did not offer any specialized or in-service training in undercover techniques (p. 480), and all the training provided was on the job. From the corruption-control perspective, resources can be cut at another critical juncture: education in ethics. If the resources are limited, training can be unrealistic, boring, too short, outdated, or led by too few instructors or by instructors with questionable skills (see, e.g., Knapp Commission, 1972).

Finally, as discussed earlier, lack of resources can make supervisory conditions difficult: The ratio of supervisors to line officers can be high, supervisors can be overburdened, they can be assigned to perform line officers' jobs (e.g., responding to the calls for service), or they can receive no in-service training once they are promoted (see, e.g., Mollen Commission, 1994, p. 82).

Control the Police Department's Efforts to Control Corruption

The investigations conducted by independent commissions clearly show that police agencies plagued by serious corruption suffer from extensive failures of their internal control systems. Although particular details differ from case to case and from agency to agency, the many common themes lead toward a broad conclusion: The decision to assign the policing of the police primarily to the police agency itself turns out to be counterproductive precisely when this control is needed the most. Thus, it is crucial to provide another layer of protection and empower other institutions or agencies to control the police agency's control efforts. Other institutions or agencies can engage in such efforts of their own will (e.g., the media, citizen groups) or have this task assigned to them by the government (e.g., independent commissions, the mayor), in which case the task could be temporary or permanent, continuous or sporadic, and a dominant or a peripheral activity. Their focus can be limited, targeting a particular aspect of the control system, or general, examining the control system as a whole.

The police are a part of the government apparatus: Their chief executive officer—the police chief—is responsible for the operation of the police agency (including the operation of the control system) to the government official, the mayor or the city manager, who has a serious interest and duty to foster the *overall* performance by the police. Although the mayor or city manager can hold the chief accountable through budgets and annual reviews for both the use of resources and the general exercise of authority entrusted to them (Moore & Stephens, 1991, p. 37), the head of the city has

neither an explicit duty nor the resources to engage in systematic and continuous control over every element of the agency's control system. This,
however, does not preclude the possibility that the mayor or city manager
could be extremely interested in the investigation and outcome of a few
selected cases of high visibility or a particular aspect of the agency's operation (e.g., training), albeit for potentially different reasons (e.g., the media
spotlight or a brewing scandal).

The relationship between the head of the city and the police chief is
partly predetermined by the selection type and the type of chief's contract
(see Guyot & Martensen, 1991). If the police chief is not motivated to vol-
unteer information about police corruption or the status of the control apparatus, little additional information is provided to the mayor or city manager, other than the annual reports and budget proposals. Even a head of the
city who would like to obtain more systematic feedback from the police
about any particular aspect of their control efforts, especially the disciplinary system, may be reluctant to do so because of the fear that such behavior could be perceived as interference (see Moore & Stephens, 1991, p. 36)
or that the general public, which may possess a great degree of trust in the
police, would find it unnecessary. Furthermore, the mayor is an elected public official who may hesitate to bring such issues into a relatively peaceful
political arena. The city manager, potentially with weaker political allies
than the chief (see Guyot & Martensen, 1991, p. 438), can be even more
averse than the mayor to rocking the boat and disrupting an existing relationship with the police chief.

It seems, then, that the mayor or city manager primarily has either a
very broad agenda in mind (the overall performance) or a very narrow one
(a particular case or a particular issue). Even the mayor who focuses on a
particular case or a set of cases may still assign the task of systematic control to another institution. In particular, if the mayor's attention is devoted
to these issues as a consequence of a growing scandal and political pressure,
one possible outcome is establishing an independent commission and charging it with the task of examining the police department's control system,
while control over the department remains in the hands of the mayor or
city manager. Therefore, the goal of independent commissions is not to control the agency's control system but to audit it and provide feedback to those
in charge of controlling it.

There is an inherent limitation of independent commissions, however. Although the purpose of independent commissions—typically to investigate the existing allegations of corruption and to examine the operation of the agency's control system (see Knapp Commission, 1972, p. 273; Mollen Commission, 1994, p. 1; Pennsylvania Crime Commission, 1974, pp. 40–41)— allows sufficient authority for a detailed examination of the way an agency fulfills each of its control functions, its temporary nature provides only a detailed snapshot, which limits the commission's suitability as a continuous control mechanism over the control system.

A snapshot can be quite effective if it is sharp and taken from the right angle, as the descriptions of various elements of the control system provided by the three independent commissions readily illustrate. All three recent commissions—the Knapp Commission, the Pennsylvania Crime Commission, and the Mollen Commission—seem to have been successful in providing evidence of the problems associated with various elements of the police agency's control system. They reported failures in the recruiting system, inadequate training, absence of supervision and accountability, a strong culture of silence, rare and limited investigations of corruption, and no punishment or light punishment for discovered corrupt activities.

However, such a snapshot can be far from perfect; as discussed earlier, it can be blurred by the commission's internal political struggle or lack of political independence (see, e.g., Pennsylvania Crime Commission, 1974). Depending on the political compromises reached in the process of establishing the commission, it can suffer from inadequate legal authority (see, e.g., Knapp Commission, 1972, p. 44) or experience serious difficulties in finding the investigators, administrative support, and equipment necessary to perform its work (see, e.g., Pennsylvania Crime Commission, 1974, p. 762). All these obstacles and their potential resolutions can affect the commission's ability to perform its task: "The continued pattern of harassment against [Pennsylvania Crime] Commission agents by the City police had two effects. While the investigators' resolve was hardened by the opposition, significant amounts of investigative and staff time were being devoted to combating various crises created by the Philadelphia Police Department" (Pennsylvania Crime Commission, 1974, p. 791).

In the end, even if a commission is established and endowed with adequate resources, and it succeeds in accurately describing the state of affairs

of each of the elements of the control system and in compiling a set of recommendations on how to improve the existing system, the control-over-
control function has not been fulfilled completely. Once the commission
proposes a set of recommendations, it is now up to the mayor or city manager to decide what to do with it. The best possible option from the control
standpoint is to engage in a thorough reform, but whether the events will
take such a turn depends on a number of issues. However, even if political
muscle and support is obtained for an extensive reform, as was the case with
the NYPD's education in ethics in the 1970s (in the aftermath of the Knapp
Commission), the temporary nature of independent commissions presents
an obstacle. Controlling the police control efforts requires constant monitoring, which independent commissions, because of their temporary nature,
simply cannot provide. The report filed by the Mollen Commission (1994,
pp. 107–108) contained an example of outdated integrity training: Asking
officers to watch a flickering black-and-white film from the 1970s about corruption hazards that no longer existed was a result of the lack of continuous monitoring of NYPD's integrity training by an outside agency.

The role played by the media, despite its sporadic and temporary nature,
is complex and challenging. It includes collecting information about police
corruption, conducting occasional yet thorough investigations (potentially
challenged by lack of access to files or individuals), disseminating information about allegations of corruption, monitoring the performances of public
actors (such as the mayor or city manager or the police chief), and pressur-
ing them to carry out their roles. Furthermore, because newspapers and
other media are in the business of selling information, their interest may be
more intense in the times preceding the scandal (resulting in front-page
breaking news about the revelations of police corruption; see, e.g., Burnham, 1970) than in the postscandal period (i.e., the reform era).

Another institution to which the mayor or city manager can assign the
responsibility of controlling the police control efforts is a citizen review. The
reality is that, with the exception of the two citizen reviews (the Philadelphia Police Advisory Board and the New York City Civilian Complaint Review Board) established by their respective mayoral executive orders in the
1960s, "all but a handful of the oversight agencies [in the 1990s] were created by ordinance or referendum" (Walker, 2001, p. 41). Citizen reviews have
been established in very few municipalities or other local units: Of the esti-

mated 20,000 police agencies in the United States (Pastore & Maguire, 1999, p. 36), despite a rapid emergence of citizen reviews in the 1980s and the 1990s, in 2000 only 100 jurisdictions (mostly larger cities) utilized some form of citizen review (see Walker, 1995, p. 6; 2001).

The term *citizen review* or *citizen oversight* incorporates a heterogeneous set of institutions, only a small subset of which are engaged in the control of the police agency's control efforts. Walker classified citizen reviews into four categories (Walker, 1995, 2001). In particular, Class I systems, such as the Minneapolis Citizen Review Authority or the San Francisco Office of Citizen Complaints, have the responsibility of investigating individual complaints and, therefore, conduct the reactive investigation *instead* of the police agency (Walker, 2001, p. 62).

Class II systems, such as the Kansas City Office of Citizen Complaints, are characterized by the fact that "citizen complaints are investigated by the police department and citizens have some input in the review of the investigative reports" (Walker, 2001, 62). In other words, citizen reviews of this type depend on investigations conducted by the police investigators. Their recommendation is forwarded to the chief, who in turn makes the final decision. Therefore, although they have some input, that input is a part of the process within the police agency and has at best only advisory capacity.

Class III systems, such as the Omaha Citizen Review, serve as appellate boards for complainants unsatisfied with decisions made by the police agency. These review boards focus on a particular case, and then only if the complainant is dissatisfied with the police department's decision. Theoretically, then, if the department hides the case and issues no decision, the complainant would have no grounds to initiate the appellate review.

In sum, neither the examination of broader patterns of misconduct and shortcomings in the agency's process of investigation and discipline nor the investigation into the overall control efforts or other elements of the control system is part of the tasks assigned to either Class I, Class II, or Class III systems.

Class IV systems, such as the San José Independent Police Auditor and the Portland Police Internal Investigations Auditing Committee (Walker, 2001, p. 62), are also known as auditor systems because they "do not investigate individual complaints, but are authorized to review, monitor, or audit the police department's complaint process." Although they are most comprehensive because of their focus on larger patterns, they constitute a rather small percentage of all citizen reviews (3%; see Walker, 1995, p. 10).

The San José Independent Police Auditor, one of the very few in the country, was established in 1992 to "provide an independent review of the citizen complaint process, to promote public awareness, and increase greater police accountability to the public by the San Jose Police Department" (Office of the Independent Police Auditor, 2000). Although the auditor's focus is on citizen complaints and the department's reaction to those complaints (and *not* on the other parts of the control system), the analysis of complaints and the search for patterns enable the auditor to expand the inquiry into certain other elements of the control system and make policy change recommendations (Guerrero-Daley, 2000, p. 90). However, the official task assigned to the Office of the Independent Auditor is not to control the overall system of control, but only one aspect of it—the investigation of misconduct—with possible recommendations for changes in other areas if they affect this particular aspect.

In sum, the current system of control of police agency's control suffers from multiple shortcomings. It is assigned to institutions that are temporary (e.g., independent commissions) or sporadic (e.g., the media), institutions whose focus is either too wide or too narrow (e.g., the mayor), or institutions that at best have the authority to examine only some elements of the agency's control system (e.g., citizen reviews). No agency has the task of controlling the police agency's control system as a whole on a continuous basis.

Detect and Investigate Corruption Not Investigated by the Police Department

Although no institution carries a permanent, continuous responsibility to detect and investigate corruption the police department is not investigating, some institutions are assigned the permanent responsibility of investigating and prosecuting corruption in general (e.g., prosecutors) or the temporary responsibility of investigating the extent of corruption within the police department and the effectiveness of the agency's apparatus (e.g., independent commissions), both of which entail an implicit responsibility to check the "dark numbers."

Prosecutors, both federal and local, have the basic duty of investigating and prosecuting cases of police corruption and not necessarily a specific duty of controlling the work of the police agency and investigating corruption not investigated by the agency. Because their task is different—investigating cases with the purpose of collecting evidence and building cases that can be prosecuted successfully—the prosecutors' efforts can also discover corruption not investigated by the agency, but the choice of the cases is affected by their primary task. Consequently, they tend to select more serious cases, cases with stronger evidence and a higher probability of winning, and cases that, as a result of plea bargaining, will lead toward the big fish. Their choice of cases will reflect selection bias and the resources available and, even in the best of circumstances, their work will not be performed in a systematic and continuous way.

A serious problem prosecutors face at the outset is obtaining information about corruption not investigated by the police agency. Of course, the police agency itself, regardless of whether it engaged in a serious investigation of corruption in the first place, would yield no information about the corruption hidden or omitted by the agency. Citizens and police officers can be very reluctant to provide any information about corruption (especially the corruption the department is not aware of or does not intend to investigate) for a variety of reasons, ranging from their own involvement in corruption to their fear of retaliation and lack of confidence in the police. The media also have disadvantages, including the difficulty of engaging in investigative journalism, focusing on the stories that are likely to attract attention, and depending on a good working relationship with the police, and cannot be relied on to provide information about the corruption not investigated by the police agency in a systematic way.

The prosecutors themselves could have reasons to be reluctant to investigate cases of police corruption in general, especially corruption not investigated by the police agency. They could face a heavy caseload and focus primarily on the prosecution of cases that originated elsewhere (i.e., in another police agency or attorney's office), as did the local prosecutors in New York in the 1970s (see, e.g., Knapp Commission, 1972, p. 257). They could also perceive putting a high priority on the investigation of any case of police corruption, especially a case swept under the rug by the police agency, as potentially damaging for the good working relationship between the police and the local prosecutors.

As argued before, local prosecutors—elected public officials dependent on public support—may perceive that the public is willing to tolerate corruption by their blue knights (see Moore, 1997, p. 62; Krauss, 1994) and that the public would disapprove of their focus on police corruption cases while other cases, considered more important by the public, are being put on hold or completely neglected. Federal prosecutors, on the other hand, need neither fear the political pressure nor guess the public's wishes to the same extent. However, as outsiders, they have a more difficult time gaining access to the police culture, unless they rely on local investigators (which in turn introduces another set of problems; see chapter 5).

Another candidate with the potential of providing answers about corruption not investigated by the agency is an independent commission. As discussed earlier, because of the way independent commissions are established—in the aftermath of a scandal and under political pressure to investigate allegations of corruption—they typically have sufficient powers and authority to engage in systematic detection and investigation of corruption, but, much like Cinderella, even if they do have the power, it expires soon after midnight. They are established with a particular purpose in mind, and, once they fulfill that purpose, their work is complete and they are dissolved.

Setting aside the usual problems with independent commissions (e.g., lack of political independence, insufficient resources, inadequate legal power and authority notwithstanding), they have the potential of providing information in a systematic yet temporary manner. Because of their purpose— the detection of the *overall* level of corruption (see, e.g., Mollen Commission, 1994, p. 1; Pennsylvania Crime Commission, 1974, pp. 40–41)—they have a tendency to search for corruption not detected by the agency. As documented in their reports, the three recent U.S. commissions quite successfully detected and investigated corruption intentionally hidden, neglected, or unknown to the agency. The extent of corruption discovered by these commissions, especially the Knapp Commission and the Pennsylvania Crime Commission, is diametrically opposite to the image presented by the administration of these agencies and the extent of corruption in the official statistics at the time.

Although citizens, both as individuals and as organized groups (e.g., the American Civil Liberties Union or the National Association for the Advancement of Colored People), lack the authority, the resources, and perhaps the motives to engage in extensive investigation of corruption not investigated by the police agency itself, a specific form of citizen group—citizen reviews—can be established and assigned the sole or primary task of conducting such investigations. However, as discussed earlier in this chapter, a small number of the very few existing citizen reviews are in a position to engage in such a task (for details, see Walker, 2001).

Relying once again on Walker's classification (2001, p. 62), because by their very nature Class I systems participate as a part of the regular administrative process, they at the same time cannot investigate the cases not investigated by the police agency. Although in theory Class II systems could provide input or criticism, their focus is on the cases investigated by the police agency (rather than the cases *not* investigated by the police agency). Class III systems, which serve as appellate boards, examine only the cases in which the complainant is unsatisfied with the police department's original decision. This, of course, implies that, if the department does not issue a decision in a case or there is no complaint to begin with, these Class III systems have no mechanisms at their disposal to examine the particular case or a set of cases in pursuit of corrupt activities not investigated by the agency.

Finally, the effectiveness of Class IV systems depends significantly on the ultimate purpose of detection and investigation. If the investigation is conducted with the purpose of building court cases, these Class IV reviews will not help because they "do not investigate individual complaints, but are authorized to review, monitor, or audit the police department's complaint process" (Walker, 2001, p. 62). If the purpose is merely to learn about the nature and extent of corruption not investigated by the police agency, these monitors could be assigned such a responsibility and carry it out successfully.

Though their focus is sporadic, the media have the potential for detecting and investigating corruption the police agency is not detecting. Unlike other institutions, such as the prosecutors or the citizen reviews, which typically have the task of investigating corruption in general, the media, like independent commissions, can focus primarily on the extent and nature of corruption *not* investigated by the police agency itself. Publishing stories that summarize the official agency reports about corruption will not spark nearly as much interest or sell nearly as many copies of newspapers as publishing stories about corruption hidden or neglected by the agency. A story becomes more interesting, and consequently more likely to be published, when there is a considerable discrepancy between the agency's official statement about corruption and the perceived reality by the public.

However, reliance on the media has its share of limitations and problems. As discussed earlier, high-quality investigative journalism requires time, skill, and resources, as well as the ability to obtain information and break the code of silence or convince the general public to provide information. In addition, the strategy and practice of editors' publication decisions could also have an impact on the journalists' decision to engage in the time-consuming, challenging, and potentially dangerous task of investigating police corruption. The editors' decisions, the political orientation of the newspapers, the strength of the code of silence, and the level of public tolerance are among the crucial factors determining whether the media will be able to investigate corruption not investigated by the police agency at all and, if so, whether it is going to be sporadic or continuous.

Improve the Existing System of Corruption Control

The overall system of control consists of many institutions. Because they are not hierarchically ordered, they are rarely in a position to be responsible for the way other institutions within the same system operate, despite the fact that the performance of other institutions could have a dramatic impact on their own operation. There is one crucial exception to the rule: the police agency. A number of institutions, such as the mayor or city manager, independent commissions, and citizen reviews, could be responsible for diagnosing the problems and proposing solutions related to the existing mechanisms of control within the police department. Their tasks need not be identical; while independent commissions will tend to examine the overall system, as well as each of its separate elements, citizen reviews could focus primarily on improvements to the complaint system—that is, only one element of the overall system of control.

The primary carrier of the responsibility to improve the existing system of control within the police agency, of course, is the police agency itself. Although police agencies rarely examine the operation of their overall system of control and contemplate possible improvements, they could use the information collected from various sources, including unsubstantiated and substantiated complaints (Sparrow et al., 1990). Although it is possible that clean agencies work on improving their existing systems with regularity, the more crucial test of the notion that police agencies continuously monitor their system and work on its improvement lies with the agencies characterized by widespread corruption. None of the three U.S. independent commissions—the Knapp Commission, the Pennsylvania Crime Commission, and the Mollen Commission—explicitly wrote that the police agencies failed to engage in the continuous improvement of their existing system of control. However, it is clear from the commissions' general descriptions of the state of the respective agencies' control systems and indications of serious problems with the control apparatus that these police departments were not seriously and consistently engaged in monitoring the system and proposing improvements to it.

Although citizens, individual police officers, and the media, all of whom are in a position to experience the system and observe the associated problems, have no authority to engage in improving the existing system directly (unless their constitutional rights have been violated), they can serve as valuable sources of information about potential problems with the existing system. Based on this information, institutions such as the mayor or city manager or the police agency, assuming that they are genuinely interested in learning about corruption and acting on such information, could act accordingly and thus exercise the authority vested in them. For various reasons enumerated previously, ranging from the fear of political interference and political suicide to lack of resources, the mayor could be reluctant or unable to step in and disturb the status quo of the agency's monitoring efforts or personally perform the monitoring on an ongoing basis.

An approach that a mayor or city manager (unable to personally perform the task but determined to obtain answers) can take, especially in the midst of a growing scandal, is to issue an order and establish an independent commission to conduct an investigation and to summarize its findings in a written report. For example, David Dinkins, former mayor of New York City, established the Mollen Commission by an executive order on July 24, 1992 (Mollen Commission, 1994, p. 1), much as did another former mayor,

John Lindsay, in the early 1970s by taking an "unprecedented step, as Mayor of a city, of creating an independent commission [the Knapp Commission] to investigate a police department responsible to [him]" (see Knapp Commission, 1972, p. 2). However, because of, among other reasons, the lack of public interest, inactive media, or ongoing political battles, one of the most fundamental questions related to independent commissions is whether they will be established in the first place.

Because the commissions focus on patterns of corruption (rather than on building individual cases of corruption) and evaluation of the department's overall system, they are well placed to observe the problems and propose recommendations for reform. Therefore, when mayors assign commissions to suggest recommendations for reform, as was the case with the Knapp Commission and the Mollen Commission, the commissions have potential for providing a description of the actual situation and, depending on their views about the police and the causes of misconduct, for proposing subsequent recommendations.

Indeed, all three commissions proposed numerous detailed changes, from those limited in scope such as raising the minimum entry age requirement from 20 to 22 years of age (Mollen Commission, 1994, p. 116) to changes considerably broader in scope, such as legislative proposals in regard to gambling, the Sabbath laws, and prostitution (Knapp Commission, 1972, p. 18). Suggested improvements of the existing system within the police agency addressed, among others, the following issues:

- the restructuring of the internal control mechanisms (Knapp Commission, 1972; Mollen Commission, 1994)
- the enforcement of responsibility to provide integrity training to recruits (Pennsylvania Crime Commission, 1974, pp. 829–840)
- holding line commanders accountable for the behavior of their subordinates (Pennsylvania Crime Commission, 1974, p. 830)
- publicly rewarding supervisors with demonstrated commitment to integrity (Mollen Commission, 1994, p. 132)

In addition to the extent and nature of police corruption and the state of the agency's control apparatus, the breadth and the magnitude of the proposed improvements are also dependent on the commission members' political views, prior experience, and education; shared understanding of corruption and willingness to propose dramatic changes; and the resources and support available to investigate corruption. For example, if the commission is primarily composed of lawyers, their recommendations will reflect their experiences, and, as Maher (2001) illustrates in the case of Los Angeles, the proposed improvements will tend to be legalistic (e.g., the imposition of a new set of rules and systems), rather than steps characteristic of a hands-on management approach (e.g., strengthening supervision, long-term changes in police culture).

Disregarding for the moment whether the recommendations proposed by an independent commission are appropriate and sufficient to provide a systematic and continuous change in a police agency's treatment of corruption, a weak spot with respect to commissions' recommendations is the question of their implementation. Because of the temporary nature of commissions, the actual implementation of these changes, monitoring of further developments, and readjustments of the established mechanisms are not part of their task. Ideally, the mayor, who established the commissions and charged them with such tasks, should be in a position to determine how to handle the proposed recommendations. For a variety of reasons already detailed, however, the mayor might not be as interested in pursuing all the crucial recommendations as in implementing the quicker, more "cosmetic" ones. Even worse, a mayor who opposes the commission established by some other authority can side with the police, be defiant, and even actively sabotage the investigation (see, e.g., Pennsylvania Crime Commission, 1974).

Improving the existing system consists of three tasks: the diagnosis of the problem, the proposal of the recommendations for reform, and the implementation of the recommendations—all of which are critical for success. This is illustrated nicely by the example of the Los Angeles Police Department.[1] The findings of the Christopher Commission (1991), the focus of

1. Although the independent Christopher Commission was established by the mayor in April 1991 (in the aftermath of the Rodney King incident) with the purpose of examining the issues related to a different type of police misconduct (use of excessive force), the investigation

which was primarily the LAPD's use of excessive force, clearly suggest a substantial breakdown in the LAPD's system of internal control, including management, supervision, and accountability. The commission wrote that full implementation would require action from the mayor, the city council, the police commission, the police department, and the voters (p. 225). The commission recommended the creation of the Office of the Inspector General within the police commission overseeing the department (p. 225). However, the commission was aware that the police commission had neither sufficient powers nor resources to successfully exercise its oversight role over the LAPD. The situation did not change over time. Finally, a major corruption-related scandal, uncovered in 1999, indicated the same severe problems with supervision, accountability, and discipline within the department (see Los Angeles Police Department, 2000). The police commission thus not only failed to implement the recommendations proposed by the Christopher Commission but also failed to perform its oversight role effectively.

One of the crucial recommendations issued by the Christopher Commission—the establishment of the Office of Inspector General in charge of auditing, investigating, and overseeing the LAPD's own efforts to handle complaints—was delayed until 1995, and Katherine Mader began performing her role as inspector general as late as mid-1996. Mader faced opposition from the LAPD and the police commission itself, and eventually resigned in late 1998, after the chairman of the police commission attempted to restrict her authority (Walker, 2001, p. 39).

Another institution that might be in a position to suggest improvements is the citizen review. Although the number of citizen reviews rapidly increased in the last two decades (Walker, 1995), they have been established primarily as a consequence of police misconduct other than corruption (most notably use of excessive force); the revelations of corruption, if resulting in a scandal, will more likely lead to the establishment of independent commissions.

---

performed by the commission focused on the LAPD's overall control mechanisms, most of which are important for the control of police corruption as well (e.g., increasing accountability, strengthening supervision, investigating complaints, and curtailing the code of silence).

Another limitation is that the overwhelming majority of citizen reviews are performing a role in the complaint investigation process and, consequently, have very limited interest and authority to engage in continuous improvement of the overall system. In fact, Samuel Walker—a leading expert on citizen reviews—defined citizen oversight as a "procedure for providing input into the complaint process by individuals who are not sworn police officers" and wrote that their basic goals are "to open up the . . . complaint process, to break down the self-protective isolation of the police, and to provide an independent, citizen perspective on complaints" (2001, p. 5). Therefore, their focus is the complaint process: a case-by-case review and/or a review of existing agency policy (see Walker, 1995, p. 8).

With the exception of Class IV reviews (Walker, 1995, pp. 9–10), even when citizen reviews are assigned the responsibility of examining the existing official policy and proposing changes to it, their scope is within the range of issues raised by the complaints. In police agencies characterized by widespread corruption, citizens and police officers alike rarely submit corruption complaints. The subsequent reliance on their complaints, of course, will provide a tainted, narrow, and often distorted view. This bottom-up approach will not provide a thorough and systematic examination of the entire control system because the complaints will typically be silent on the issues crucial for corruption control, such as the administration's failure to provide adequate resources for control, lack of accountability by the police chief and the administration, or promotion of supervisors who are too inexperienced or are corrupt themselves.

Class IV systems, however, "do not investigate individual complaints, but are authorized to review, monitor, or audit the police department's complaint process" (Walker, 2001, p. 62). Consequently, although they have the greatest potential among the four types of citizen reviews to provide feedback relevant to the improvement of the system, their focus, by definition, still is primarily the complaint process. For example, the focus of the San José Independent Police Auditor is citizen complaints and the department's reaction to those complaints. The analysis of complaints and the search for patterns enabled the auditor to expand the inquiry into certain other elements of the control system and propose quite a number of policy changes (e.g., enact the policy for collecting physical evidence in the use of force cases and immediate investigation by supervisors, change the forcible blood-taking policy, implement a procedure for responding to citizens' requests for officer identification; see Guerrero-Daley, 2000, pp. 88–90) and changes in the way certain parts of the system operate (e.g., provide report-writing training for "drunk in public" cases; see Guerrero-Daley, 2000, p. 90).

Typically, the auditors share the fate of citizen reviews by being limited to the issues raised in citizen complaints. For example, the San José Police Auditor described the auditor model as one in which the "focus [is] on identifying and changing the underlying causation factor that give rise to complaints" (Guerrero-Daley, 2000, p. 1). Similarly, the recently established auditor in Omaha "will be permitted to review all records of the Police Department's investigations, sit in during interviews, request follow-up investigations and analyze trends in citizen complaints" (Spencer, 2001). In other words, the auditor will monitor investigations into citizens' complaints and recommend policy changes (Ruggles, 2001). Unlike other auditors, the special counsel to the Los Angeles Sheriff's Department, Merrick Bobb, was hired in 1993 with the purpose of reducing costs of civil litigation resulting from the misconduct of deputy sheriffs. Bobb perceived his mandate in broad terms and "investigated virtually every aspect of the sheriff's department, including recruitment and training, officer assignment patterns, and sex discrimination in the department as well as use of physical and deadly force" (Walker, 2001, p. 39).

Auditors' performance could be adversely affected by a number of problems. If established as a small group, auditors could be composed of community members with often conflicting political interests, whose primary purpose might be to serve those interests rather than systematically evaluate the police agency. Furthermore, as auditors tend to be rather small offices, the quality of the leadership is extremely important. In fact, according to Walker, the differences between strong auditor systems, such as those in Portland or San José, and the weak ones, such as the one in Seattle, are often "the result of political leadership, which in turn reflected the civic culture of a community, and the quality of the leadership in the agency itself" (2001, p. 41). Finally, if the auditor is challenged either legally or politically, the ability to perform the work decreases. On the other hand, as the example of the San José auditor suggests, if these challenges are overcome successfully, the auditor's credibility increases.[2]

Just like citizen reviews that focus exclusively on one aspect of the control system—the complaint procedures—and can propose only changes related to the complaints, prosecutors are in a position to propose changes limited to the scope of their work. In particular, they can propose legislative changes of substantive and procedural laws they use during investigations and prosecutions. Moreover, notwithstanding the usual set of potential obstacles, such as lack of interest, heavy caseloads, and political connections, prosecutors are among the players best suited to notice the problems with the existing normative solutions and propose their improvements.

Recently, Florida engaged in a thorough examination of the current statutes and laws concerning public corruption. Governor Jeb Bush created the Public Corruption Study Commission by his executive order in September 1999 and entrusted it to "make recommendations related to statutory revisions on the issue of public corruption and official misconduct in Florida" (State of Florida, 1999). The 23-member commission, composed of lawyers and other designees from the Attorney General's Office, the chief inspector general, the comptroller, the chairman of the Ethics Commission, the president of the Senate, and the speaker of the House, met four times and proposed a number of changes (Florida Public Corruption Study Commission, 1999). Although the changes, such as increasing the severity of punishment for criminal violations by public servants (Florida Public Corruption Study Commission, 1999) and putting the rules concerning public servants under the same section (M. T. Cagle, personal communication, May 25, 2000), have the potential to improve the legal means available to the prosecutors, despite the prosecutors' best efforts, as well as efforts by

---

2. Teresa Guerrero-Daley, San José's police auditor, faced resistance by the police chief, who threatened to resign. Her moment of truth happened when she proposed policy changes related to off-duty work, such as prohibiting wearing official uniforms to off-duty work and establishing the affirmative obligation to report the off-duty hours to the police department. The police union demonstrated at the city hall, but the city council approved her recommendations and put the auditor's position into the city charter the next year (Ruggles, 2001). Similarly, the mayor opposed the establishment of the auditor office in Omaha. When Mayor Hal Daub vetoed the establishment of the office, however, the city council overrode his veto (Ruggles, 2001).

other commission members, their improvements are only *recommendations* to the legislature. Whether the recommendations will become the letter of the law is beyond their reach. In this particular case, the Senate passed all the recommendations, while the House passed only some (M. T. Cagle, personal communication, May 25, 2000).

Limit Opportunities for Corruption

Monitoring actual police work, learning about the types of opportunities available, and introducing appropriate changes are unavoidable elements of control efforts. These changes can range from legislative ones (e.g., elimination of a duty to enforce certain laws from the police jurisdiction) and from changes in the organizational structure of the police (e.g., more frequent rotation of assignments, stricter supervision) to changes in actual enforcement policies (e.g., provide sufficient funds for undercover work and develop ways to measure police officers' performance other than relying on arrest quotas). However, with the exception of the police department itself, none of the agencies is assigned this task on a continuous and systematic basis. Yet, a recurring paradox is that in the extensively corrupt police agencies, which most need this task to be performed, the administration has no incentive to engage in a thorough examination of the existing system and propose changes that would limit opportunities for corruption.

The problem at the outset is that the legal environment can provide additional opportunities for corruption by requiring police officers to enforce "problematic" laws or by providing vague descriptions of prohibited behavior in the statutes. In the words of Patrick Murphy, a former commissioner of the NYPD, "By charging our police with the responsibility to enforce the unenforceable, we subject them to disrespect and corruptive influences, and we provide the organized criminal syndicate with illicit industries upon which they thrive" (Pennsylvania Crime Commission, 1974, p. 420). Changing the legal rules requires an orchestrated effort by a number of players, from those who have the opportunity to notice where the problems are (such as law enforcement officials, prosecutors, and the general public), as well as those who have sufficient clout to push for change (such as governors and state representatives).

One of the crucial stages in the process of introducing the changes in the existing set of laws is initiation. This is especially problematic in communities in which the public tolerates corruption and no scandal results as a consequence of its public revelations. Although the police officers, the police agency, the citizenry, the mayor, the media, and/or the prosecutors could initiate the process, and each of them has a somewhat different set of considerations (as discussed earlier), the ultimate effect is the same: reluctance to get involved. Independent commissions, typically established at the peak of an ongoing corruption scandal, have, on the one hand, the attention of the media, the public, and the mayor and, on the other hand, sufficient resources to learn about the agency, notice the weak spots in terms of opportunities for corruption, and propose changes to the system. Therefore, notwithstanding the usual problems experienced by independent commissions, they can be equipped to succeed in the second stage in the process—providing the diagnosis of the problem and proposing improvements to the system.

For example, the two independent commissions in the 1970s noted a number of laws that provided opportunities for corruption and proposed subsequent changes (see Knapp Commission, 1972; Pennsylvania Crime Commission, 1974). The law regulating the sale of food and other necessities on Sunday (the Sabbath Law) was a very complex statute (Knapp Commission, 1972, p. 149) that included rules store owners violated frequently. Similarly, construction regulations required so many permits that a typical contractor could not obtain all of them and was thus compelled to cross the line to proceed with the project (Knapp Commission, 1972, p. 125).

The Pennsylvania Crime Commission (1974, p. 413) and the Knapp Commission (1972, p. 90) also pointed out that prohibitions of certain behaviors, such as vice-related or gambling laws, are disapproved of by a sizable fraction of the general public. Although police officers should have enforced the laws that prohibit gambling activities, for example, the public and the police officers shared the belief that gambling is not harmful and that there is nothing wrong with it (Knapp Commission, 1972, pp. 72–73).

Laws can also be worded in ways that allow for ambiguous interpretations. The Knapp Commission found examples of vague laws that police officers were asked to enforce in the 1970s; the rules governing the operation of bars were "sound in principle but are so vague and ill-defined that they lend themselves to abuses in practice" (1972, pp. 147–148). Regardless of whether they are legal statutes or official agency rules, the rules that regulate the conduct of police officers can be vague as well, thus providing for misinterpretations of the rules or for enforcement practices different from the official rules, both of which could open doors for additional opportunities for corruption.

The last two stages in the process—the legislative change and its actual implementation—are no less problematic, especially if the recommendations for legislative changes are made by independent commissions, temporary in nature and having no authority over their implementation. Moreover, despite the changes in the laws introduced in the aftermath of the Knapp Commission with the purpose of limiting opportunities for corruption, the Mollen Commission, studying the same police agency two decades later, reported that the new opportunities for corruption that developed in the 1990s were neither anticipated nor affected by the changes in the laws. Thus, as the case of the NYPD illustrates, unless new opportunities for corruption are monitored and the changes affecting opportunities for corruption are introduced on a continuous basis, police officers with high levels of propensity for corruption will find alternative new ways of obtaining illegal gain.

In addition to the existence of clear official rules and their actual enforcement, opportunities for corruption can also be minimized indirectly through organizational changes, such as the increased accountability of supervisors, tighter supervision, provision of adequate resources for control, or more frequent rotation of police officers across different assignments. However, as noted earlier, part of the problem why police corruption spread in agencies such as the NYPD (see Knapp Commission, 1972) and the Philadelphia Police Department (see Pennsylvania Crime Commission, 1974) in the 1970s was the lack of accountability of the supervisors, who were involved in corruption themselves and/or who, by tolerating the corruption of their subordinates, failed to exercise effective supervision.

Another organizational change that can affect the opportunities for corruption is the way the resources for undercover drug buys and informants are allocated and provided to police officers. For example, the Pennsylvania Crime Commission (1974, p. 691) heard testimony from police officers, substantiated by the commission's examination of the department's budget allocation, that the Philadelphia Police Department did not provide sufficient financial resources for police officers to pay informants or buy drugs in undercover operations (p. 416). Consequently, police officers covered these expenses from money that might not have come directly from their own pocket, but from someone else's: "I put it out myself with the money that I received for my regular notes" (Pennsylvania Crime Commission, 1974, p. 415).

Furthermore, internal monitoring systems that would monitor police officers' propensity for corruption could ensure at the very least that the police officers with higher propensity for corruption (see chapter 4) are not designated for assignments characterized by plentiful opportunities (e.g., the vice unit) and that they are rotated from assignment to assignment frequently. However, as discussed earlier and documented by the Knapp Commission and the Pennsylvania Crime Commission, agencies characterized by widespread corruption typically do not maintain effective monitoring systems.

The measures described so far, both direct and indirect, try to limit the opportunities for corruption on the police officers' side by increasing the costs of corrupt behavior and by eliminating conditions that allow corruption to flourish. Because some of the basic forms of corruption involve both the bribe taker and the bribe giver, a logical choice would be to try to affect the *supply side* as well—that is, the citizenry. After all, citizens who passively tolerate police corruption, as was the case in Philadelphia and New York in the late 1980s and early 1990s (see Moore, 1997, p. 62; Krauss, 1994), and especially those who actively participate in corruption, as was the case with restaurant owners, owners of gambling establishments, small store owners, and contractors in New York and Philadelphia in the 1970s (Knapp Commission, 1972; Pennsylvania Crime Commission, 1974), are just the other side of the same corruption coin.

Judging from the findings of the Knapp Commission and the Pennsylvania Crime Commission, such widespread and organized corruption could not have survived without strong support from at least a substantial minority of the public. For example, according to the Knapp Commission (1972, p. 170), the practice of providing gratuities to police officers was "widely accepted by both the police and the citizenry, with many feeling that it wasn't corruption at all, but a natural perquisite of the job." The Mollen Commission (1994, p. 146) also noted the role of the public in the continuation of corruption: "The 30th Precinct investigation demonstrated that citizens, whether they be drug dealers, show owners, building superintendents, or local residents, participate in and assist officers in corruption schemes."

Having in mind the lack of motivation to reduce their opportunities for corruption by increasing the costs on the side of the bribe givers, the few steps that these corrupt police agencies and the larger society carried out, if any, to educate the public were evidently fruitless. Under the guidance of the Knapp Commission, the NYPD engaged in a public education campaign. Bribery arrests increased dramatically in a period of 3 years, although the absolute arrest numbers were still minuscule and included primarily the small fish (Knapp Commission, 1972, p. 21).

Disseminate True Information About Corruption

Because the primary agent for most control efforts is the police agency itself, it may be reasonable to expect that the agency would be interested in collecting information about corruption for its own purposes of control, regardless of whether it would be willing to share that information. However, because of the prevalence of the rotten-apple approach and the resulting effects—emphasis on individual responsibility and denial of any systematic corruption within the agency—a simple regularity seems to have evolved: the more corrupt the agency, the less likely it is to be interested in collecting information about corruption and sharing it with the public. Indeed, the findings of the Mollen Commission (1994, pp. 95–96) indicate that the NYPD in the 1990s not only failed to provide accurate information about the extent of corruption but also actually hid complaint-generated cases of police corruption.

Information an agency does disseminate about corruption is still almost exclusively only the official rates of corruption, that is, the number of police officers disciplined for corruption-related behavior. However, the official corruption rates, especially in corrupt agencies, are typically based on reactive investigations and represent just the tip of the iceberg. The reality of this discrepancy between the official agency rates and the actual extent of corruption becomes apparent when the official rates of police corruption in the NYPD and the Philadelphia Police Department in the 1970s are compared with the findings about the extent of police corruption by the Knapp

Commission and the Pennsylvania Crime Commission. In these two agencies, characterized by widespread corruption, only a few police officers were punished each year for corrupt behavior. Similarly, the Mollen Commission (1994) described the gap between the extent of corruption the commission was discovering and the extent of corruption presented by the police administrators:

> From the beginning of our investigation, we were struck by the difference between what the Commission was uncovering about the state of corruption and corruption control within the Department, and what the Department was publicly— and privately—stating about itself. The Department maintained that police corruption was not a serious problem, and consisted primarily of sporadic, isolated incidents. It also insisted that the shortcomings had been disclosed about the Department's anti-corruption efforts reflected, at worst, insufficient resources and uncoordinated organization of internal investigations. The Commission found that the corruption problems facing the Department are far more serious than top commanders in the Department would admit. (p. 2)

Those who have the best access to information are frequently motivated either not to collect it or to hide it even if it is collected. The question, then, is whether there are other feasible sources willing to collect information and disseminate it. The prosecutors, both local and federal, are also quite close to the source of information, and investigating cases of corruption is part of their duties. However, because they are frequently included in the second stage of the process, unless they engage in their own investigations, they largely rely on the information collected by the police agency itself (which may fail, especially dealing with highly corrupt agencies) and on the information provided by the general public and police officers (who know about corruption and can have stronger reasons not to report corruption than to report it). As discussed earlier, there may be a variety of reasons for prosecutors to be reluctant to investigate corruption and thus obtain accurate information regarding its nature and extent. In the end, if prosecutors do collect and disseminate such information, it is still sporadic and focused on individual cases.

Although the mayor or city manager—an official made responsible to the city counsel for the performance of the police and endowed with the authority to hold the police chief accountable—could have strong motives not to share information about corruption, especially if it is unfavorable, a mayor faced with political pressure or an erupting scandal or driven by a personal zeal for integrity might decide to obtain this information. One way the mayor could attempt to learn about the actual state of affairs is to establish an independent commission and empower it to provide the answers and share them with the public.

Notwithstanding the usual problems associated with the success of independent commissions, the findings of the three recent commissions—the Knapp Commission, the Pennsylvania Crime Commission, and the Mollen Commission—were thorough, vivid, and quite graphic illustrations of corrupt police activities at the time. The fact remains, of course, that the commissions are established on a sporadic and temporary basis and that the snapshot they document is at best accurate at the moment.

The media could also provide and disseminate true information about police corruption. Because journalists' interests, activities, and incentives are governed in no small part by the fact that they are in the business of selling information, they are likely to pursue the stories that are more extreme in at least one aspect (such as the severity of the misconduct, the extent of the gain, the degree to which it affects the whole department, the arrogance of its actors, or the rank of the actors) for the purpose of selling more newspapers or attracting more viewers. Consequently, unlike mayors and police chiefs, who may tend to downplay the seriousness of corruption allegations, journalists could be motivated to embellish the story and leap to more general conclusions.

The journalists' quest for stories apt to attract public attention may not be an effective tool of information dissemination for two further reasons: First, the public might fail to react to revelations of even very serious allegations of police corruption; second, despite all the zest, the public may lose interest over time. Furthermore, individual, personalized stories are easier to build and have a tendency to attract more attention than stories using aggregate data. In sum, although newspapers may actually disseminate accurate information about certain individual cases or the nature and extent of police corruption in general, as was the case with Burnham's shocking story about the NYPD (see Burnham, 1970; Knapp Commission, 1972), they do not perform this task on a systematic and regular basis.

A Look Ahead

The police agencies themselves should carry the heaviest burden of control efforts. They have been assigned to perform or share a number of control functions, including detecting and investigating corruption, punishing corrupt police officers, monitoring the propensity for corruption, cultivating a culture intolerant of corruption, establishing supervision and accountability, setting official policies and enforcing them, providing resources for control, proposing improvements to the existing system, and disseminating true information about corruption. However, 20-year cycles of scandals and reforms in New York over a period of at least a century (Curran Committee, 1913/1997; Helfand Investigation, 1954/1997; Knapp Commission, 1972; Lexow Committee, 1894/1997; Mollen Commission, 1994; Seabury 1932/ 1997) and revelations of police corruption and subsequent scandals in other parts of the United States (e.g., Los Angeles Police Department, 2000) tell us that the police simply cannot be trusted to exclusively police themselves.

Yet, it becomes obvious that, much like a typical police agency itself, none of the external institutions of control—the mayor, the independent commissions, the prosecutors—are concerned with continuous, systematic monitoring of corruption within the agency and of control efforts performed by the agency. One common feature of the current control mechanisms is that their focus is either too wide (e.g., annual reports, budget) or too narrow (e.g., individual cases), with the exception of independent commissions and the media. The mechanisms are typically set in motion by reactive, incident-driven events, rather than by proactive methods. Their actual operation and output are more likely to be sporadic than continuous and systematic.

What can be done to ensure systematic and continuous control of police corruption? Guided by the functional perspective (rather than by the organizational perspective), in the next chapter—the concluding chapter in this book—I propose a comprehensive control mechanism aimed at effective corruption control. It is complex, yet intuitive. Its complexity stems from the involvement of many organizations that have to act in concert to successfully carry out the functions that the control mechanism requires. It is nevertheless intuitive because it clearly lays out what needs to be done and by whom and what incentive structure should be set in place to align the interests of various actors and focus them toward a common goal—attainment and maintenance of a healthy police agency free of widespread, systematic, and serious corruption.

7

A Step Ahead

A Multifaceted System of Comprehensive Corruption Control

Although in an ideal world a number of organizations in the current corruption-control system—from the mayor and the police agency itself to the prosecutors and courts—should perform their control functions continuously and systematically, the last two chapters show that the real world is very different. In the current setup, most existing mechanisms often operate in isolation, with insufficient resources, and are bound to fail where they are needed most—in profoundly corrupt agencies. At best, an occasional scandal or growing public pressure for change may compel the mayor or other public figures to react and try to address the problem of pervasive police corruption. However, even in the examples of powerful punitive scandals and subsequent successful reforms—such as the Knapp Commission investigation and the resulting reforms affecting the NYPD—the effects of the scandal begin to wear off shortly, typically within a year, as the attention of the public and the focus of other political players turn toward other issues (Sherman, 1978).

The proposed model rests on the premise that satisfactory control of police corruption can be achieved only through coordinated, continuous, and systematic efforts by both internal and external control mechanisms. Control tasks would be divided among the police agency itself and a number of other institutions, such as the mayor, prosecutors, and courts. Although the primary responsibility for corruption control would still rest with the police agency, external oversight mechanisms would oversee the police agency's internal mechanisms. As an embodiment of the external oversight mechanism, this chapter introduces a new oversight agency—the integrity-enhancing agency (IEA)—and makes it an integral part of the model of corruption control.

One of the IEA's key features is that it can—and should—operate without reliance on scandals and dramatic events. Although the very establishment of the IEA might be preceded by a major reform (most likely triggered by a scandal), once the IEA is operational, scandals and drastic reforms, although they may occur with the IEA already in place and the IEA could well be a catalyst, would be neither necessary nor particularly important.

In this chapter, I concentrate on issues related to the IEA: its establishment, powers, organization, and membership, as well as the associated costs. In the second part of the chapter, I revisit the topic of control functions and examine the division of labor among various agencies once the IEA is built into the system. Finally, I evaluate how acceptable the citizens and police officers would find the IEA and outline how its effectiveness should be measured.

The New Kid on the Block: The Integrity-Enhancing Agency

The mission of the proposed integrity-enhancing agency (IEA) should not be to investigate complaints; rather, the IEA should be established with the exclusive purposes of securing oversight over the police agency, continually monitoring its performance, and providing feedback about it. The IEA thus would serve simultaneously as a management tool for the police chief and as a watchdog for the public.

Because the IEA's primary purpose would be to provide continuous monitoring of the police agency and disseminate its findings on a regular basis, a scandal is not a necessary ingredient for its success. In fact, the IEA should work successfully without relying on the uncertain development of headlines. Consequently, although the extent and nature of corruption can change from one period to another, these changes are unlikely to be as dramatic as a sudden discovery of serious corruption. The modus operandi of the IEA would be exactly the opposite: to provide regular updates about corruption and the police department's efforts to deal with it, rather than rely on occasional spurts of media attention and the might of potential subsequent scandals to control corruption.

The Establishment of the IEA

Although the IEA might well be established in the aftermath of a scandal, when sufficient political power is generated to push for the reform of the existing control system, the emergence of a scandal is not a necessary condition for its creation. Despite its substantial pressure to change the existing system, a scandal may not be the setting for making the wisest decisions. Under political pressure, the mayor may be inclined to resort to quick fixes and thus satisfy growing public pressure (e.g., establish a citizen review, dismiss a few police officers), while neglecting to search for a superior long-term solution (e.g., the creation of the IEA).

One of the very few citizen reviews—the closest cousins to the IEA—that were not established in the aftermath of a police crisis is the Office of the Independent Police Auditor for the San José Police Department (Guerrero-Daly, 2000, p. 1). Rather, its creation was a result of accumulated dissatisfaction with the police expressed by several different segments of the community (e.g., students, members of the Bar Association, and the ACLU) through peaceful but loud demonstrations in front of City Hall (Guerrero-Daley, 2000). Such public pressure ultimately prompted political leaders to pay attention. After examining several existing models of citizen reviews, the city of San José selected the auditor model.

The IEA could be established as an independent city agency by a city ordinance or a referendum. The overwhelming majority of the nearly 100 existing citizen reviews have been established that way (Walker, 2001, p. 41). For example, the Portland auditor, the Minneapolis Civilian Review Authority, and the Kansas City Office of Citizen Complaints were all established by city councils, and the Berkeley Police Review Commission, the Detroit Board of Police Commissioners, and, more recently, the San Francisco Office of Cit-

izen Complaints were established by referendum (Walker, 2001). Walker
(2001) argues that "this [the establishment by city ordinance or referendum]
represents a major shift from the 1960s, when both the Philadelphia PAB
and the citizen-dominated CCRB in New York were established by mayoral
executive order in the face of opposition or indifference from city councils"
(p. 41). This shift in public support for citizen reviews has been the result of
numerous social and political changes, ranging from the success of the civil
rights movement and the strengthening of the political power of African
American and other minority citizens, to the outrage over several extreme
cases of police misconduct and the growing interest in developing partner-
ships between the police and the communities (see Walker, 2001, pp. 41–43).

Once established by either a city ordinance or a referendum, the IEA
would become a city office. Although there are many options in the process
of designing a successful IEA, and it is not immediately clear how to proceed
with the details of its implementation, two unsuccessful stories about auditor systems clearly suggest what options should *not* be pursued. The problem
with the Albuquerque Independent Counsel was that, despite strong legal
grounds for the counsel's authority, the police oversight role was assigned by
contract to a law firm as merely one of the firm's activities. The public had no
office of an auditor to identify with, and the counsel did not establish a connection with the public (Guerrero-Daley, 2000). Walker (2001) concluded
that the Albuquerque auditor "failed to fully utilize its authorized powers
or play much of a public role" (p. 40). The problem with the Seattle auditor
was of a different nature but with the same consequences: A retired judge
would read the investigation files and perform a cold review of the cases
(Guerrero-Daley, 2000). This approach did not build trust and confidence in
the community. Furthermore, the Seattle auditor had no authority to review the police department's policies and practices (Walker, 2001, p. 40).

One of the more successful citizen review stories—the independent police auditor (IPA) in San José—was first created in 1993 by San José City
Council ordinance as a city office (Guerrero-Daley, 2000, p. 1). Three years
later, the residents voted to make the IPA a permanent city office (Guerrero-
Daley, 2000, p. 1). The auditor, Teresa Guerrero-Daley, argued that, by virtue
of being chartered as a permanent city office, the Office of the Auditor is politically better protected now. In fact, "measure E amended the City Charter to require a vote of the residents of San José before the IPA office can be

abolished and provided insulation to the Police Auditor by requiring a super majority vote of the city council [at least 10 members] before removal mid-term" (Guerrero-Daley, 2000, p. 4). Analogously, because political independence constitutes one of the crucial prerequisites for its successful operation, the IEA would be better protected against changes in the political scenery if it were established as a *permanent* city office.

Naturally, establishing the IEA would be subject to certain economies of scale. Although IEAs could readily be established for larger city police agencies, the budgets of smaller cities and townships would probably be seriously strained if each town established a separate IEA. Thus, the potential need to decrease costs and increase the independence also suggests the formation of IEAs that oversee a number of smaller agencies within the same geopolitical unit (e.g., county).

The Powers of the IEA

To perform successfully, the IEA would need a number of legal powers. Like the successful independent commissions, the IEA would need to be able to provide immunity to police officers willing to supply information, to have the subpoena power to compel the testimony of police officers or citizens if necessary, and to have access to police records. In the 1999 year-end report, the San José auditor wrote about the importance of having these legal powers.

> Currently, neither the PSCU [Professional Standards and Conduct Unit] nor the IPA [the Auditor] has the authority to compel a citizen witness to be interviewed or release and/or provide physical evidence such as medical records that may be an integral part of an investigation. Because of this, subpoenas are needed for citizen witnesses . . . subpoenas would be very useful in cases where a witness is reluctant to get involved for whatever reason, but may be more inclined to cooperate if they are summoned. In addition, subpoenas duces tecum, which are used to subpoena records are very necessary and often provide the most reliable evidence. (Guerrero-Daley, 2000, p. 6)

Furthermore, to obtain police officers' testimony, the IEA should also have some of the powers given to the police agency: cooperation with the IEA would be a condition of police officers' continued employment and lying to the IEA, just like lying to the official structures within the police agency itself, should be a firing offense.

Although the IEA should be endowed with these legal powers, it would be unlikely to exercise them frequently or rely on them exclusively. The reason is simple: The IEA's relationship with the police agency would be different from the relationship between a typical independent commission and the police agency. The police perceive an independent commission as a headhunting agency, established to conduct a thorough one-time investigation and recommend excessive changes. By contrast, the IEA would be established as a permanent city office, entrusted to provide continuous monitoring and positioned to draw the attention of the police chief, mayor, city council, and media to the recommended changes and the ways to implement them. Its purpose would be to work *with* the police agency and the city council to enhance the quality and integrity of the police service provided to the community.

An example of successful coordinated efforts by a monitoring agency, the police, and the city government is the San José Office of the Independent Police Auditor. San José's police auditor works with the police chief, the city council, and the city manager to address the problems and issues noted by the auditor (Guerrero-Daley, 2000). The auditor notifies the chief about weak areas and asks him to come up with solutions. At meetings with city council and the city manager, the auditor presents her findings and recommends changes. The chief, having had the opportunity to think about these issues in advance, takes the lead in proposing changes and explaining how the situation should be improved. Although the problem is pointed out by the auditor, the solution to the problem is the chief's. Such a division of labor makes the changes more acceptable to the rank and file. At the same time, the chief does not feel put on the spot or publicly intimidated by the auditor, yet the presence of the city manager and the city council adds credibility.

The Organization of and Membership in the IEA

Unlike traditional citizen reviews that spend a substantial portion of their time in some aspect of investigation and adjudication of actual complaints (see Walker, 1995), the IEA would operate like a research group. This difference stems from the difference between the tasks assigned to the IEA and those assigned to a typical citizen review: Whereas the IEA would primarily focus on patterns and underlying causes, a typical citizen review focuses on individual cases. IEA meetings would be research oriented and problem solving, rather than investigative or focused on isolated cases.

The IEA would be headed by its director and would include several other members, active and determined individuals of high integrity. The potential success of the IEA would depend not only on the formal structure of the IEA and the level of political support but also on the quality of its members. As the conclusions of Walker's study on citizen review boards indicate, leadership quality is a crucial factor in differentiating between success and failure.

> There were also clear differences in the effectiveness of the various forms of oversight that were not related to formal structure. Some review boards with independent investigatory power had credible records, such as Minneapolis and the reinvigorated San Francisco OCC. Others, such as the New York CCRB, had little to show for themselves. There were strong auditor systems, as in Portland and San José, and weak ones, as in Seattle. The differences were more often the result of political leadership, which in turn reflected the civic culture of a community, and the quality of the leadership in the agency itself. (Walker, 2001, pp. 40–41)

The IEA would require trained professionals, such as lawyers and social scientists. Indeed, some of the more successful citizen review boards have engaged in complex types of analyses that went beyond analyzing individual cases (Walker, 2001). For example, Merrick Bobb, special counsel to the Los Angeles Sheriff's Department, analyzed a high number of shootings by officers assigned to the department's Century Station. While the internal study by the LASD focused exclusively on the individual shooting incidents, Bobb's analysis was more thorough. His investigation included "a review of all relevant documents, interviews with LASD personnel, ride-alongs with officers, and a helicopter fly-along" (Walker, 2001, p. 98).

Members of the IEA would work as a team on designing the methods to be used and selecting the issues to be examined, developing relationships with the police officers within the agency, conducting interviews with police officers, and examining the agency's official records. Some specific issues would require a more intense application of social science methods (such as surveys of community members, focus group interviews with police officers, observation of police work), and others would require either greater reliance on the knowledge of the law (such as the determination of whether the police officer had a valid reason for a search) or both (such as the analyses of police records for patterns of misconduct or corruption-conducive situations). A heterogeneous group of social scientists and lawyers would be in a much better position to perform all of these tasks successfully and would also generate more credibility in the eyes of the general public than if these same tasks were conducted by the police agency itself.

The use of social scientists also could introduce novel approaches to the issues crucial in corruption control. For example, although previous attempts to survey police officers about the extent and nature of the code of silence in police agencies—a crucial step in corruption control—have failed or suffered serious drawbacks because of the police officers' reluctance to talk about misconduct (i.e., precisely because of the code of silence; see Fabrizio, 1990; Martin, 1994), a novel approach probes police officers with a series of questions related to facts and opinions about corruption in general rather than about their own corrupt activities or others' corrupt activities (Kutnjak Ivković & Klockars, 1995). This methodology minimizes police officers' resistance and thus allows researchers to study and quantify a range of corruption-related issues.

The Integrity-Enhancing Agency Versus Citizen Review Boards

An integrity-enhancing agency (IEA) would perform primarily a monitoring role. It outgrows the usual complaint-examination focus of most existing citizen review boards. Indeed, citizen review boards have not been established with the purpose of controlling police corruption and are not considered part of the corruption-control apparatus but rather are a wake-up call and a way to fix the problem in the aftermath of highly publicized cases of police brutality (see, e.g., Perez, 1994, p. 125). The integrity-enhancing agency is fundamentally different along two crucial dimensions.

First, the IEA's task extends far beyond the usual involvement with complaints. Unlike some other types of police misconduct (such as police brutality or verbal abuse), except in special circumstances that involve the use of excessive force as the means of achieving corrupt ends or in especially widespread or organized corruption, police corruption yields very few complainants willing to report corruption. Thus, very few corruption-related complaints are officially recorded, and it is meaningless to build complex machinery to investigate these few complaints. Furthermore, unless utilized as part of a larger organized and systematic strategy of corruption control that deals with the underlying causes of corruption, the focus on complaints will not yield the long-term organizational changes that improve corrupt police departments.

Even the citizen oversights that incorporate monitoring as a substantial part of their role, such as the independent auditor for the San José Police Department (Guerrero-Daley, 2000), are not assigned the task of controlling the *overall* system of control, just one aspect of it—the investigation of misconduct. Recommendations for changes in other areas are possible but only if they are related to investigations based on complaints. Indeed, the San José Independent Police Auditor was established in 1992 to "provide an independent review of the citizen complaint process, to promote public awareness, and increase greater police accountability to the public by the San José Police Department" (Guerrero-Daley, 2000).

Second, members of the proposed IEA should not be volunteers or citizens who have secured a spot on the IEA through their political position or their close association with powerful political players in the community. Although complete ignorance of political opinions and utmost separation of the existing political climate in city hall from the offices of the IEA are probably impossible, the impact of politics can be substantially limited. In principle, attaining this goal would be simple: IEA members should be selected on the basis of their professional expertise (rather than political activity and political views). Professionalism would enable members to submit their expert opinions to pertinent political figures, including members of the city government, mayors, and police chiefs, as well as the media, citizen organizations, and other watchdog groups. Moreover, even changes in the political balance should not affect the membership on the IEA.

In addition, unlike traditional citizen review board members, who typically had no inside knowledge of the operation of the police agency and the everyday work of police officers before becoming board members, members of the IEA would have gained systematic knowledge about the police throughout the course of their studies, as well as by research projects and legal cases on which they had worked. That exposure to problems in policing would probably make them more acceptable to police officers, who traditionally resist any citizen interference into "police matters" and argue that "people who have never experienced the police officer's lot *cannot* review police conduct fairly" (Perez, 1994, p. 3). At the same time, members of the IEA would not become "native" or "one of them," which would satisfy a requirement important to the public—that they would be nonpolice personnel.

Costs

The effectiveness of the IEA critically depends on the resources available. The estimated cost would depend on the city budget, city size, size of the police force, size of the IEA, and the current level of police integrity in the police agency. Although the exact cost cannot be determined in abstract, a rough estimate can be obtained from the expenses of San José's Office of the Independent Police Auditor.

The auditor has three primary functions: "(1) it serves as an alternate office where people may file a complaint, (2) it reviews the investigations of citizens' complaints conducted by the SJPD, and (3) it promotes public awareness of a person's right to file a complaint" (Guerrero-Daley, 2000, p. 2). The auditor also reviews all investigations of use-of-force cases. In addition to the auditor, the auditor's office also employs an assistant auditor, complaint examiner, complaint analyst, community outreach coordinator, and the office specialist, for a total of six employees (Office of the Independent Police Auditor, 2005). The auditor oversees the San José Police Department, which employs approximately 1,400 sworn officers (Reaves & Smith, 1999) and serves a community of 918,000 (the 11th largest city in the United States). Approximately 400 to 600 formal allegations against the police are received annually (Guerrero-Daley, 2000, p. 42). In the San José city budget of $ 3.34 billion for the year 2002–2003, the city allocated $216,394,450, or 6.5% of its budget, to the police; at the same time, the city devoted merely $647,866 or 0.016% of its overall budget to the auditor (City of San José, 2004). However, the IEA's tasks and the San José auditor's tasks are not identical; compared with the San José auditor, the IEA would not investigate cases (e.g., use-of-force ones) on a regular basis, which would decrease the costs, but it would initiate research projects not necessarily related to the issues raised in the complaints, which would increase the costs.

The IEA would be a new city office and thus by definition would generate additional costs for the city. However, the IEA could actually turn out to be a far less expensive and more efficient management tool than the traditional mechanism of corruption control, especially if its duties extended to include other types of police misconduct. The losses from corruption can be not only exorbitant in monetary terms but also high in terms of the resulting injustice; they can generate perceptions of injustice and decrease trust in the government. One of the most drastic examples is that of the New York Police Department in the 1970s, where "police corruption, a secret tax totaling millions of dollars a year, is a constant in the lives of most New Yorkers" (Burnham, 1974, p. 305).

If the jurisdiction of the IEA included other forms of police misconduct, the savings in the resources devoted to civil litigation and settlements with aggrieved citizens might well be worth the effort. The cost of police liability in large cities is typically millions of dollars annually. For example, from 1991 to 1994 Chicago paid $29 million for excessive force and false arrest lawsuits, Los Angeles paid $179.2 million from 1991 to 1995 (excluding traffic-related lawsuits), and New York paid $44 million from 1994 to 1995 (Kappeler, 2001, p. 10). Merrick Bobb, the special counsel to the Los Angeles Sheriff's Department, indicates that such costs can be reduced substantially with diligent efforts.

> The reduction of civil litigation costs was one of the main reasons for the creation of the Special Counsel to the Los Angeles Sheriff's Department. Between 1992–1993 and 1998–1999, the litigation docket of active use-of-force cases fell from 381 to 70, while the costs of judgments and settlements dropped by half. (Walker, 2001, p. 155)

In addition, the actual cost of the IEA would depend on its size. Even if it is double the size of the San José's auditor (six employees) that serves a community of close to 1 million inhabitants, the overall amount of $1 million allocated to the IEA would still constitute less than 0.1% of the overall city budget of $3.34 billion. However, a fair calculation of the financial aspects of the IEA should also include the benefits, especially the possible savings to the city budget. Equipped with a relatively simple recommendation, for example, to improve the written policy on the use of force, the city might prevent and almost completely avoid millions of dollars worth of expensive lawsuits and settlements with citizens each year. The ongoing dynamic of emergence of new, unanticipated police problems suggests that there would be ample room for a steady flow of beneficial recommendations.

The Division of Labor: Who Does What?

The control of police corruption involves a multitude of interconnected functions, from monitoring the propensity for corruption and detecting and investigating corruption to controlling the police agency's internal efforts to control corruption (Table 7.1). Although the basic control functions need to be incorporated into a comprehensive control action plan for any police agency, particular aspects and the weight placed on each of the functions depend on the concrete conditions facing the agency and its environment. Thus, it is pointless and maybe impossible to generate a detailed list of all control-related research questions and social science methods without taking into account the police agency's own specifics and those in the larger environment.

The analysis that follows is not a to-do list. Rather, it rests on examples of the issues and approaches that could be addressed within the basic control functions. Filling in the blanks is a matter of implementation that needs to revolve around the following fundamental questions:

1. Is the agency in charge of performing a particular control function in reality doing what it is supposed to do?
2. If not, why not, and how could the problems be fixed?
3. If the agency is doing what it is supposed to be doing, is what it is doing adequate?
4. What is the level of quality and thoroughness of the agency's conduct?
5. Is someone monitoring the performance of the agency, and, if so, what do the results suggest?
6. Are the specific individuals performing this function adequately trained and sufficiently disinclined toward corruption?

Table 7.1 Control Functions and Agencies

Control functions	Agencies	IEA participates	
		Directly	Indirectly
Monitor propensity	Police department (PD)		Yes
Provide resources	Public/mayor, PD		Yes
Set official policies and enforce	PD, legislature, mayor		Yes
Establish supervision and accountability	PD, mayor, citizen review, courts, media, public		Yes
Cultivate intolerant culture	PD		Yes
Detect and investigate corruption	PD, prosecutors, media, independent commissions (ICs)		Yes
Discipline/punish corrupt POs	PD, courts		Yes
Detect/investigate corruption not investigated by the PD	Prosecutor, ICs, citizen reviews, media	Yes	
Control PD's efforts	Mayor, ICs, media, public	Yes	
Improve existing system	PD, mayor, ICs, citizen reviews, prosecutors	Yes	
Limit opportunities for corruption	PD, legislature, public, media, courts, mayor		Yes
Disseminate true information	PD, mayor, ICs, media, citizen reviews, courts	Yes	

7. Are the resources at the agency's disposal adequate to cover the costs of control?

Monitor Propensity for Corruption

Monitoring propensity for corruption is a distinctly preventive measure. The agency performing this function identifies potentially problematic areas and, using the least invasive methods, addresses or ameliorates the conditions causing the problems *before* they escalate. Thus, monitoring efforts targeting individual police officers, groups, organizational units, or the entire agency could be helpful in detecting the existing problem areas (e.g., a particular service area, enforcement of particular laws, specific conditions surrounding a narrow set of work-related activities) or individual officers with potentially problematic behavior, as well as in noticing the development of capacity not only to pinpoint the potential problems on the basis of the agency snapshot taken at a specific time but also to identify the changes from a series of such snapshots and project future trends.

Because police corruption shares the fate of other "invisible offenses" (see Moore, 1983)—invisible to traditional law enforcement methods— reactive methods of investigation (i.e., waiting for a victim or a witness to complain and then initiating an investigation) are not very effective. One of the consequences is that "we might end up using enforcement methods whose degree of intrusiveness is characteristic of investigations, but using them for broad surveillance purposes spanning a large area of possible offenses and offenders" (Moore, 1983, pp. 30–31). Some of these more intrusive methods of investigation, such as integrity testing, examination of financial records, analysis of reports submitted by police officers, and review of all criminal arrests and investigations conducted by police officers, can be used in the processes of learning about the extent and nature of police corruption in an agency and identifying specific problem areas or causes of corruption.

The proposed model of corruption control places the basic monitoring efforts in the hands of the police agency. To keep the agency from slipping in its performance or completely failing to monitor its efforts, the model assigns the task of overseeing the agency's performance of these efforts to the IEA (Table 7.1). Although police agencies should assess individual police officers' propensity for corruption before they become police officers with recruitment and selection criteria and should also continue to monitor it once police officers are hired through the eyes of the supervisors and early-warning systems, the IEA would perform the task of overseeing the quality and thoroughness of their efforts at each of these stages.

Provide Resources for Control

Although the public and the city government determine the size of the police budget, the actual determination of the portion of this budget devoted to corruption-control issues rests with the mayor and the police chief. The allocation of specific funds for smaller subsections of the police agency then typically follows a tree structure, in which each unit commander decides about the specifics in that unit.

Decisions depend on the nature and needs of a particular unit. Nevertheless, a common theme across all units is that resources are limited and that it is up to the unit heads to create criteria to prioritize the allocation of funds. Although the heads of smaller units within the police agency are accountable to their immediate supervisors for their conduct and decisions, including financial ones, the fact remains that their decisions need not be optimal from the corruption-control perspective. The reasons for suboptimal decisions may be varied: First, heads of smaller units may not be properly informed about the nature and severity of the problems under consideration; second, they may be motivated to make different decisions to protect their own failure to keep their units under control or not to tarnish the agency's public image; or, third, they may want to allocate a larger portion of resources to regular law enforcement tasks.

The IEA could step in at both levels: the decision about allocating funds from the city budget to the police and the decision about the structure of the police budget. Because it would be responsible for monitoring the performance of the police agency's own control efforts, including analyses of how individual elements of the overall system are carrying out their tasks and recommendations for improvement, the IEA would be in a position to learn about the potential financial problems faced by each unit. It would be able to provide feedback about the personnel working in the system (e.g., the adequacy of their training, level of their skills) and finance-related problems (e.g., the ratio of supervisors to line officers, supply of unmarked vehicles or money for undercover operations). The IEA's periodic report could contain such findings along with a clear warning regarding possible problems and consequences (e.g., if the ratio of supervisors to line officers does not decrease substantially in the near future, the level of police misconduct is likely to increase at an alarming rate).

Set Official Policies and Enforce Them

Directly or indirectly, setting official agency policies and enforcing them involve several entities: the legislature, professional associations, the police agency itself, the mayor, and the IEA. By proscribing certain behaviors such as bribery or extortion (18 U.S.C. Section 201; 18 U.S.C. Section 1951), the legislature imposes boundaries for setting the agency's official policies. The boundaries are also partly predetermined by the Commission on Accreditation for Law Enforcement Standards, which explicitly requires police agencies seeking accreditation to develop a written set of rules specifying the standards of conduct and appearance, including those covering the acceptance of gratuities, bribes, or rewards (Commission on Accreditation for Law Enforcement Agencies, 1994, 26.1.1). Within these boundaries, the police chief and administration and the mayor set up the official agency policies and are in charge of their subsequent changes and improvements.

The IEA would perform primarily a monitoring role over the police agency. A substantial portion of its task would be to propose modifications of the existing rules, based on findings from their research projects examining the nature of the underlying problems, changes in the patterns of misconduct and criminogenic situations, and the agency's responses to them.

From the control perspective, enforcement of the official rules is at least as crucial as establishment of the rules themselves; if the gap between the official agency rules and the unofficial rules is wide, the unofficial rules completely overshadow the official ones. The task of enforcing the official rules would be entirely in the hands of the police agency, but its enforcement would be monitored by the IEA. The function of enforcing official rules includes numerous aspects of the agency (e.g., supervision, investigation of misconduct, discipline of corrupt police officers) and intertwines with a number of other functions (e.g., establishment of supervision and accountability, detection and investigation of corruption, punishment of corrupt police officers). Thus, the IEA's examination of the enforcement of official rules would need to focus on supervision, investigation of corruption, discipline of corrupt officers, curtailment of the code of silence, personal conduct of the administrators, and the adequacy of the resources provided for corruption control. For each of these issues, the IEA could develop research questions (e.g., the role of supervisors in undermining the value of official rules), conduct an empirical study, and generate a set of appropriate recommendations.

Establish Supervision and Accountability

The accountability of line officers lies with their immediate supervisors, who are accountable to the administration, which is accountable to the police chief. These aspects of accountability are primarily internal, whereas the accountability of the police chief, as the top administrator in the agency, is primarily external. The police chief answers directly to the head administrator of the city or to city council and indirectly to the public. The police chief can be removed from that post for failure to maintain accountability in the agency.

All employees in a police agency, including the chief, also can be held accountable by external agencies if an employee's conduct reaches criminal or illegal levels (hence the role of prosecutors and courts in the performance of this control function) or if misconduct is so severe and widespread that it leads to scandal and subsequent reform (hence the role of the media and the public in the performance of this control function). In terms of criminal responsibility, although the prosecutors' choices of cases requiring further processing in the criminal justice system should be independent, local prosecutors are more susceptible to external accountability because chief prosecutors are elected public officials, responsible to their constituencies for their conduct and decisions.

The IEA could play a valuable role in pursuit of external accountability by drawing the attention of the media, the public, political figures, and the prosecutors' supervisors if its investigation uncovers unacceptable discrepancies between its estimates of the nature and extent of serious corruption in the police agency and the cases with which prosecutors decided to proceed.

In comparison with the traditional model of corruption control, which neglected to monitor how the police agency established and operationalized its internal mechanism, some of the IEA's tasks would be to oversee the actual operation of the internal mechanisms of accountability, to study the underlying obstacles to and causes for its successful operation, and to propose modifications. The IEA could use social science methods of inquiry to examine, on a continuous basis, how internal mechanisms of accountability have been operationalized, the degree of discrepancy between the operation of the internal mechanism de facto and de iure, whether those in charge of holding others accountable are held accountable themselves (e.g., are the supervisors punished for failures in supervision and rewarded for maintaining accountability in their units?), what conditions undermine the system (e.g., supervisors who are unskilled, overworked, or unmotivated), and how these conditions can be improved.

Cultivate a Culture Intolerant of Corruption

This task, assigned primarily to the police agencies themselves (see Table 7.1), includes the adoption of organizational values by the agency's police officers and curtailment of the code of silence. Although the message sent by the administration may reach every police officer in the agency, it will not be received equally by all. It will probably have sufficient impact on the police officers who are "true positivists"—those at the high end of the scale of integrity—and encourage those in the middle of the scale to put the code of silence aside, stop tolerating other police officers' misconduct, and report it.

A police agency may try to develop a police culture intolerant of corruption by developing official rules and keeping the gap between the official and unofficial rules narrow. First, the agency may select applicants with low levels of propensity toward corruption and provide adequate training in ethics. Second, the agency may establish effective supervision and appropriate discipline for failures to report misconduct. Third, the agency may reward reporting and guarantee anonymity to the whistleblowers. Fourth, the agency may use proactive and reactive methods of corruption investigation and punish corrupt police officers. To help the agency avoid pitfalls in the performance of these tasks, the IEA would need to monitor them and report its findings.

To learn what the values of the police culture are, what the extent of the code of silence is, what misconduct (severity and type) is covered by the code, and how the police culture is changing, the IEA could conduct surveys and interviews, as well as observe police officers' actual behavior and study official corruption cases. Based on these findings, the IEA could infer the degree of discrepancy between the official values and rules and those entrenched in police culture. A more detailed analysis can assess the agency's success in cultivating a culture intolerant of corruption, the extent and adequacy of the agency's efforts, the adequacy of the personnel performing these control efforts, and the sufficiency of the resources devoted to these tasks.

The IEA could also help bring the police agency's inner strength to the surface through its own efforts. In particular, by putting the topic of police corruption on the radar screen, monitoring the agency's internal control efforts, and suggesting improvements, the IEA could articulate its unwavering commitment to corruption control. Such a message could encourage not only the true positivists but also the police officers in the middle of the integrity scale to report misconduct and thus narrow the extent of the code of silence.

Control efforts also need to focus on the society at large, whose cultural norms can be tolerant of police corruption. Because society-wide tolerance of corruption minimizes the risks of corrupt behavior, nourishes perceptions that the costs of engaging in corruption are not high, and creates a pool of citizens willing to participate in corruption, control efforts should try to change public opinion. In the traditional system of control, no institution has been assigned this task directly; some institutions can have a strong indirect impact on public perceptions about the seriousness of corrupt behavior and on its tolerance through their actions, such as changes in the existing bribery laws (the legislator) or punishment of corrupt individuals (courts, prosecutors, police agencies).

One of the IEA's most important functions would be public education. Its regular reports would cultivate a culture intolerant of corruption by raising awareness of the topic, providing detailed analysis of the severity and gravity of the consequences resulting from corrupt behavior, disseminating information about the increased societal costs and risks of engaging in corruption, and describing the changes in the agency's control apparatus.

Detect and Investigate Corruption

Detection and investigation of corruption are primarily assigned to the police agency itself; if the conduct is potentially criminal as well, the task may be shared by prosecutors. A police agency that actually performs some work in this area usually initiates an administrative investigation to determine whether the implicated police officers have violated official agency rules and, if the misconduct calls for it, a criminal investigation as well. Prosecutors can participate in the agency's criminal investigation or conduct their own investigations.

At present, the police agency and prosecutors focus almost exclusively on individual cases; the agency is either too busy dealing with individual cases or lacks interest in examining wider patterns of misconduct and the underlying conditions leading to corruption. The IEA, by contrast, could take a step back and focus on the patterns and issues (e.g., lack of supervision) stemming from the complaints and existing cases. Unlike typical citizen review boards (Walker, 2001), the IEA would neither be a part of the official agency system of internal formal control nor have any role in the process of detection and investigation.

The reality of corrupt police agencies (those most in need of detecting and investigating corruption) is that they frequently fail to investigate corruption (see chapter 5). To ameliorate the great reluctance of police agencies to engage in the task of detecting and investigating corruption among their own, rather than taking over some of the police agencies' responsibilities (by accepting complaints or investigating them), the IEA would *oversee* the police agency's internal operation. Its task would be to systematically monitor the thoroughness and quality of the police agency's internal efforts, examine the wider patterns and issues generated by the police agency's work, address them in its periodic reports, and disseminate its findings.

Discipline or Punish Corrupt Police Officers

The success and effectiveness of disciplining or punishing corrupt police officers through administrative sanctions by the agency and, in criminal cases, sentences by the courts are inextricably linked with the extent and sincerity of the effort exerted in the detection and investigation of cases of corruption in the previous stage.

Although the IEA would play no direct role in either applying administrative discipline or securing a conviction, it might have an important indirect role. As part of its task to monitor the police agency's internal system of control, the IEA would gather information required to draw conclusions about the similarities between the estimated extent and nature of actual corruption and the picture painted by the individual officially investigated cases. One of the IEA's most important roles would be to disseminate information to outside agencies, especially when the agency routinely fails to discipline or punish corrupt police officers.

Detect and Investigate Corruption Not Investigated by the Police Agency

No institution in the traditional model of corruption control has a permanent and continuous responsibility to detect and investigate corruption not investigated by the police department (i.e., look for the dark numbers), but several agencies are involved in some aspects of this function. Prosecutors have the permanent and general responsibility of investigating and prosecuting corruption, regardless of whether it was investigated by the police agency in the first place. Similarly, independent commissions established to investigate corruption in a particular police agency have a temporary and general responsibility of investigating the extent of corruption within the police department under scrutiny. Because of the difference in the ultimate nature of their own work, independent commissions are in a better position than prosecutors to focus on corruption the police agency is not investigating. However, their temporary existence and their dependence on those who established them to provide sufficient resources and authority make them unable to provide a continuous check on corruption the police agency is not investigating.

Citizen review boards, which are not part of the traditional mechanism of corruption control, are mostly unsuited for this task of investigating corruption omitted by the police agency. Simply put, the duty of most existing citizen review boards (Class I to Class III; see Walker, 2001, p. 62) is to participate in or replicate the investigative processes run by the police agency, which inherently limits their ability to investigate cases *not* investigated by the agency. Finally, those few citizen reviews that are not intrinsically connected with the police agency's internal system of controls (Class IV; see Walker, 2001, p. 62) are bound by their overall task—"to review, monitor, or audit the police department's complaint process" (Walker, 2001, p. 62)—and are thus not allowed to go beyond the police agency's official process.

The IEA, by contrast, would be authorized and even required to engage in such investigations. However, the primary purpose of the exercise would not be to prepare a case for prosecution or for an internal departmental administrative hearing. Rather, the IEA would seek to measure the discrepancy between the nature, extent, and severity of corruption as reported in the official agency reports (i.e., official cases) and the estimates of the nature, extent, and severity of actual corruption. Applying a combination of legalistic and social science methods of investigation would help to measure accurately both sides of the scale: the official reports versus estimates of actual corruption. The summary of these issues in the IEA's reports would also have the potential to draw to the problem the attention of the media, the public, and political leaders.

Control Police Agency's Efforts to Control Corruption

The traditional mechanism of corruption control recognizes that police officers cannot be trusted to police themselves but assigns no agency to monitor the police agency's overall control efforts on a regular basis. Rather, as a part of their role, various agencies—the mayor or city manager, independent commissions, the media—have been assigned or chosen to perform the task of supervising one aspect of the agency's control efforts. Common problems are that agencies (e.g., the media, citizen review boards) either focus on individual cases (e.g., the reactive approach or the complaint-driven approach) and disregard the wider patterns and underlying causes or, when they do examine larger patterns and conditions causing corruption, their mandate is temporary (e.g., independent commissions).

Even the very few citizen review boards—transplants from the control mechanisms for other types of misconduct—that do not necessarily participate only in the complaint process and may provide a continuous oversight of the control efforts exerted by the police agency are limited to the issues and problems generated by the complaints. This may be an appropriate approach for some other forms of police misconduct, but it is definitely not appropriate for corruption. The nature of corruption is such that very few complaints are generated, and reliance on complaints to detect serious problems in the agency's internal control mechanisms would be ineffective.

One of the IEA's most important tasks, if not *the* most important task, would be to monitor the police agency's overall control efforts on a continuous and systematic basis. This task extends far beyond the regular reactive, case- or complaint-driven approach and covers all aspects of the police agency's internal control system. Because the police agency's control system is composed of various elements—from selection and recruitment to detection and investigation of corrupt behavior—the IEA would need to monitor the effectiveness of each of these elements. However, monitoring the majority of these separate elements would already be incorporated into the IEA's agenda, as the satisfactory monitoring of other control functions, from cultivating a culture intolerant of corruption to monitoring the propensity for corruption, would require the IEA to examine the operation of these separate yet constituent elements of the overall control mechanism.

Improve the Existing System of Corruption Control

As discussed earlier, the overall system of corruption control is a combination of many different agencies and control functions (see Table 7.1). Within this mixture, various agencies engaged in control are primarily and almost exclusively responsible for their own performance and for improvements to their own control-related operation.

Of the agencies responsible for the improvement of the police agency's internal system of control, technically only the police agency itself (which has the advantage of knowing its own limitations and problems best) is assigned to improve its system on a continuous basis. Although citizens, individual police officers, and the media may not directly engage in improvements to the agency's internal system, they have the power to create public pressure and force the mayor to examine the issue and/or establish an independent commission to study the police agency and recommend improvements. Yet, all these efforts, with the exception of those exerted by the police agency itself, experience difficulties in identifying the problems that need to be addressed, suffer from a haphazard approach, and are oriented toward case- or incident-driven responses. The police agency, on the other hand, can fail not only to think about the improvements of its control system but also to utilize the control system.

The IEA, also charged with the task of continuously monitoring the police agency's overall control efforts, would be in an excellent position to develop and propose recommendations for improvement. In particular, as part of its other functions, the IEA would already have engaged in a detailed examination of the agency's overall system of control and thus would already have information about potential problems. Furthermore, it would have the capacity and skills to propose improvements or, in the more complex or unusual cases, know whom to ask for advice.

Limit Opportunities for Corruption

A police agency can increase the costs of corrupt behavior, thus making corruption less attractive to police officers. It can increase the probability of detection through more intense corruption control, stricter enforcement of official rules prohibiting corrupt behavior, tighter supervision, and more resources devoted to control. It can also increase the certainty of punishment and possibly its severity. In parallel, prosecutors and the courts can increase the certainty and severity of punishment for police officers in the cases that qualify as criminal.

Police agencies themselves are in the best position to know what conditions induce corrupt behavior among police. Changes in police departments could include clarification of the official policies, more consistent enforcement, monitoring propensity for corruption, rotating police officers more frequently, changes in the set of rules that are enforced, and changes in enforcement priorities for state laws and city ordinances. The legislature may need to step in and abolish vague or problematic laws, assign the enforcement of challenging laws to a different agency, or increase the severity of punishment for corruption, thus lessening the citizens' need to engage in corruption or substantially increasing the costs of a corrupt transaction.

As discussed earlier, because citizens are the other party in external corruption—the party that provides bribes—a thorough effort in limiting the opportunities for corruption could include efforts to reduce the supply of people willing to pay a bribe through educational efforts (to lower the level of tolerance and raise the level of hostility toward corruption) and increased costs for corruption (e.g., higher probability of being caught, more severe punishment, stronger stigmatization by society, more serious consequences of labeling by the official system).

The IEA could participate in the process of limiting opportunities for corruption in multiple ways. For example, the IEA would be in a position to suggest to the police agency and/or the legislature which legal rules should be clarified, appended, changed, or even abolished. Similarly, the IEA could measure changes in the citizen level of integrity or susceptibility to corruption.

In the traditional model of corruption control, the decision on whether a particular police agency will engage in all these activities to increase the costs of a corrupt transaction and decrease the impact of conditions breeding corruption is left to the police agency itself, with certain exceptions that could lead to a public scandal. Thus, to avoid the failure to limit opportunities for corruption, the IEA would monitor the agency's efforts, evaluate its success, analyze how the agency adopts to changes in the scope of corrup-

Table 7.2 Agencies Collecting Information About Police Corruption

	Continuous	Sporadic
Systematic	Police agency	Independent commission
	Mayor/city manager	
	Prosecutors/courts	
Haphazard		Media

tion opportunities, estimate the level of tolerance for corruption among the general public, and write a report summarizing its findings.

Disseminate True Information About Corruption

An indispensable step in the process of disseminating information is to collect the appropriate information in the first place. In the traditional system of corruption control, a number of entities participate in this process, including the police agency itself, the mayor, prosecutors, the courts, the media, and independent commissions (Table 7.2).

The police agency, the mayor or city manager, the prosecutors, and the courts are all assigned responsibility for collecting information about police corruption on a continuous and systematic basis. Yet, disregarding for a moment their possible lack of motivation to collect the information about the *true* extent of corruption, the type of information they collect—the official data—can tell more about the efficiency of the agencies generating the information than about the actual nature and extent of police corruption in the agency. In particular, the police agencies and the mayor have the data on corruption complaints and internal disciplinary cases involving corruption, and prosecutors and the courts record the actual cases involving police officers they have prosecuted, convicted, and sentenced. Although these official data can be useful, they do not have the power to project the true image of corruption in the police agency.

The problem with independent commissions and the media, on the other hand, is that their data collection is sporadic. Independent commissions depend on the political will to be established and for the resources and powers to perform their work, and the media, in the business of selling newspapers or information in general, may tend to select cases that would sell news-papers by virtue of their extraordinary circumstances, such as the severity of the crime or the rank of those involved.

As part of its other control-related tasks, the IEA would have already collected information about various stages of the funnel of police corruption (see Figure 3.2 in chapter 3). To perform several of its functions, the IEA would survey, interview, and observe, with the purpose of estimating the true nature and extent of corruption in the police agency. As part of its task of overseeing the police agency's internal system of control, especially its detection and investigation of corruption, it would also keep track of the characteristics of the internal official corruption-related cases processed by the police agency. Furthermore, in the process of monitoring the execution of the control function of detection and investigation of corruption, the IEA would touch on the prosecutorial data as well because prosecutors are also assigned the task of detection and investigation of corruption cases that fulfill the requirements of being criminal.

In addition to monitoring and helping the police agency control corruption, the IEA would provide regular (e.g., semiannual) reports about its own activity and the challenges, problems, and improvements experienced by the police agency. The reports would disseminate information about the operation of the agency's internal efforts to control corruption as well as the nature and extent of corruption in the agency. They would be sent to the police agency, the political figures responsible for control of the police (e.g., the mayor, city council), the prosecutor, and the media. Of course, the reports would also be available to individual members of the public in the IEA's office and on the IEA's Web site.

These reports should induce a range of reactions. They should alert prosecutors and prompt them to compare the nature and extent of police corruption reported by the IEA to their own perceptions of corruption (probably based largely on their files); they should also direct the mayor's and city council's attention to these issues and lead them to discuss whether the findings indicate a change in a satisfactory direction and, if not, what should be done about it.

The reports might not be received equally well by various political groups. Because a political struggle could have preceded the establishment of the IEA and continued while appointments to the IEA were made, the politicians, citizen groups, and media supporting its establishment and the IEA appointments would use these reports to publicize the need to resolve problematic issues, push for the solution proposed by the IEA, and further promote the agency and advance its status. On the other hand, opponents of the IEA would try to discredit the IEA and downplay its findings. The quality and thoroughness of the IEA's work, the actual implementation of its recommendations despite potential political opposition, consequent improvements to the existing systems, and the appropriate visibility of the reports over time may have an impact even on the initial opponents' opinions about the IEA, its work, and the necessity of its existence.

Reports sent to the media and available to the public would draw public attention to police corruption and its control. A possible consequence of such public dissemination might be a scandal that would pressure political figures to deal with the problem if they had neglected to do so. Nevertheless, although the IEA would depend on the public at large, politicians, and the media, its successful operation does not depend on scandals. Instead of operating in cycles of scandal and reform, the IEA would continuously monitor and disseminate information on a regular and systematic basis and could use the momentum created by a scandal to push for a thorough reform of the agency. The IEA might be in a position to provide information to the mayor, politicians, media, and the public about the serious integrity-related problems within the police agency they uncovered and, consequently, initiate a successful scandal. However, regardless of whether scandals always require revelations of individual cases of corruption within the agency or whether they can be created on the basis of the systematic supply of information about serious integrity-related problems, they have the potential to draw attention to the larger issues of police accountability and the underlying causes of existing problems. Although the media and the public probably would be more captivated by the accounts of actual cases and have a shorter attention span, the role of the other players, primarily the IEA, should be to use the momentum created, move the discussion beyond individual cases, and focus on the underlying causes and their solutions.

The IEA's reports, because they contain data on police corruption and integrity collected in a systematic and continuous fashion, could serve an additional purpose. The IEA, unlike some of the other agencies that have clear stakes to do the opposite (e.g., mayor, police chief; see chapter 6), would have incentives to disseminate true information about police corruption. Consequently, its findings could be used as a basis for comparison when revelations of corruption hit the media and a public scandal develops. The IEA and its findings could help manage the situation if they suggest that the cases reported in the media are outliers. On the other hand, if the cases discussed in the media are representative of typical corruption events in the agency, the IEA could make the media's case even stronger, draw attention to the burning problem, and generate support for reform.

Finally, the impact of these reports on the police agency should be twofold: First, the IEA could serve as an unbiased fact finder that either independently confirms what the administration knew already or provides new information about the problems or issues that the administration should address. Indeed, if the administration is carrying out its job thoroughly and meticulously, very few of the basic findings should be unanticipated or completely novel, yet if certain parts of the organization or the whole organization is slipping, these reports can pinpoint problem areas and capture the attention of those who can facilitate changes.

Second, the IEA would send the information about possible improvements and policy changes to the police chief for advisement. Such a step would provide a chief interested in running an organization of high integrity with an opportunity to be the first in line to propose improvements and thus save face. At the same time, because ultimately the suggested improvements would at least partially come from the chief—the insider—police officers would be more likely to accept such changes.

For example, the San José independent police auditor and the police chief of the San José Police Department deliver presentations at the meeting of the San José City Council and the city manager, the auditor recommends the changes, and the chief replies on what has been done in connection with the recommendations. Teresa Guerrero-Daley argues that notifying the chief about the problems and providing him with an opportunity to think about the solutions in advance is beneficial because "the Chief takes a lead in making the change; it is not seen as a threat, nor a public intimidation at this point [furthermore,] it is his solution—his directive, so rank and file will accept it" (Guerrero-Daley, 2000).

The report going out to the mayor and the rest of the political players would typically contain the response from the police chief or a comment that the chief provided no response. A meeting of the IEA director, police chief, and mayor could be routinely scheduled before the report is due to go to the presses to discuss the issues raised in the report and the chief's response. Thus, if the police chief were unresponsive or would have serious objections to the IEA's recommendations and propositions, it would be up to the mayor or city council and the public to react. As argued earlier, the role of the IEA would be fact finding and advisory, not decision making. Its task would stop here; once the relevant information was made available, it would be up to the public and the elected officials to determine the course of action.

The Acceptance of the IEA

A sensible question at this point is: What makes us think that the idea of the IEA and its implementation would be accepted? This question is all the more pressing with respect to corrupt agencies and communities more tolerant of corruption.

The initial acceptance of the IEA would depend on the circumstances under which it was created. If a major scandal erupts, the momentum for change will be created, and pressure will be put on the elected officials—from mayor and city council members to the police chief—to do *something* about corruption. Although typical reactions to powerful, punitive, corruption-related scandals have included the formation of independent commissions and prosecution of corrupt police officers, a possible reaction in the future might be formation of the IEA, either initially, at the peak of the scandal, or subsequently, based on recommendations by the independent commission.

If the IEA were created under such conditions, the public would probably support it. Similarly, if the IEA were established without a scandal but instead after a series of smaller incidents that built pressure over time, resulting in, for example, a public referendum, the public at large generally would be supportive of the IEA. Generally, while the strength of the actual support by various political groups will depend on the nature and extent of the political struggle that preceded the establishment of the IEA, by definition, the public at large would back the IEA *as an idea*. If that were not the case, the IEA would not come into existence to begin with; there would be insufficient political support for its establishment.

However, how long and with what intensity the support will persist depends on a number of factors, including the reputation and quality of the people appointed to the IEA, the IEA's actual operation, its degree of independence, and its success in performing its tasks. Indeed, although the nature of the tasks given to a typical review board and those the IEA would handle differ (participate in the investigation of complaints versus monitor the police agency), some supporting evidence can be found in Perez's study of citizen review boards (1994): Continued support for a particular citizen review board is strongly related to its performance. Moreover, although a typical citizen review board, by the very nature of its tasks, is sentenced to a declining level of public support (it simply cannot substantiate a sizable proportion of all complaints; see Perez, 1994), future support for the IEA would depend neither on substantive justice (e.g., the percentage of complaints it substantiates) nor on procedural justice it provides to individual complainants. Rather, the IEA's level of support is likely to be strongly related to its success in performing its monitoring role and the integrity of the procedures it utilizes.

Changes to city government usually do not happen without a reason; a scandal or a series of smaller incidents creating the necessary momentum would probably produce the political push necessary for the establishment of the IEA and draw the attention of the media, the public at large, and political groups to the issue. The establishment of the IEA should obviously signal the mayor's support of the IEA. If the IEA were established by a city council's ordinance, then the political climate in the city (clearly strong enough to generate the majority vote) supports the establishment of the IEA. In such a situation, opposing and openly resisting the IEA as an idea would not be politically smart. If the IEA were established by a referendum, then the mayor would merely be the top city executive implementing the public wish for independent oversight of the police agency, expressed through the referendum and supported by a strong political coalition.

Although the mayor or city manager and the city council members could initially support the IEA, the IEA could also have been established as a consequence of a political struggle that the mayor and/or some of the city council members lost. In that case, the mayor or city manager and the unsatisfied city council members may exercise their political muscle and try to sabotage the work of the IEA by, for example, trying to appoint people who will not do a satisfactory job. However, the fact remains that the same political players who successfully pushed for the establishment of the IEA would dominate the political scenery, at least for a while. Thus, initially, because of the political pressure created before and during the establishment of the IEA and the focus of media and public attention (at least temporarily) on the issue of police misconduct and police accountability, even an unwilling mayor would be put in a position in which it would be politically smarter to support the IEA, at least for the time being. Alternatively, a mayor who would openly obstruct the establishment of the IEA despite the wishes of the clear majority (expressed through the referendum or the city ordinance) could pay the ultimate political price: As an elected public official dependent on public support, the mayor might lose the next election or be voted out of office.

Although the IEA might be supported by a police chief who inherited a corrupt police agency, who views the police agency as a "learning organization," and who perceives police accountability as a key agenda item, a typical chief is more likely to initially regard the IEA as a threat to the independence of the police agency. However, there are strong reasons for the police chief to think twice before openly condemning the IEA. First, even as the head of one of the most independent city agencies, the police chief is nevertheless a city employee who is accountable to supervisors (the mayor or city manager and/or the city council) who can, with a greater or lesser degree of difficulty, depending on whether the chief serves at the pleasure of the city administration or has a fixed-term appointment, remove the police chief from office. Second, a police chief or sheriff who is an elected official is accountable to the public and therefore relies on voters for reelection. Given the public and media attention devoted to the issue, the elected law enforcement official who openly opposes the IEA—in the situation in which either the majority of the public and/or the powerful political groups would support the IEA—might well be jeopardizing reelection. Third, as policing moves from the political era into the community policing era, community satisfaction, community input, and accountability to the community become the key words. As the views and values evolve within the police organization to fit this new paradigm (see Sparrow et al., 1990), the police chiefs could (and should) become more open to the idea of the IEA. Fourth, an endorsement of the idea of external accountability by the organizations at the epicenter of contemporary policing, such as the Commission on Accreditation for Law Enforcement Agencies and the International Association of the Chiefs of Police, could provide a new professional standard and ease the acceptance of external bodies such as the IEA by the police chiefs and police officers.

Over time, if and when the IEA distinguished itself as a body of high integrity and professionalism and had strong supporters among politicians and the public, the police chief would have greater incentives to react before the political pressure grows and accountability questions are raised. The experience of Teresa Guerrero-Daley, one of the few successful police auditors in the United States, supports this notion. Immediately upon the establishment of the Office of the Independent Police Auditor in San José in 1993, the model of police auditor was relatively unfamiliar to police and citizens alike. Although the model was "tested" by both the chief and the police union, the auditor's determination, her regular reports, and joint meetings of the San José City Council, the city manager, the auditor, and the police chief made the police chief a more eager participant over time.

The mayor and police chief who initially opposed the IEA might eventually want to support it and appoint high-quality professionals to it. First, the mayor and police chief may want to prevent scandals: The IEA could identify the problem areas of systematic failures early and provide valuable advice on how to handle these issues. Second, the mayor and the police chief could benefit if they could rely on the IEA's findings in situations in which scandal is about to emerge, and they would thus be better equipped to diffuse it. The findings presented in the IEA's regular reports could serve as a basis for the statement, for example, that the released cases of corruption are primarily a consequence of the agency's increased investigative efforts rather than a growing severity or intensity of actual corruption. The reports could also be used to confirm that the underlying causes of pending corruption cases have already been detected and the efforts are now turned toward finding the solutions and implementing them. Third, the police chief and the mayor could engage in a vigorous pursuit of corruption in the agency without being concerned that other politicians, citizen groups, and the public at large would attribute the resulting cases of corruption to their inability to manage the agency and thus run the risk of jeopardizing their own careers. Fourth, the mayor and the police chief as elected officials accountable for the performance of the police department and the misconduct of its police officers could use the reports to substantiate the claim that they are successful administrators able to control the misconduct of their subordinates. Fifth, the mayor and the police chief could go a step further and use their ability to run the agency in their reelection campaign. Naturally, to be able to do that, they need to appoint to the IEA people of high integrity and quality who could be relied on to produce results.

Initially, police officers would probably openly oppose the idea of the IEA and resort to the typical arguments already offered against citizen review boards, ranging from the notion that the police are well able to police themselves to the opinion that only those who had actually experienced police work could make meritorious decisions about the split-second situations police officers face (see Walker, 2001). However, research studies pertaining to citizen review boards suggest that police officers' opinions are quite likely to change over time. After 17 years of studying citizen reviews, Perez (1994) concluded that police officers in agencies with no citizen reviews resist them but police officers in agencies with an established citizen review accept them as part of the "rules of the discipline game."

> One crucial finding of this study is that police officers in jurisdictions that *have* experienced civilian review are not opposed to it. The police officers who have been educated to the realities of civilian review will often take issue with some of the specifics of its application. They will argue with the politics of particular individuals and interest groups involved in civilian process. But a majority of police officers who have direct experience with civilian review neither fear it nor believe it to be illegitimate. On the contrary, police officers educated to the potential legitimizing functions of civilian review believe it to be a viable, workable concept. (p. 239)

The police chief's stance about the IEA might significantly ease the police officers' acceptance of it. For example, the meetings of the San José City Council, the city manager, the auditor, and the police chief over time showed the police chief and other police officers that the City of San José is serious about its auditor. The way it is set up—with the chief proposing and imple-menting the changes—makes the whole system more acceptable to the line officers. The changes are not perceived as a threat, but rather as the chief's directive (Guerrero-Daley, 2000).

Although police officers might find it difficult to accept the public as their boss (see Guerrero-Daley, 2000) and the IEA as an entity there to stay, over time, as the IEA would start to operate and they would realize that the IEA is not there to have their heads rolling, they would likely change their opinion. After all, the IEA's decisions would have an impact on their lives and could improve not only the quality of policing but also their everyday working conditions.

Evaluating the Effectiveness of the IEA

The IEA is at present a unique and hypothetical agency. There is neither an empirical body of research evaluating its effectiveness nor established crite-ria for its evaluation. As an independent agency with the primary task of monitoring the police agency, the IEA has some similarities with the citizen review boards. Despite the differences between the two in regard to their purpose, scope, functions, and organization, the criteria for the evaluation of citizen review boards, although still developing, can be used as a rough benchmark.

Walker (2001, p. 61) uses three criteria of independence to evaluate cit-izen review boards: structural, process, and perceived independence. As a permanent city agency, the IEA, which most closely resembles the Class IV citizen review boards—the more independent forms of citizen reviews (Walker, 2001, p. 63)—fulfills the structural independence requirement: It would be structurally, organizationally, and financially separate from the police agency. The IEA also fares well with respect to the second criterion: process independence. In particular, the control functions performed by the IEA would focus on overseeing the police agency and rest on the IEA's own collection of information and the analysis of the data provided by the police agency. Finally, in terms of perceived independence, the IEA has the poten-tial of scoring high. Unlike citizens, police officers may not wholeheartedly support the IEA. However, their initial judgment would depend on their general impressions of the IEA (e.g., the way it was established, the political support it generated, the qualifications and reputation of the IEA members). Depending on the IEA's subsequent performance, the initial judgment would be reinforced or reversed.

Another set of plausible criteria, used by Perez to evaluate citizen review boards, includes integrity, legitimacy, and learning (Perez, 1994). The integrity criterion refers to the thoroughness and fairness of the complaint investigation process. If applied to the IEA (which would not perform the complaint investigation process), this criterion would correspond to the thoroughness and fairness of the IEA's overall efforts, and how these functions actually would be performed cannot be evaluated before the IEA is even established. Legitimacy rests on the perceptions of legitimacy developed by the police officers, citizens, and the public in general. It is thus similar to Walker's criterion of perceived independence, and all the related discussion applies. Finally, learning refers to "the extent to which the process provides meaningful feedback to responsible officials in such a way that allows them to make improvements in both the complaint process and the police department" (Walker, 2001, p. 60). Two of the tasks assigned to the IEA fulfill this requirement: The IEA would have the duties of proposing improvements to the existing system and providing detailed feedback not only to the police agency but also to other parties (e.g., the mayor, political leaders, the public).

A Final Remark

Scandals from New York to Los Angeles and from Chicago to Miami clearly demonstrate that existing control mechanisms do not provide as effective and continuous corruption control as we expect and need. Their focus is either too wide (e.g., annual report, budget) or too narrow (e.g., individual cases). They rely on a reactive approach, and, for various reasons, information about corruption does not reach the decision makers. In the end, police corruption remains largely uncontrolled.

Recognizing its own temporary nature and the success of the reforms starting under its watch, the Knapp Commission struggled with the issue of what to do to ensure permanent and continuous corruption control. Will

the positive trend "continue after the Commission has disbanded and public attention has ceased to be focused on police reform?" (Knapp Commission, 1972, p. 261). The commission reasoned that the answer should be
affirmative.

> Once these attitudes [supportive of police integrity and criti-
> cal of corruption] become securely established, the Commis-
> sion feels, the momentum toward integrity will have a chance
> to become self-generating and the Department's internal anti-
> corruption machinery, assisted by the district attorneys and
> other regular law enforcement agencies, should be adequate
> to cope with corruption. (p. 261)

However, continued momentum for reform necessitates an independent anticorruption effort. Yet, taking steps that, although well intended, are not
comprehensive enough (such as establishing the office of the independent
prosecutor in the aftermath of the Knapp Commission investigation and the
related reform) does not lead toward long-term success in corruption control.

In the concluding chapter of their book about the corruption control efforts, Anechiarico and Jacobs also argued for the need to provide continuous
control:

> Controlling corruption is a dynamic part of governing that
> requires constant attention. There is simply no magic list or
> formula of corruption control that academics, commissions,
> consultants, or other pundits can hand over to public admin-
> istrators. Good policy will need to grow out of a sophisticated
> data-collecting effort, a rich discourse on the problem, the iden-
> tification of alternative solutions, experimentation, evaluation,
> and estimates of the costs of various controls. (1996, p. 198)

The story of police corruption and its control could have a happy ending.
The system of corruption control developed in this book has strong potential
for filling the void in the traditional model: It opens the doors to continuous
control efforts that focus on patterns and causes of corruption. Although the
web of causes and correlates of police corruption is quite complex, the solutions need not be: A relatively simple addition to the existing model of cor-

ruption control, the integrity-enhancing agency (IEA), could have a substantial impact on the overall level and patterns of police corruption.

The IEA, a group of professionals, would have three principal duties: to monitor the performance of the police agency's control functions, to propose improvements to the system of control, and to disseminate its findings. Its success would depend not only on the degree and quality of the support it would have from the politicians, the public at large, the police, and the media but also on the structural, organizational, and financial rules regulating its operation and the associated legal powers. Although initially its credibility and legitimacy would be determined by the quality and professionalism of the IEA members themselves, over time the quality of its own work would leave a long-lasting mark. In the era characterized by the pursuit of accountability and transparency, such a mechanism, one that a police agency can embrace to enhance its accountability and improve transparency, should be welcome.

References

Adler, F., Mueller, G. O. W., & Laufer, W. S. (1995). *Criminology* (2nd ed.). New York: McGraw-Hill.

Alvazi del Frate, A., van Dijk, J. J. M., van Kesteren, J., Mayhew, P., & Zvekic, U. (1999). *International crime victim survey (ICVS), 1989–1997*. Retrieved March 3, 2005, from http://webapp.icpsr.umich.edu/cocoon/ICPSR-STUDY/02973.xml

Anderson, J. (1998). *Report: Corruption in Latvia: Survey evidence*. Retrieved July 11, 2000, from http://www.worldbank.org/wbi/governance

Anechiarico, F., & Jacobs, J. B. (1996). *The pursuit of absolute integrity: How corruption control makes government ineffective*. Chicago: University of Chicago Press.

Bahn, C. (1975). *The psychological costs of police corruption*. New York: John Jay College of Criminal Justice.

Barker, T. (1977). Peer group support for police occupational deviance. *Criminology*, 15(3), 353–366.

Barker, T. (1983). Rookie police officers' perceptions of police occupational deviance. *Police Studies*, 6(2), 30–38.

Barker, T., & Carter, D. L. (1991). Police lies and perjury: A motivation-based taxonomy. In T. Barker & D. L. Carter (Eds.), *Police deviance* (2nd ed., pp. 139–152). Cincinnati, OH: Anderson.

Barker, T., Friery, R. N., & Carter, D. L. (1994). After L.A., would your local police lie? In T. Barker & D. L. Carter (Eds.), *Police deviance* (2nd ed., pp. 153–163). Cincinnati, OH: Anderson.

Barker, T., & Wells, R. O. (1981). Police administrators' attitudes toward the definition and control of police deviance. *FBI Law Enforcement Bulletin, 51*(3), 8–16.

Baueris, V. (1997). *New York Police Department: Preventing crime and corruption*. Retrieved March 10, 2005, from http://www.icac.nsw.gov.au/files/pdf/pub2_30cp.pdf

Bayley, D. (1974). Police corruption in India. In L. W. Sherman (Ed.), *Police corruption: A sociological perspective* (pp. 74–93). Garden City, NY: Anchor Press.

Bittner, E. (1999). The quasi-military organization of the police. In V. E. Kappeler (Ed.), *The police and society* (2nd ed., pp. 170–180). Prospect Heights, IL: Waveland Press.

Bracey, D. H. (1995). Police corruption. In W. G. Bailey (Ed.), *The encyclopedia of police science* (2nd ed., pp. 545–549). New York: Garland.

Britz, M. (1997). The police subculture and occupational socialization: Exploring individual and demographic characteristics. *American Journal of Criminal Justice, 21*(2), 127–146.

Brockhaus, R. (1980). Risk taking propensity of entrepreneurs. *The Academic Management Journal, 23*, 509–513.

Brown, L. P. (1967–1968). Handling complaints against the police. *Police, 12*, 74–77.

Buckley, S. (2000, February 29). In Brazil, the state police are a killing force; thousands of brutal slayings attributed to corrupt civil and military officers. *The Washington Post Foreign Service*, p. A1.

Buder, L. (1982, July 21). 7 officers indicted for corruption. *The New York Times*, p. B3.

Burnham, D. (1968, December 16). Some policemen are found to be sleeping on duty. *The New York Times*, p. 1.

Burnham, D. (1970, April 25). Graft paid to police here said to run into millions. *The New York Times*, pp. 1, 18.

Burnham, D. (1974). How police corruption is built into the system—And a few ideas for what to do about it. In L. W. Sherman (Ed.), *Police corruption: A sociological perspective* (pp. 305–314). Garden City, NY: Anchor Press.

Burnham, D. (1978). *The role of the media in controlling corruption.* New York: John Jay College of Criminal Justice.

Burnham, D. (1996). *Above the law: Secret deals, political fixes and other misadventures of the U.S. Department of Justice.* New York: Scribner.

Burns, P., & Sechrest, D. K. (1992). Police corruption: The Miami case. *Criminal Justice and Behavior, 19*(3), 294–313.

Carter, D. L. (1990). Drug-related corruption of police officers: A contemporary typology. *Journal of Criminal Justice, 18*(2), 85–98.

Chambliss, W. J. (1971). Vice, corruption, bureaucracy, and power. *Wisconsin Law Review, 4*, 1150–1173.

Chen, J. B. L. (with Devery, C., & Doran, S.). (2003). *Fair cop: Learning the art of policing.* Toronto, Ontario, Canada: University of Toronto Press.

Chevigny, P. (1995). *Edge of the knife: Police violence in America.* New York: New Press.

[Christopher Commission.] Independent Commission on the Los Angeles Police Department. (1991). *Report of the Independent Commission on the Los Angeles Police Department.* Los Angeles: Author.

City of San José. (2004). *2003–2004 operating budget: Summary information.* Retrieved May 1, 2004, from http://www.sanjoseca.gov/index.html

Cloward, R. A., & Ohlin, L. E. (1960). *Delinquency and opportunity*. Glencoe, IL: Free Press.

Cohen, B. (1972). The police internal system of justice in New York City. *Journal of Criminal Law, Criminology, & Police Science, 63*(1), 54–67.

Coleman, S. (2004). When police should say "no!" to gratuities. *Criminal Justice Ethics, 23*, 33–44.

Commission on Accreditation for Law Enforcement Agencies. (1994). *Standards for law enforcement agencies: The standards manual of the law enforcement agency accreditation program*. Fairfax, VA: Author.

Crawford, T. J. (1973). Police perceptions of ghetto hostility. *Journal of Police Science & Administration, 1*(2), 168–174.

[Curran Committee.] (1997). Special Committee of the Board of Aldermen of the City of New York Appointed August 5, 1912 to Investigate the Police Department. (1913). Report of the Special Committee of the Board of Aldermen of the City of New York Appointed August 5, 1912 to Investigate the Police Department. Reprinted in G. J. Chin (Ed.), *New York City police corruption investigation commissions, 1894–1994* (Vol. 2, pp. 1–147). Buffalo, NY: William S. Hein. (Original work published 1913)

DeFrances, C. J. (2002). *Prosecutors in state courts, 2001*. Retrieved June 2, 2003, from http://www.ojp.usdoj.gov/bjs/pub/pdf/psc01.pdf

Dennis, E. S. G., Jr., & Wilson, D. O. (1988). Investigation and prosecution of police corruption cases. In W. E. Weld (Ed.), *Prosecution of public corruption cases* (pp. 65–75). Washington, DC: U.S. Department of Justice.

Dombrink, J. (1994). The touchables: Vice and police corruption in the 1980s. In T. Barker & D. L. Carter (Eds.), *Police deviance* (2nd ed., pp. 61–85). Cincinnati, OH: Anderson.

Fabrizio, L. E. (1990). *The FBI national academy: A study of the change in attitudes of those who attend*. Chicago: Office of International Criminal Justice, University of Illinois at Chicago.

Felstiner, W. L. F., Abel, R. L., & Sarat, A. (1980). The emergence and transformation of disputes: Naming, blaming, claiming. *Law and Society Review, 15*, 631–654.

Finnane, M. (1990). Police corruption and police reform: The Fitzgerald inquiry in Queensland, Australia. *Policing and Society, 1*, 159–171.

Fishman, J. E. (1978). *Measuring police corruption*. New York: John Jay College of Criminal Justice.

[Fitzgerald Commission.] Commission of Inquiry into Possible Illegal Activities and Associated Police Misconduct. (1989). *Report of a commission of inquiry pursuant to orders in council*. Brisbane, Queensland, Australia: Author.

Florida Public Corruption Study Commission. (1999). *Report to the governor.* Tallahassee, FL: Author.

Franz, V., & Jones, D. M. (1987). Perceptions of organizational performance in suburban police departments: A critique of the military model. *Journal of Police Science & Administration, 15*(2), 153–161.

Gallup International. (1996). [Gallup international 50th anniversary survey]. Unpublished data.

Gardiner, J. A. (1970). *The politics of corruption: Organized crime in an American city.* New York: Russell Sage Foundation.

Garrity v. State of New Jersey, 385 U.S. 493; 87 S. Ct. 616 (1967).

Giuliani, R. W., & Bratton, W. J. (1995). *Police strategy no. 7: Rooting out corruption. Building organization integrity in the New York Police Department.* New York: New York City Police Department.

Goldstein, H. (1975). *Police corruption: A perspective on its nature and control.* Washington, DC: The Police Foundation.

Green, M. (1999). *Investigation of the New York City Police Department's response to civilian complaints of police misconduct — interim report.* New York: Office of the New York City Public Advocate.

Greisinger, G. W., Slovak, J. S., & Molkup, J. J. (1979). *Civil service systems: Their impact on police administration.* Washington, DC: U.S. Department of Justice.

Griswold, D. B. (1994). Complaints against the police: Predicting dispositions. *Journal of Criminal Justice, 22*(3), 215–221.

Guerrero-Daley, T. (2000). *Office of the independent police auditor: 1999 year end report.* San José, CA: Office of the Independent Police Auditor.

Guyot, D., & Martensen, K. R. (1991). The governmental setting. In W. A. Geller (Ed.), *Local government police management* (3rd ed., pp. 437–462). Washington, DC: International City Management Association.

Hailman, J. R. (1988). Corruption in government contracts: Bribery, kickback, bidrigging and the rest. In W. E. Weld (Ed.), *Prosecution of public corruption cases* (pp. 15–27). Washington, DC: U.S. Department of Justice.

Haller, M. (1976). Historical roots of police behavior: Chicago, 1890–1925. *Law and Society Review, 10*(2), 303–323.

Heidorn, R., Jr. (1986, October 21). A tough challenge faces Tucker: Cleaning house, inside out. *The Philadelphia Inquirer,* p. B6.

[Helfand Investigation.] (1997). District Attorney of Kings County. Report of special investigation by the district attorney of Kings County, and the December 1949 grand jury. Reprinted in G. J. Chin (Ed.), *New York City police corruption investigation commissions, 1894–1994* (Vol. 4, pp. 1–154). Buffalo, NY: William S. Hein. (Original work published 1954)

Hirschi, T. (1969). *Causes of delinquency*. Berkeley: University of California Press.

Hobbs Act, 18 U.S.C. Section 1951.

ICVS Working Group. (1997). *Codebook main database from the International Crime Victim Surveys*. Retrieved March 3, 2005, from http://webapp.icpsr.umich .edu/cocoon/ICPSR-STUDY/02973.xml

Jacobs, J. B. (1999, May 18). *Dilemmas of corruption control*. Paper presented at the Perspectives on Crime and Justice 1998–1999 lecture series before the Department of Justice, National Institute of Justice. Retrieved March 10, 2005, from http://www.ncjrs.org/pdffiles1/nij/178244.pdf

Jarrett, M. (1988). Charging decisions. In W. E. Weld (Ed.), *Prosecution of public corruption cases* (pp. 209–215). Washington, DC: U.S. Department of Justice.

Jones, B. D., Greenberg, S. R., Kaufman, C., & Drew, J. (1977). Bureaucratic response to citizen-initiated contacts: Environmental enforcement in Detroit. *American Political Science Review, 71,* 148–165.

Kania, R. E. (1988). Should we tell the police to say "yes" to gratuities? *Criminal Justice Ethics, 7*(2), 37–49.

Kappeler, V. E. (2001). *Critical issues in police civil liability* (3rd ed.). Prospect Heights, IL: Waveland Press.

Kappeler, V. E., Sluder, R. D., & Alpert, G. P. (1999). Breeding deviant conformity: Police ideology and culture. In V. E. Kappeler (Ed.), *The police and society* (2nd ed., pp. 238–264). Prospect Heights, IL: Waveland Press.

Keefer, W. (1988). Additional covert techniques in corruption investigations. In W. E. Weld (Ed.), *Prosecution of public corruption cases* (pp. 135–143). Washington, DC: U.S. Department of Justice.

Kelling, G. L., & Moore, M. H. (1988). *The evolving strategy of policing*. Perspectives on Policing 4. Washington, DC: National Institute of Justice.

Kellner, L. B. (1988). Narcotics-related corruption. In W. F. Weld (Ed.), *Prosecution of public corruption cases* (pp. 39–53). Washington, DC: U.S. Department of Justice.

Kleinig, J. (1996). *The ethics of policing*. Cambridge, UK: Cambridge University Press.

Klitgaard, R. (1988). *Controlling corruption*. Berkeley: University of California Press.

Klockars, C. B. (1991). The Dirty Harry problem. In C. B. Klockars & S. B. Mastrofski (Eds.), *Thinking about police* (2nd ed., pp. 413–423). New York: McGraw-Hill.

Klockars, C. B., Kutnjak Ivković, S., Haberfeld, M. R., & Uydess, A. (with contributions by Geller, W. A.). (2001). *Enhancing police integrity*. Final report to the National Institute of Justice, U.S. Department of Justice. Unpublished report.

Klockars, C. B., Kutnjak Ivković, S., Harver, W. E., & Haberfeld, M. R. (1997). *The measurement of police integrity*. Final report to the National Institute of Justice, U.S. Department of Justice. Unpublished report.

[Knapp Commission.] Commission to Investigate Allegations of Police Corruption and the City's Anti-Corruption Procedures. (1972). *Knapp Commission report on police corruption*. New York: George Braziller.

Knowles, J. J. (1996). *The Ohio police behavior study*. Columbia, OH: Office of Criminal Justice Services.

Krauss, C. (1994, June 19). Poll finds a lack of faith in the police. *The New York Times*, p. A1.

Kutnjak Ivković, S. (2000). *Prosecuting the blue knights: An analysis of federal police corruption records*. Manuscript in preparation.

Kutnjak Ivković, S., & Klockars, C. B. (1995, November 15–18). *A cross-cultural study of police corruption*. Paper presented at the annual meeting of the American Society of Criminology, Boston.

Kutnjak Ivković, S., & Klockars, C. B. (2001, November 7–10). *The code of silence in a comparative perspective*. Paper presented at the annual meeting of the American Society of Criminology, Atlanta, GA.

Lasley, J. R. (1994). The impact of the Rodney King incident on citizen attitudes toward police. *Policing & Society, 3*(4), 245–255.

Lawless, J. M. (1988). Learning the players and identifying targets: Tactics for smaller offices. In W. F. Weld (Ed.), *Prosecution of public corruption cases* (pp. 269–275). Washington, DC: U.S. Department of Justice.

[Lexow Committee.] (1997). Special Committee Appointed to Investigate the Police Department of the City of New York. Report of the Special Committee Appointed to Investigate the Police Department of the City of New York. Reprinted in G. J. Chin (Ed.), *New York City police corruption investigation commissions, 1894–1994* (Vol. 1, pp. 1–76). Buffalo, NY: William S. Hein. (Original work published 1894)

Los Angeles Police Department. (2000). *Board of inquiry into the Rampart area corruption incident: Executive summary*. Retrieved June 2, 2001, from http://www.lapdonline.org

Lundman, R. J. (1980). *Police behavior: A sociological perspective*. New York: Oxford University Press.

MacQuarrie, B. (1996, February 12). Probe of police belies relatively good record. *The Boston Globe*, p. 1.

Maher, P. T. (2001, April). *The LAPD Ramparts Bureau corruption case: Why it was inevitable!* Paper presented at the annual meeting of the Academy of Criminal Justice Sciences, Washington, DC.

Main, F. (2003, February 7). Retired cop charged with stealing cocaine. *Chicago Sun-Times,* p. 12.

Malec, K. L., & Gardiner, J. A. (1987). Measurement issues in the study of official corruption: A Chicago example. *Corruption and Reform, 2,* 267–278.

Malouff, J. M., & Schutte, N. S. (1986). Using biographical information to hire the best new police officers: Research findings. *Journal of Police Science & Administration, 14*(3), 175–177.

Manning, P. K., & Redlinger, L. J. (1977). Invitational edges of corruption: Some consequences of narcotics law enforcement. In P. Rock (Ed.), *Drugs and politics* (pp. 279–310). Rutgers, NJ: Transaction Books.

Martin, C. (1994). *Illinois municipal officers' perceptions of police ethics.* Chicago: Illinois Criminal Justice Information Authority, Statistical Analysis Center.

Mastrofski, S. (1988). Varieties of police governance in metropolitan America. *Politics and Policy, 8,* 12–31.

McCormack, R., & Ward, R. H. (1987). An anti-corruption manual for administration in law enforcement. In R. McCormack & R. H. Ward (Eds.), *Managing police corruption: International perspectives* (pp. 29–187). Chicago: Office of International Criminal Justice, University of Illinois at Chicago.

McMullan, M. (1961). A theory of corruption. *Sociological Review, 9*(2), 181–201.

McNamara, J. H. (1967). Uncertainties in police work: The relevance of police recruits' background and training. In D. J. Bordua (Ed.), *The police: Six sociological essays* (pp. 163–252). New York: Wiley.

Merton, R. K. (1938). Social structure and anomie. *American Sociological Review, 3,* 672–382.

Meyer, J. C., Jr. (1973). A descriptive study of police corruption. *Police Chief, 40,* 38–41.

Meyer, J. C., Jr. (1976). Definitional and etiological issues in police corruption: Assessment and synthesis of competing perspectives. *Journal of Police Science and Administration, 4*(1), 46–55.

Miller, B. (1999, April 27). Shakedown gets ex-officer 15 months: Former district detective credited with prompting investigation of FBI agents. *The Washington Post,* p. B2.

Misner, G. E. (1975). The organization and social setting of police corruption. *Police Journal, 48,* 45–50.

[Mollen Commission.] New York City Commission to Investigate Allegations of

Police Corruption and the Anti-Corruption Procedures of the Police Department. (1994). *Commission report*. New York: Author.

Moore, M. H. (1983). Invisible offenses: A challenge to minimally intrusive law enforcement. In G. M. Caplan (Ed.), *Abscam ethics: Moral issues and deception in law enforcement* (pp. 17–42). Washington, DC: Police Foundation.

Moore, M. H. (1997). Epilogue. In Gaffigan, S. J., & McDonald, P. P. (Eds.), *Police integrity: Public service with honor* (pp. 59–70). Washington, DC: U.S. Department of Justice.

Moore, M. H., & Stephens, D. W. (1991). Organization and management. In W. A. Geller (Ed.), *Local government police management* (3rd ed., pp. 22–55). Washington, DC: International City Management Association.

Murphy, P., & Caplan, G. (1991). Fostering integrity. In W. A. Geller (Ed.), *Local government police management* (3rd ed., pp. 239–271). Washington, DC: International City Management Association.

Murphy, S. P. (1992, October 4). Wave of abuse claims laid to a few officers. *The Boston Globe*, p. 1.

Neuffer, E., & Freedenthal, S. (1989, July 27). Jury convicts former Boston detective of extortion. *The Boston Globe*, p. 26.

Newman, G. (1999). *Global report on crime and justice*. New York: Oxford University Press.

The New York Times. (1986, May 16). 2 policemen convicted of taking a bribe, sex involving a girl, 16. p. A15.

The New York Times. (1993, May 29). Officer is charged with accepting bribe. p. 23.

The New York Times. (1995, October 18). 2 ex-officers plead guilty in bribe case. p. B6.

Oettmeier, T., & Wycoff, M. A. (1997). *Personnel performance evaluations in the community policing context*. Washington, DC: Police Executive Research Forum.

Office of the Independent Police Auditor, City of San José. (2000). *Introduction*. Retrieved November 11, 2000, from http://www.ci.san-jose.ca.us/ipa/ipaintro.html

Office of the Independent Police Auditor, City of San José. (2005). *IPA organizational chart*. Retrieved March 10, 2005, from http://www.sanjoseca.gov/ipa/IPA%20Appendix%20E.pdf

O'Neill, G., Zuckoff, M., & and Lehr, D. (1996, February 10). Corruption probe shakes up Boston police detective unit. *The Boston Globe*, p. 1.

O'Sullivan, J. T. (1988). Organizing a public corruption investigations and prosecutions unit. In W. E. Weld (Ed.), *Prosecution of public corruption cases* (pp. 257–268). Washington, DC: U.S. Department of Justice.

Pastore, A. L., & Maguire, K. (2000). *Sourcebook of criminal justice statistics, 1999*. Washington, DC: U.S. Government Printing Office.

Pate, A. M., & Fridell, L. A. (1993). *Police use of force: Official reports, citizen complaints, and legal consequences.* Washington, DC: Police Foundation.

Pate, A. M., & Hamilton, E. E. (1991). *Big six: Policing America's largest cities.* Washington, DC: Police Foundation.

Paternoster, R. (1987). The deterrent effect of the perceived certainty and severity of punishment: A review of the evidence and issues. *Justice Quarterly, 4,* 173–217.

Paternoster, R., Saltzman, L. E., Waldo, G. P., & Chiricos, T. C. (1982). Casual ordering in deterrence research: An examination of the perceptions ↔ behavior relationships. In J. Hagan (Ed.), *Deterrence reconsidered* (pp. 55–70). Beverly Hills, CA: Sage.

Pennsylvania Crime Commission. (1974). *Report on police corruption and the quality of law enforcement in Philadelphia.* Saint Davids, PA: Author.

Pennsylvania Crime Commission. (1980). *A decade of organized crime.* Harrisburg, PA: Author.

Perez, D. W. (1994). *Common sense about police review.* Philadelphia: Temple University Press.

Pileggi, N., & Pearl, M. (1973, July 23). What happens when cops get caught. *New York Magazine,* p. 23.

Prenzler, T., & MacKay, P. (1995). Police gratuities: What the public think. *Criminal Justice Ethics, 14*(1), 15–25.

President's Commission on Law Enforcement and Administration of Justice. (1967a). *The challenge of crime in a free society.* Washington, DC: U.S. Government Printing Office.

President's Commission on Law Enforcement and Administration of Justice. (1967b). *Task force report: The police.* Washington, DC: U.S. Government Printing Office.

Reaves, B. A., & Smith, P. Z. (1999). *Law enforcement management and administrative statistics, 1997.* Washington, DC: U.S. Department of Justice.

Reiss, A. J., Jr. (1971). *The police and the public.* New Haven, CT: Yale University Press.

Reiss, A. J., Jr. (1974). Officer violations of the law. In R. J. Lundman (Ed.), *Police behavior: A sociological perspective* (pp. 253–259). New York: Oxford University Press.

Roebuck, J. B., & Barker, T. (1973). *An empirical typology of police corruption.* Springfield, IL: C. C. Thomas.

Roebuck, J. B., & Barker, T. (1974). A typology of police corruption. *Social Problems, 21*(3), 423–437.

Rose-Ackerman, S. (1978). *Corruption: A study in political economy*. New York: Academic Press.

Rose-Ackerman, S. (1999). *Corruption and government: Causes, consequences, and reform*. Cambridge, UK: Cambridge University Press.

Rosoff, S. M., Pontell, H. N., & Tillman, R. (1998). *Profit without honor: White-collar crime and the looting of America*. Upper Saddle River, NJ: Prentice Hall.

Royal Commission into the New South Wales Police Service. (1997). *Final report*. Sydney, Australia: NSW Police Integrity Commission.

Ruggles, R. (2001, April 2). Colorado lawyer hired as first police auditor. *The Omaha World-Herald*, p. 1.

Ruiz, J., & Bono, C. (2004). At what price a "freebie"? The real cost of police gratuities. *Criminal Justice Ethics, 23*, 44–54.

Russell, K. V. (1978). Complaints against the police: An international perspective. *Police Journal, 51*, 34–44.

Seabury, S. (1997). Final report of Samuel Seabury, referee, in the matter of the investigation of the magistrates' courts in the first judicial department and the magistrates thereof, and of attorneys-at-law practicing in said courts. Reprinted in Chin, G. J. (Ed.), *New York City police corruption investigation commissions, 1894–1994* (Vol. 3, pp. 1–256). Buffalo, NY: William S. Hein. (Original work published 1932)

Sherman, L. (1978). *Scandal and reform*. Berkeley: University of California Press.

Sherman, L. W. (1974). Becoming bent: Moral careers of corrupt policemen. In L. W. Sherman (Ed.), *Police corruption: A sociological perspective* (pp. 191–208). Garden City, NY: Anchor Press.

Sigler, R. T., & Dees, T. M. (1988). Public perception of petty corruption in law enforcement. *Journal of Police Science & Administration, 16*(1), 14–20.

Simpson, A. E. (1977). *The literature of police corruption: Vol. 1. A guide to bibliography and theory*. New York: John Jay Press.

Skolnick, J. H. (1966). *Justice without trial: Law enforcement in democratic society*. New York: Wiley.

Skolnick, J. H., & Fyfe, J. J. (1993). *Above the law*. New York: Free Press.

Souryal, S. S. (1975). Stages of police corruption. *Police Chief, 42*, 63–65.

Sparrow, M. K., Moore, M. H., & Kennedy, D. M. (1990). *Beyond 911: A new era for policing*. New York: Basic Books.

Spencer, K. (2001, May 7). Daub, Fahey differ on police auditor candidates' stand on the creation of a police auditor's office. *The Omaha World-Herald*, p. 1.

State of Florida, Office of the Governor. (1999). *Executive order regarding public corruption* (Executive Order Number 99–237). Tallahassee, FL: Author.

Stoddard, E. R. (1974). A group approach to blue-coat crime. In L. W. Sherman (Ed.), *Police corruption: A sociological perspective* (pp. 277–304). Garden City, NY: Anchor Press.

Struck, D. (2000, March 3). Japan's police wear tarnished badge of honor. *The Washington Post Foreign Service,* p. A23.

Sutherland, E. H., Cressey, D. R., & Luckenbill, D. F. (1992). *Criminology* (11th ed.). Ft. Worth, TX: Harcourt Brace.

Torpy, B. (1996, February 21). Officers set to testify against colleague: Prosecution depends a lot on testimony of three who admit corruption. *The Atlanta Journal and Constitution.*

Transparency International. (1999). *Transparency international 1999 corruption perceptions index.* Retrieved March 10, 2005, from http://www.transparency.org/cpi/1999/cpi1999.html

Trott, S. S. (1988). The successful use of informants and criminals as witnesses for the prosecution in a criminal case. In W. E. Weld (Ed.), *Prosecution of public corruption cases* (pp. 115–133). Washington, DC: U.S. Department of Justice.

U.S. Commission on Civil Rights. (1981). *Who is guarding the guardians: A report on police practices.* Washington, DC: Government Printing Office.

U.S. Department of Justice. (1989). *Building integrity and reducing drug corruption in police departments.* Washington, DC: Government Printing Office.

U.S. Department of Justice. (1994). *Criminal victimization in the United States, 1992.* Washington, DC: Bureau of Justice Statistics.

U.S. Department of Justice. (1995). *Sourcebook online.* Retrieved July 11, 2000, from http://www.albany.edu/sourcebook/1995/pdf/t578.pdf

U.S. Department of Justice, Criminal Division, Public Integrity Section. (1999). *Report to Congress on the activities and operations of the Public Integrity Section for 1998.* Retrieved June 5, 2001, from http://www.ojp.usdoj.gov

United States v. Brewster, 506 F.2d 62, 72, Section 201(c), (D.C. cir. 1974).

van Dijk, J. J. M. (1997). *The international crime victims surveys 1989–1997.* Leiden, Netherlands: Leiden University.

Viviano, J., & Kaempffer, W. (1999, July 13). Cop fined $200, resigns with $55,000 pension. *The New Haven Register,* pp. A1, A4.

Walker, S. (1992). *The police in America* (2nd ed.). New York: McGraw-Hill.

Walker, S. (1995). *Citizen review resource manual.* Washington, DC: Police Executive Research Forum.

Walker, S. (2001). *Police accountability: The role of citizen oversight.* Belmont, CA: Wadsworth Thompson.

Walker, S., & Bumphus, V. W. (1992). The effectiveness of civilian review: Observations on recent trends and new issues regarding the civilian review of police. *American Journal of Police, 11*(4), 1–26.

Warmbir, S. (2001, April 25). Cop's bragging was his downfall. *Chicago Sun-Times,* p. 6.

Watts, E. J. (1981). St. Louis police recruits in the twentieth century. *Criminology, 19*(1), 77–113.

Weingarten, R. H. (1988). Legislative corruption. In W. E. Weld (Ed.), *Prosecution of public corruption cases* (pp. 55–63). Washington, DC: U.S. Department of Justice.

Weisburd, D., & Greenspan, R. (with Hamilton, E. E., Williams, H., & Bryant, K. A.). (2000). *Police attitudes toward abuse of authority: Findings from a national survey.* Washington, DC: National Institute of Justice.

Weld, W. E. (1988). Introduction: Why public corruption is not a victimless crime. In W. E. Weld (Ed.), *Prosecution of public corruption cases* (pp. i–v). Washington, DC: U.S. Department of Justice.

Whyte, W. F. (1955). *Street corner society: The social structure of an Italian slum* (2nd ed.). Chicago: University of Chicago Press.

Williams, K. L., & Hawkins, R. (1986). Perceptual research on general deterrence: A critical review. *Law & Society Review, 20*(4), 545–572.

Wilson, J. Q. (1968). *Varieties of police behavior: The management of law and order in eight communities.* Cambridge, MA: Harvard University Press.

Wilson, J. Q., & Herrnstein, R. J. (1985). *Crime and human nature.* New York: Simon & Schuster.

World Bank. (2000a). *Cambodia governance and corruption diagnostic: Evidence from citizen, enterprise and public official surveys.* Retrieved September 1, 2000, from http://www.worldbank.org/wbi/governance/pdf/guide_pdfs/06-survey_report.pdf

World Bank. (2000b). *Evidence of corruption: Main lessons.* Retrieved September 1, 2000, from http://www.worldbank.org/wbi/governance/pdf/guide_pdfs/albania.pdf

Zimring, F., & Hawkins, G. (1973). *Deterrence.* Chicago: University of Chicago Press.

Zuckoff, M. (1997, September 17). An outside review for hub police. *The Boston Globe,* p. A1.

Index